Neighbours
and Networks

Neighbours and Networks

THE BLOOD TRIBE IN THE SOUTHERN ALBERTA ECONOMY, 1884–1939

W. KEITH REGULAR

UNIVERSITY OF
CALGARY
PRESS

University of Calgary Press
2500 University Drive NW
Calgary, Alberta
Canada T2N 1N4
www.uofcpress.com

LIBRARY AND ARCHIVES CANADA CATALOGUING IN PUBLICATION

Regular, W. Keith (William Keith), 1952-
     Neighbours and networks : the Blood tribe in the southern
Alberta economy, 1884-1939 / W. Keith Regular.

Includes bibliographical references and index.
ISBN 978-1-55238-243-1
Issued also in electronic format:
ISBN 978-1-55238-483-1
ISBN 978-1-55238-654-5
ISBN 978-1-55238-655-2

1. Kainai Indians–Commerce–History. 2. Kainai Indians–Economic conditions. 3. Blood
Indian Reserve No. 148 (Alta.)–Commerce–History. 4. Blood Indian Reserve No. 148
(Alta.)–Economic conditions. 5. Indian business enterprises–Alberta–History. 6. Alberta–
Commerce–History. 7. Alberta–Economic conditions. 8. Kainai Indians–History. 9.
Blood Indian Reserve No. 148 (Alta.)–History. I. Title.

E99.K15R43 2009   330.90089'97352071234   C2008-908080-7

The University of Calgary Press acknowledges the support of the Alberta Foundation for
the Arts for our publications. We acknowledge the financial support of the Government
of Canada through the Book Publishing Industry Development Program (BPIDP) for our
publishing activities. We acknowledge the financial support of the Canada Council for the
Arts for our publishing program.

Alberta Foundation for the Arts   Canada   Canada Council for the Arts / Conseil des Arts du Canada   Alberta Historical Resources Foundation

Cover design, page design and typesetting by Melina Cusano.

Dedicated to my mother and father

ELIZABETH (NOFTALL) REGULAR
1930-2005

&

RYBURN BAXTER REGULAR
1927

And to my mother-in-law and father-in-law

ANN 'NANCE' (COOKE) PUMPHREY
1923-1985

&

WILLIAM THOMAS PUMPHREY
1919-2007

CONTENTS

TABLES

MAPS

PREFACE

This history focuses on the economic association between the Blood Indians and their neighbours in southern Alberta from the 1880s through the 1930s. Canadian historiography has yet much to detail regarding the economic associations between Natives and non-Natives sharing an environment and experiencing an integrated economic. I posit the argument that the Bloods and their reserve, contrary to general perceptions of Native reserves, have at times played more than a minor role in the regional development of southern Alberta. The Bloods have influenced the economic circumstances in which Natives and newcomers found themselves in the post-treaty period on the Canadian Plains.

The Blood tribe and their large reservation were a significant factor in the southern Alberta region in which they were located. Their land base was important to the nascent and established ranching industry near the reserve during the 1880s through the period of the Great Depression. The products of the Blood reserve, especially coal and hay, were commodities in demand by settlers, and the Bloods were encouraged to provide them as needed. The Bloods became expert freighters and the local community sought them out to transport the much-needed produce from the reserve and to transship goods for non-Native entrepreneurs. Blood field labour in the Raymond area sugar beet fields was at times critical to the functioning of that industry. Their availability and willingness to work was a deciding factor in the operations of the Knight Sugar Company, especially during the first decade of operations. Finally, the Bloods' ties to the merchant community, particularly in Cardston and Fort Macleod, resulted in a significant infusion of money into the local economy. Importantly, much of this cash resulted from the personal wealth of the Bloods and was not a consequence of Department of Indian Affairs charity. The Bloods were not a drain on the local resources but were important contributors to the developing economy of the region. The relationship that the Bloods had with local merchants was very much like that of their White neighbours – interdependent.

Unfortunately the Department of Indian Affairs did not recognize the potential of the reserve to serve the needs of the Bloods, or at least did not let this recognition mitigate their policies of restriction and paternalism. Had they done so the fortunes of the Bloods, and many other Native reserves, might be now much different. So too might there be greater recognition of the part played by Natives in regional economies.

Scholarly inquiry is not a lonely endeavour and my efforts in this case are no exception. Many individuals and organizations are owed a debt of gratitude for their valuable assistance and contribution to this project. The archivists and staff of the Library and Archives of Canada, Provincial Archives of Alberta, and the Glenbow Archives were very helpful. My friend Douglas Cass at the Glenbow Archives is deserving of special mention. He readily fielded my inquiries, offered advice and did footwork when I was stymied by lack of access to documents and books imposed by my rural setting. Thanks are also due to the helpful and efficient staff at the University of Calgary Press. I owe a special debt of gratitude to two scholars who epitomize the scholarly teacher. Dr. Herman Ganzevoort of the University of Calgary provided constant encouragement and advice from the initial stages of this project. Many thanks are also due to Dr. Joseph Cherwinski, now retired, Memorial University of Newfoundland. It during a teacher and student conversation with Dr. Cherwinski that this project had its genesis. He was encouraging and keen to see its completion. Three anonymous readers gave very helpful suggestions for improving this work. It is my hope that I have at least met some of their expectations. Their suggestions were much appreciated and I am grateful. This work is better for their insights. Clearly, however, sins of omission and commission are strictly my own. Last but not least I wish to thank my wife Anne for her understanding, encouragement, and patience throughout this project. Without such this work could have never been brought to fruition. Thanks also to Ryburn and Nancy, who seemed to have understood that their dad was preoccupied with some historical matter, as is usually the case.

W.K.R.
December 2008

1: Introduction

There is a long-standing and firmly entrenched belief among Canadians in general that holds that Indian reservations are culturally confused, economically emaciated, physically isolated 'islands' of poverty. Buckley has called reserves *terra incognita* to all but their own people, while another has concluded that the majority of reserves produce nothing but people.[1] Robertson has posited that, overall, reserve economies have been colossal failures from their inception until as recently as the 1960s.[2]

While some Native reserves do fit this description, the predisposition to accept such a judgment for all is, in part, informed by the pseudo-scientific theories that were in vogue at the turn of the twentieth century and results that issued from the theory *cum* policy embodied in the Indian Act.[3] Duncan C. Scott, Superintendent General of Indian Affairs from 1913 to 1932 and, arguably, the most influential individual to hold that post, best summed up the aims and the inherent contradictions of the Act when he stated:

> This system was designed to protect them from encroachment and to establish for them a sort of sanctuary where they could develop unmolested, until advancement had rendered possible their absorption with the general citizenship. The Reserve System was intended to ensure the continuation of the tribal life and the life of the individual as an Indian, as well as to render possible a continuous and consistent administrative policy directed toward civilization.[4]

Ultimately, of course, 'civilization,' as envisioned by Scott and the government, was incompatible with the continuation of Native economic and social traditions. The Plains Indians' loss of the buffalo by 1880 was, for the Government of Canada, a fortuitous circumstance. The demise of entrenched economic patterns necessitating cultural adaptations created significant temporary confusion in Native life, thus assisting the government's assimilationist policy aimed at erasing Native identity through re-education and the curbing of certain social and religious practices.[5]

This policy of isolation was vigorously promoted and zealously applied to Canada's Aboriginal peoples by an army of Indian agents and other government servants. The Indians, however, challenged both the policy and its repressive application, from day to day and generation to generation. The Act was intended to protect and assimilate, while at the same time severing Native homelands from the economic, social, and political milieu which surrounded them and to which they were attached. That the Act succeeded absolutely in this intent has, to a large degree, been uncritically accepted by Canadian historians, both Native and non-Native alike. Thus the 'fact' of Native exclusion and isolation, with all the attendant disadvantages that this entails, has seemingly been sustained. The consequence of Canada's hegemony over Indians, historians have concluded, has resulted in a less than marginal existence for Native people, their only victory being 'survival.'[6]

Native Canadians have been presented as a culturally primitive people and works largely now dated have sustained this view. During the early reserve period Natives were believed to have an unsustainable economic and population base and were, therefore, dependent on Canadian government beneficence. The nineteenth-century belief that Indian societies had lost their cultural and economic vibrancy and were a people headed for extinction has helped perpetuate the view of Native irrelevance that is reflected in Canadian historical and literary writings, especially those dealing with the post–World War I period.[7] Discussion of Native and non-Native interactions is generally cast in a negative mould because Natives were viewed as irrelevant to Canadian economic and social development.[8] Historian James St. G. Walker has noted that Indians have made little impression on how historians write Canadian history. In fact, Native peoples are denied a historic role except for that which the dominant society chooses to give them.[9] It is telling, perhaps, that to date they have been accorded very little.

THE LITERATURE

The view that Natives have played no significant part in Canada's modern history was set out by an earlier generation of scholars, one of the most influential being G.F.G. Stanley. In his work *The Birth of Western Canada*, first published in 1936, Stanley established the premise of a dichotomy between 'civilized' and primitive peoples and cast the latter or Aboriginal peoples at a predictable disadvantage. How could it be otherwise for societies described as 'simple' and 'inflexible'? In essence he argued that Canadian plains Native cultures were not viable in the face of Euro-Canadian advancement.[10] There were apparently then only two possible outcomes. Native societies had to adjust, such adjustment requiring total cultural reorientation, or fortune and disease would dictate whether or not they were doomed as a race.

Stanley also firmly entrenched the idea of the permanent disastrous effect of the loss of the buffalo to plains Native cultures.[11] The consequences according to both Canadian and American historians were an economic and cultural destabilization from which the Plains Indians have never recovered.[12] Inherent in Stanley's outlook is the supposition that Anglo-Canadian individualism in both economic enterprise and social behaviour is superior to individual Native initiative and to Native communities acting in economic and social concert. Although surrounded on their reserves by an immigrant culture, there was apparently nothing they could contribute to or gain from this association. Thus the stage was set for the Indians to fade to the back of both the real and perceptual landscape. A new generation of historians, although no longer viewing Natives and their affairs through a Euro-centric cultural lens, has found little to celebrate in Native attempts to prosper, basing their views on a core body of literature with interpretations largely ingrained.

Hugh Dempsey, one of the most prolific writers on the nineteenth and twentieth centuries southern Alberta Plains environment, for example, has focused, chiefly in the form of biography, on the valiant if vain efforts of individual Native leaders to lead their people after the decline of the buffalo and the move to reserves. His work is a calendar of cultural turmoil centred on the Native struggle to remain economically and culturally relevant. Though his biographies of leaders and individuals, such as Crowfoot, Red Crow, James Gladstone, and Tom Three Persons in particular, are tributes to individual endurance, adaptation, fortitude, and ultimately personal success, they are nonetheless presented against a backdrop of collective tribal economic and social dysfunction and despair.[13]

Helen Buckley's 1992 study *From Wooden Ploughs to Welfare* is a chronicle of the long despairing descent by prairie Indians into welfare. Buckley's is a damning indictment of a federal government Indian policy that, she claims, was shortsighted in its planning, repressive in its application, and largely sterile in its results. Buckley is clear, however, in holding the government and its policy to account, and not the Natives themselves, for their victimization and failure. Dealt with differently, that is, offered the same opportunities as non-Native farmer-settlers, the Indians might have succeeded. But fail they did and that is her ultimate bleak conclusion, a current stasis that has no predictable end except in Native self-government. Unfortunately there has been a general acceptance by Canadians of what Buckley has termed the "melancholy reality" of Native and reserve existence as all-embracing and for all time.[14]

Historian Hana Samek's *The Blackfoot Confederacy 1880–1920* scrutinized the similarities and differences in the administration of Canadian and American Indian policy by focusing on the reserves of the Blackfoot Confederacy. Samek accepts 'the failure of reservation economies' among the Blackfoot, including the Bloods, a failure which she sees as rooted in the loss of the buffalo, geography, climate, and government policies. She claims the latter were bound to fail because of the "cultural chasm" that existed between government officials and the Indians they administered. Her study, however, ends in 1920 and her discussion of the most recent years is brief and unsatisfactory. Samek believes that Canada continues to pursue a policy that will continue the cycle of dependency.[15]

In their *Town Life: Main Street and the Evolution of Small Town Alberta, 1880–1947,* Wetherell and Kmet focus considerable attention on the southern Alberta towns of Fort Macleod and Cardston. Key developments in town genesis, political life, economic activities, physical planning and structure, and community living are analyzed. Except for occasional references, however, significant Native influences on community development are ignored. There is no recognition of Natives as transient visitors or permanent residents. Natives are noticeably absent in discussions on doing business and street life. They are accorded little or no influence in the important phases of town genesis and growth. The view of a contentious and confused relationship between resident Aboriginals and the towns established in their traditional territory, a relationship in which Natives were rejected as out of place, is discussed by New Zealand historian David Hamer in his *New Towns in the New World.*[16] Yet even the most cursory glance at local newspapers for Fort Macleod and Cardston leads to starkly different conclusions. In some ways, as will be discussed, Natives were an essential determinant of the kind of urban and rural setting that emerged in southern Alberta.

The origins of the perception that Native economies have developed in isolation are uncertain. Early ethnographic works seem not to have laid this foundation. Goldfrank, for example, suggests that the Bloods took to haying simply because a market existed and "onerous cultivation was unnecessary" and "work for the agency or white ranchers, for the money wages received ... offered a greater measure of independence."[17] Significantly, Goldfrank declares that for the decade from 1910 to 1920, "for the first time in the history of the Blood, a money economy, entirely divorced from the traditional horse economy, flourished exuberantly and with success in this competitive society."[18] Goldfrank may have under-stressed the importance of earlier decades. Similarly Hanks and Hanks note a similar proclivity among the Blackfoot to engage in contract work, although the focus of their efforts is mainly on the reserve economy.[19] The acceptance of an isolated Native economy, therefore, simply seems to fit with the government's stated policy of isolation on reserves, the desired social and physical control and the assumption that the policy succeeded.

American historians have delved more deeply into the nature of the processes and place of the 'frontier,' 'borderland,' or 'middle ground' experience and how to interpret the interplay occurring in the economic and cultural meeting area has led to spirited exchanges.[20] The various works, however, point to one certainty: Natives were *not irrelevant* to the processes of integration in the earlier phases of contact, influencing as well as being influenced. At the very least it is unreasonable to expect Native people to have melted away in the face of non-Natives' unwarranted designs on their land, labour, and personages.

As both Alan Trachtenberg and Patricia Limerick have illustrated, there were no empty spaces in the American West and America's expansion into the occupied spaces resulted in a melding of peoples and fusion of economies.[21] Both historians see the West's resources and people as intimately linked to the development of the American nation. As Trachtenberg astutely observes, "The West poured its resources into the expanding productive system, contributing decisively to the remaking of that system into a national incorporated entity." Native peoples as well, of course, were sucked into the vortex of the incorporation experience but not without resistance, a fact brutally brought home to both Native and non-Native alike in a series of violent confrontations.[22] Violence aside, economic co-existence was not a rarity but it fell victim to American national political and economic exigencies, which saw in the Indians the "utmost antithesis to an America dedicated to productivity, profit, and private prosperity."[23]

Limerick concludes that after conquest was affected Indians became "a population in trouble, with massive unemployment and poor prospects for economic recovery."[24]

Historian Daniel Calhoun, in his rejection of the picture painted by both Trachtenberg and Limerick, has perhaps come closest to unmasking the reality of frontier peoples' experiences with each other. In a short but perceptive essay on Parras, Coahuila Province, Mexico, Calhoun concludes: "There were segments of the community as complex as anybody's 'middle ground,' there were other segments almost as homogeneous as somebody's ethnic 'ideal types.' Observers then and historians since have oversimplified and generalized. The various peoples worked together or defended against each other as the need arose."[25]

An exponent of this view in Canada, and a significant departure from the literature in general, is the work of Arthur J. Ray. Although his study, *Indians in the Fur Trade*, is not specific to southern Alberta, it does offer commentary on the Plains region and its economy. The significance of Ray's work is that it firmly anchors Native people as pivotal players in the fur trade economy and in a deliberate participatory fashion, reacting to the ebb and flow of goods and adjusting their relations with each other and with fur traders. Ray notes, for example, "these changes [in the fur trade] strongly influenced the evolving tribal economies of the Indians of Western Canada."[26] When the Assiniboine were undercut as middlemen, Ray suggests, they likely "shifted the primary focus of their trading activities from the exchange of furs to the bartering of dried meat and grease in a relatively short period of time."[27] Ray argues that both the Assiniboine and the Plains Cree "exerted their economic power either to obtain more favourable rates of exchange for themselves, or to prevent their enemies from trading at various parkland posts," findings supported by Thistle in his *Indian-European Trade Relations* and by Ray and Freeman in *'Give Us Good Measure'*.[28] A significant note by Ray is that, despite changing economic circumstances for the Natives, their "earlier practice of exploiting woodland, grassland, and parkland resources on a seasonal basis persisted among a large proportion of the Indian population," a testament to both persistence and adaptation, as will be discussed below.[29]

Also worthy of consideration, because of a more contemporary focus, are Hildebrandt and Hubner, *The Cypress Hills: The Land and Its People*, and Hildebrandt's *Views from Fort Battleford: Constructed Visions of an Anglo-Canadian West*. The former is a study, not so much of people in a place, but of successive transitory populations through a place, in this case the

Cypress Hills of southern Saskatchewan. Unlike the Bloods, who are, in the reserve period, resident specific, Hildebrandt and Hubner describe the attractions of the Cypress Hills for various peoples and the interactions of these peoples with the land and each other. Nonetheless, it is a well-crafted study of social and environmental interaction during a dynamic period of change in the last half of the nineteenth century. As Hildebrandt and Hubner observe, "The economy" in which Natives played a part, "changed from one preoccupied with consumption to one that concentrated on production for exchange."[30]

In his *Views from Fort Battleford*, Hildebrandt presents the theme of change and adaptation in the Battleford area, located in Plains Cree territory. In this specific place the usual colonial discourse is played out, the Natives predominate in the early history of the area only to be displaced and marginalized economically, physically, and socially by an Anglo-Canadian presence. Worthy of note here is the view that the local and regional economies of the Natives and Métis "lacked vitality" and so the traditional barter and market economy suffered in the face of externally imposed economic structures.[31]

The economic, social, and political culture of the West tends to be viewed, as Francis has illustrated, strictly in terms of a transplanting and melding of Euro-Canadian influences.[32] This is an important consideration when one realizes that Natives were, though often in a negative way, a significant part of what was perceived as the western setting. Much about Indian life and mythology also permeates our cultural and literary heritage.[33] Why Natives have apparently made no lasting impression on Anglo-Canadian interpretations of the 'image' or of the history of the region is an important question. This may, in part, explain why efforts to study Native and non-Native economic history as a regional integrated whole have been slow to occur.

Generally speaking, J.R. Miller's assessment that Canada's Natives existed in a limbo of 'irrelevance' until the post–World War II period may well be correct.[34] Although the nature of Indian participation in local economies and environments has yet, in large measure, to be determined, there is little doubt that, in the case of the Blood tribe of southern Alberta, its partial integration into the economy was multi-faceted, deliberate, sustained, and an important contribution to the local emergent economic activities in which it was involved.[35] Willingness to look at the southern Alberta area as an organic whole leads to other possible conclusions with regard to the extent of the Indian detachment from, or conversely attachment to, the physical and economic environment in which the Blood reserve existed. Accepting the above in no way excludes accepting differing, perhaps divergent, experiences for other Native and non-Native communities sharing physical and economic regions, such as the conclusion reached by Sarah Carter in *Lost Harvests: Prairie Indian Reserve Farmers and Government Policy*, her study of the Cree, or Elias in his study of the Dakota.[36] Even a heritage of sometimes uneasy cohabitation of a region need not, however, result in completely or exclusively divergent experiences when there is clearly a 'conjunction of interests.' The Bloods may well be, after all, not an isolated case.

Historian Paul Voisey assumes that "everything about a new community in an area lacking a Native host culture can ultimately be traced to environment, tradition, frontier, and metropolis."[37] I think that allowance must be made for modification and formation through interaction with a host Native community, in this case the Bloods. The intent is to detail the nature of some of the economic points of intersection of Native and non-Native in the process of forming communities. Though governments at various times attempted to isolate the Bloods and their affairs from the emerging surrounding communities, they failed to prevent the Natives' interaction with the newcomers.

The Native presence in southern Alberta, however, defies the rigid application of formulae to predict a pattern of relationships as the community developed from pioneering beginnings to the more permanent structures of the 1930s. The Bloods' presence, with their land base, likely complicated formal and informal economic and group relations so that simple dichotomies did not exist. The economic development of southern Alberta occurred in response to both on- and off-reserve conditions that prevailed from the pioneer period through the Great Depression. Clearly, any attempts to economically and physically isolate the Bloods were frustrated by the demands and needs of the Bloods and their neighbours, the reciprocity this engendered, and the governments and agencies that worked on their behalf.[38]

Historical analysis of the post–fur trade era, I believe, has led to a stilted view of the reality and extent of Canadian Indian integration into local economies. The government policy of reserve isolation, with the assumed result that there was no, or little, movement of people and materials to and from Native reserves is unrealistic. Equally, the potential for a distinct Native population and its reserve land base to influence developments among an immigrant population have not been recognized. How, for example, does the non-Native population determine its economic and social agenda, execute its economic functions, and otherwise express itself in relation to the Native presence? What attempts are made to draw the reserve and its inhabitants into the newly imported economic strategies? In this case, are the Bloods considered as liabilities or, when needed, a resource upon which to draw?

THEORETICAL CONSIDERATIONS

Discussions of economic motivations and organization for the period under discussion are usually viewed in terms of market capitalism and deals with trade, labour, and investment capital and its relationship with the state, centred on an axis of exploitation and racism. It is not the intent here to offer detailed explanations but simply to introduce concepts that, though having general economic and social applicability, need to be considered in light of specific local circumstances. American historian William Robbins argues, "The penetration of market forces ... the subjugation and colonization of native peoples" among other elements "provide the essential framework for broad historical analysis" of western American development. He concludes, however, that capitalism as a theme for understanding that development has been neglected.[39] Canadian scholarship, it can be argued, has suffered from similar neglect, despite a reality promoted by Richard White that post-contact history can be defined by "the persistent effort of whites to integrate Indian, land, labor, and resources into the market."[40] These were certainly objects of much desire among the Bloods' neighbours, but to what effect?

The above observation aside, Canadian scholars have initiated discussion of Native integration into market capitalism. Carl Beal expertly details the variety in theory and argument surrounding market economics and its application to western Canada and Native involvement and influences. Beal views economics as a set of interrelated factors, "market economy, monetization of economic relations, the economic organization of Indian reserve economies, and government policy." Importantly, Beal observes, in a market economy "market prices regulate economic activity," with regard to resource allocation and production, including "land, labour and capital" and "money functioning as purchasing power in the hands of those who possess it."[41] Germane to discussions here, however, are Beal's views that Indian involvement in the western Canadian market economy likely "figure[d] prominently in market growth" and undermines the view of their marginalization.[42]

Rolf Knight, for example, referred to British Columbia Natives as both "workers and independent producers" connected to industrial capitalism "right from the start." As well, they were entrepreneurs and players in the "general capitalist development" of British Columbia and he labels attachments to exclusive alternative interpretations of Native economic behaviours as highly romanticized.[43] In providing a capitalist framework for his brief discussion of the sugar beet industry in southern Alberta during the 1950s and 1960s, Ron Laliberté applies a structure of domination and exploitation of labour where state regulation encourages capital accumulation, with the state "intervening into the economy in order to facilitate the flow of workers into available job positions."[44] Similarly, Newell notes that such state strategies were employed in the Pacific Coast fisheries and, likewise, Bourgeault for Aboriginal labour in the North-West, specifically Saskatchewan.[45]

Bourgeault and Laliberté consider capitalism as both exploitative and racist, in that its *raison d'être* is a "continuous supply of cheap labour subjected to various means of coercion and exploitation" to achieve "maximum production of surplus value" by conscripting marginalized racial groups.[46] Bourgeault views the treaties, the Indian Act, and the reserves as aids making land available to "industrial and financial capital." He further argues that the pass system and vagrancy laws "disallowed Indian direct participation in the greater capitalist economy other than as labour. Any commodity production as in agriculture for outside sale was seriously restricted."[47] As always, however, one has to separate what was officially stated as desirable from what actually occurred, especially in the case of the Bloods. The Bloods possessed a large contiguous land area with various resources in fluctuating demand and which they disposed off often at whim. They possessed a sustainable, concentrated, adaptable population possessed of skilled leadership, and market savvy, all at some time or other and individually or in concert, calculated to mitigate the considerable weight of arbitrarily and bureaucratically imposed capitalist structure. As well, the individual personalities of the various reserve agents were an unpredictable and modifying factor regulating the integration of Natives with capitalism during much of the reserve era.

Bourgeault attributes only one *law* to capitalism, "that labour ... must be exploited in the maximum production of surplus value."[48] Consequently, as Laliberté notes, capitalist beet interests put the *squeeze* on beet labour.[49]

Contrary to what might be expected, however, the implementation of this *squeeze-law* often worked to the detriment of capitalism in the sugar beet fields during the period of Knight Sugar as it placed the industry in competitive conflict with other industrial demands on labour. As discussed below, the Bloods, on occasion, abandoned physically demanding sugar beet labour with a view to greater personal gain for less effort.

One can also argue that the active aim of the state, as opposed to official stated policy, with regard to Natives underwent transition between the early reserve period and the later half of the twentieth century. Laliberté illustrates that the Canadian state purposely removed Native peoples from relative isolation in northern Alberta and Saskatchewan to southern Alberta in the interests of capitalist labour needs. Early state policies such as the pass and permit system, the Indian Act, and the establishment of reserves, however, were calculated to have precisely the opposite effect. And even on occasions when some officials believed the enhancement of capitalism was a state obligation, the bureaucracy of the state was at cross-purposes on the occasions when agents protected Natives, in this case the Bloods, from exploitation in ranching leases, commodity resource markets, labour in the sugar beet fields, and debt retrieval. There was certainly no seamless web of efficiency tying the Bloods to their land, labour and capital, to capitalist structure with the effect of relegating them a permanently exploitable resource. Tied they were, but at times on conditions of their own determination. Tough and Ray noted that just such a self-interested tendency among Natives engaged in the northern fur trade was enough even to threaten Hudson's Bay Company monopoly profits.[50]

For much of the immediate pre-reserve period, the Plains economy, including that of the Bloods, was a dual economy, that is, Native economies and capitalist economies co-existed. This arose because the imported capitalist economy was unable to terminate or assimilate the Native economy. Thus a middleman position emerged to bridge the two, and on the Plains, Gerhard Ens concludes, the Métis filled this void. This status quo continued until the 1880s and 1890s when, with the loss of the buffalo, this dualistic economy disappeared, supplanted by developed capitalism.[51] The Bloods were thus required to continue transition from subsistence-based economics through dual economic adaptation to inclusion in a capitalist market economy, with its emphasis on profit from labour provided by free agents.[52] Friesen asserts that capitalism "re-created the entire region" between the 1840s and the 1890s with subsequent decades having the economic and "political arrangements of a democratic capitalist state confirmed."[53] Similarly, Thompson, in his synthesis of western prairie history, states that by the end of the nineteenth century, "The region had been drawn into the web of industrial capitalism, and ways of life evolved over two centuries had been swept aside; the Indian and Métis people who were once central to that way of life had been forced to the margins."[54] This was the economic environment where the Bloods applied the greatest strategies of adaptation and strategic accommodation.

The Government of Canada, as did certain elements of the local community, viewed the Bloods, and Natives generally, as obstacles to 'civilization.' Many locals, however, recruited the Indians to help create and amass wealth. Robin Fisher has determined that in British Columbia the government's policy "reflected the fact that the Indians had become largely irrelevant to the development of the province by Euro-Canadian settlers."[55] The experience in southern Alberta, however, was that the government's policies aimed at creating and sustaining that irrelevance were much diffused in transmission from the Department of Indian Affairs officials in Ottawa to the citizens of Fort Macleod or Cardston, the ranchers and farmers in the surrounding countryside, and the reserve agent. Evidence exists to show that the Bloods aggressively and sensibly participated in local economic activities because they preferred not to remain on the periphery. Often, circumstances beyond the Bloods' control such as depletion of resources, drought, depression, national economic policies, dictated that they should retreat to the confines of their reserve. Their integration into the local economy, however, was sufficient enough that their neighbours resisted the Bloods' disengagement. Indeed, the extent to which they withdrew their labour, and access to their land and capital precipitated, as we shall see, significant upset among the local business interests which in many instances found their very survival compromised.

Doxtator has charged, "the act of building Canada involved asserting a nation literally over the top of Native cultures."[56] Here we can clearly see the tendency to fit Aboriginal Canadians into Eurocentric history rather than to see certain strands of Canada's development in the late nineteenth and early twentieth centuries as a common shared heritage. By studying a small region of southern Alberta, detail will emerge to more sharply focus the non-Native and Native partnership in the development of a given locality. In the period of supposed Indian 'irrelevance,' the Bloods, at least, forged a relevant meaningful economic association with their non-Native neighbours in the period between the establishment of the reserve and the onset of World War II.

THE LOCALE

Peter Carstens has properly observed that, though Native reserves are defined spaces, they are nevertheless politically and economically tied to the broader community.[57] Historians must move beyond the view of the Natives as passive receivers, and the notion of Plains Indians, and their neighbours (homogeneously grouped as pioneers on the frontier) as having, despite their diversity, separately felt homogeneous experiences. In reality change and accommodation accompanied the realization by both Natives and non-Natives that they shared people and resources in common.

The primary focus of this work, therefore, is people and place, more specifically people in a place. The main study area is roughly the shape of a parallelogram bounded on the north with an axis connecting Lethbridge and Fort Macleod and on the south with an axis connecting Cardston with Hill Spring just west of the Blood reserve. The central focus of this territory comprises 541 square miles of Blood reserve land, centred on Townships 3 to 9, Ranges 21 to 28, West of the fourth meridian. The reserve has natural borders, bounded on the east by the St. Mary's River, on the north by the Oldman River and in the west by the Belly River. Its southern extent is an east to west line determined by the township survey system (Map 1).

During the 1880s the Bloods settled their reserve mindful of established historical economic and communications patterns and cultural ties to the surrounding area. They tended to concentrate along the western border; that is, along the eastern bank of the Belly River. Townships 5 north through Township 8 had the heaviest concentration of settlement. The south and the eastern length of the reserve along the St. Mary's River were relatively empty of settlers. This tendency to group in the west can, perhaps, be explained by the presence of Fort Macleod to the west and north of the reserve. The Blood agency buildings in the northern portion of Township 7 were only twelve miles from Fort Macleod where many Bloods shopped and where much official agency business was conducted. The presence of a North West Mounted Police post near the confluence of the Belly and Kootenai Rivers, the location of the Bloods' timber limit in the mountains to the west, and Cochrane Ranche lands to the immediate west of the reserve likely influenced reserve settlement patterns. Bands and family groupings also naturally concentrated to the north and south of the agency occupying available space. Eventually ties to Cardston became important in drawing settlement into the reserve's southern portions.

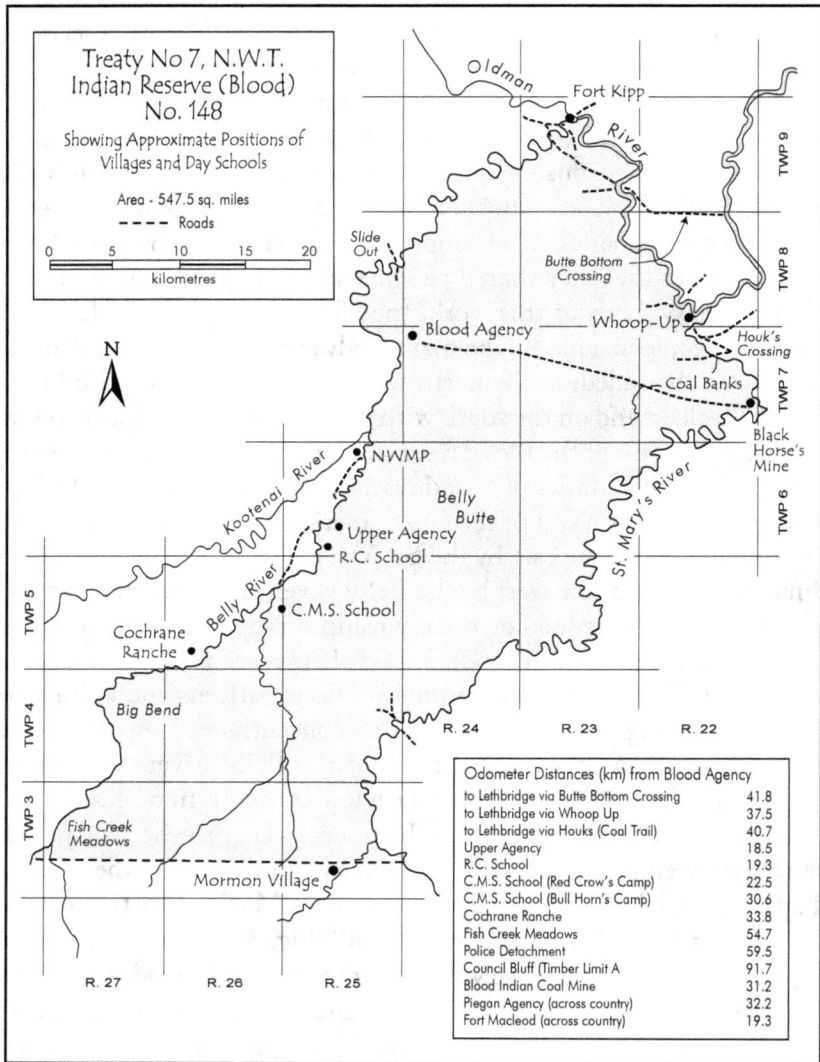

Treaty No 7, N.W.T. Indian Reserve (Blood) No. 148

Showing Approximate Positions of Villages and Day Schools

Area - 547.5 sq. miles

- - - - Roads

0   5   10   15   20
kilometres

N

Oldman River

Fort Kipp

TWP 9

Slide Out

Butte Bottom Crossing

TWP 8

Blood Agency

Whoop-Up

Houk's Crossing

Coal Banks

TWP 7

Black Horse's Mine

Kootenai River

NWMP

Belly Butte

St. Mary's River

TWP 6

Upper Agency

R.C. School

Belly River

C.M.S. School

TWP 5

Cochrane Ranche

TWP 4

Big Bend

R. 24   R. 23   R. 22

TWP 3

Fish Creek Meadows

Mormon Village

R. 27   R. 26   R. 25

Odometer Distances (km) from Blood Agency	
to Lethbridge via Butte Bottom Crossing	41.8
to Lethbridge via Whoop Up	37.5
to Lethbridge via Houks (Coal Trail)	40.7
Upper Agency	18.5
R.C. School	19.3
C.M.S. School (Red Crow's Camp)	22.5
C.M.S. School (Bull Horn's Camp)	30.6
Cochrane Ranche	33.8
Fish Creek Meadows	54.7
Police Detachment	59.5
Council Bluff (Timber Limit A	91.7
Blood Indian Coal Mine	31.2
Piegan Agency (across country)	32.2
Fort Macleod (across country)	19.3

Map 1.
Map of Blood Reserve and Area. Adapted by Marilyn Croot from a map in LAC, RG 10, vol. 3851, file 75988.

Trails also tended to cross and exit the reserve in relation to important sites such as the old Fort Slide Out and the old Fort Whoop-Up located in the western and southeast portions of Township 9 respectively. A trail from the area of the agency buildings crossed the reserve to Coal Banks, on the St. Mary's River, where Black Horse operated his mine. Another trail crossed the northern tip of the reserve in the vicinity of Fort Kipp (Kipp), continued to Butte Bottom Crossing and carried on east to Lethbridge. Trails exiting the reserve at Fort Whoop-Up and Houk's Crossing were similarly used. These trails were so placed as to eventually tie in with developed communications and transportation routes. Thus contact with Fort Macleod and Lethbridge and eventually with Cardston, Raymond, and other small communities was maintained (Map 2).

PEOPLE

The population of the study area is composed of Natives, chiefly the Bloods, and non-Native ranchers, farmers, and settlers residing in rural and urban settings. Towns have a centralized social, political, and economic infrastructure directed towards attracting resources and people from the periphery. From the start, the Bloods, by dint of numbers were poised to be significant players in the local economy, helping to both generate and sustain growth. Most of the Bloods' commercial intercourse was in trading and purchasing in both Fort Macleod and Cardston and in selling their labour in Raymond. Wetherell and Kmet surmise that phases in the growth of newly established towns in southern Alberta likely mirrored developments in the region as a whole; towns focused both population and trade and trade in particular "remained a force in knitting together a patchwork of local concerns and policies."[58]

Comparing the population figures for these towns and the Bloods, it is possible to get some perspective on the Bloods' relative position. In 1882 the government estimated the Blood population at 2,589.[59] Thereafter it declined, but in 1901 the Blood population was 1,253 or 87 per cent of that of Fort Macleod and Cardston combined. Given that the reserve was established in 1880, there were two decades in which the Bloods likely had a significant impact on the economic well-being of one or both of these places. The relative weight of the Blood population sharply declined to 1,168 or 31.5 per cent of Fort Macleod, Cardston and Raymond in 1906 and by 1911 was at 1,128 or 25 per cent. Thereafter it appears to have hit a low of approximately 20 per cent in the mid-1920s (Table 1.1).[60] But even

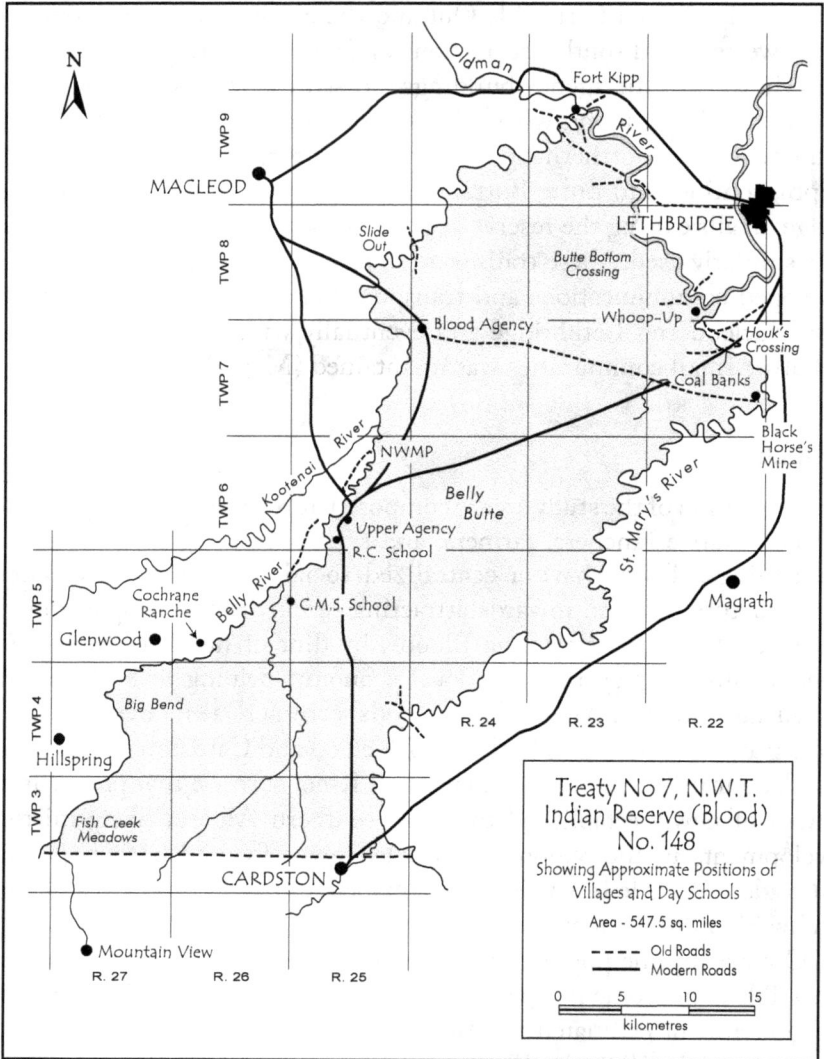

Map 2.
Map of Indian Reserve (Blood) No. 148, showing settlement and use patterns. Adapted by Marilyn Croot from a map in LAC, RG 10, vol. 3851, file 75988, and a map in the *Lethbridge Herald*, August 12, 1968.

NEIGHBOURS AND NETWORKS

Table 1.1. Population at Census Year.

Town	1901	1906	1911	1916	1921	1926	1931	1936	1946
Cardston	639	1.001	1.207	1.370	1.612	2.034	1.672	1.711	2.334
Macleod	796	1.144	1.844	1.811	1.723	1.715	1.447	1.365	1.649
Raymond	----	1.568	1.465	1.205	1.394	1.799	1.849	2.094	2.116
TOTAL	1.435	3.713	4.516	4.386	4.729	5.548	4.968	5.170	6.099
Blood	1.253	1.168	1.128	1.154		1.158*		1.325**	
Blood as % of total	87.3	31.5	25.0	26.3		20.9		25.6	

Census of Prairie Provinces, Vol. 1, 1946, p. 522. The 1881 and 1891 census reports do not differentiate on the basis of community and so were not used.
Data on the Bloods is taken from Agent's Reports contained in *Canada Sessional Papers*.
*This is the population count for 1924 taken from C.S.P., No. 14, 1925, p. 28.
**This is a reading for 1935 taken from NAC, RG 10, vol. 12645, file 205/3-2, pt. 1, M. Christianson to R.H. Coats, December 30, 1935.

at this minimal ratio the number of Bloods represented an attractive and significant market to local businesses, some of which specialized in retailing to Native peoples.[61]

The population for these communities peaked in 1926, declined during the early Depression, and recovered again in 1936. The Bloods' economic value was likely greater during this period of non-Native population decline. Given that the reserve was a home base to which the bulk of the Bloods were tied, the population was a constant presence and the people a captive market. The Blood population maintained its levels and in fact began a slow but perceptible increase. An indication of that value is illustrated by the heightened desire for Native patronage and the frantic demands for the settlement of credit accounts as discussed in Chapter 5 below.

Towns were the focus of commercial activities and the attractions they offered lured the Bloods to frequent town environs. However, the rural setting was not insignificant. The nature of land use, and government regulations, during the ranching era encouraged sparse populations.[62] The ranchers and few farmers, however, incorporated the Natives into their economy by hiring them as ranch labour, renting Native land, and purchasing fuel and fodder supplies Natives offered for sale. These commercial bonds increased as the area became more settled and as Blood labourers and entrepreneurs became more adept at marketing their resources.

STRUCTURES OF MANAGEMENT: THE RESERVE

Because it was a political entity, the Blood reserve was not independent of Canadian law or political influences. Affecting both the well-being of the Bloods and their relations with their non-Native neighbours was both the infrastructure of the Department of Indian Affairs (DIA) and its policy, as embodied in the Indian Act. The reach of the Department was extensive and was, as far as the Native peoples were concerned, a smothering embrace. Other than the often expressed and significant Native resistance, the only protection that the Indians had from the Department's grasp was the presence on the reserve of a concerned agent who placed the well-being of his charges before blind obedience to Ottawa. As for policy, it was nativist-informed and was based on the ultimate goal of assimilating the Natives, on the one hand, and making them economically self-sufficient by turning them into subsistence farmers, ranchers, or entrepreneurs, on the other.[63]

The reserve was subject to decisions made by a host of government bureaucrats, chiefly those in the Department of Indian Affairs in Ottawa. The main purpose of policies emanating from Ottawa was to isolate and control the Indians on their reserves while encouraging them to adopt White ideals of advancement and eventually assimilate with the non-Native population. Hence, it was hoped that Native peoples, as a distinct segment of the Canadian population, and their reserves as distinct political units, would ultimately disappear.[64]

The DIA was organized into an inside and outside service. The inside service was composed of the personnel at Ottawa, which included divisions for a deputy superintendent general, chief clerk, accountant, and unskilled positions. The outside service was made up of the workers in the field who dealt with the Indians on a daily basis. The most important of these was the reserve Indian agent, the ultimate government authority on the reserve. His main responsibility was the implementation of DIA directives and the Indian Act. Because of his intimate daily contact with the Indians under his charge he was in a position to influence decision making among the Native peoples. The agent's powers were increased in 1881 when an amendment to the Indian Act made him a justice of the peace with powers to effect an arrest, conduct trials, and pass sentence.[65] Other reserve personnel, such as farm instructors, worked under the agent's supervision and direction.

When the Laurier Liberals came to power in 1896, Minister of the Interior Clifford Sifton instituted cost-saving reforms that ultimately resulted in more centralized decision making. Consequently more power was concentrated in the hands of J.D. McLean, Secretary and eventually Assistant Deputy Superintendent, and accountant Duncan Campbell Scott. Scott became the Deputy Superintendent General in 1913, a post he held until 1932. McLean and Scott were the major influences and powers in Indian Affairs during their tenures in office. Harold W. McGill succeeded Scott.

Canada made its most significant contribution to the management of Indians and their affairs with the passing of the Indian Act in 1876, an act so comprehensive in scope that it regulated practically every aspect of Native life.[66] Simply put, the Indian Act of 1876 was an instrument of repression reinforcing a culture of repression with regard to Native Canadians.

In impact the Act was all-embracing and, in hindsight, it institutionalized racism as government policy, though contemporaries did not perceive it in this light. Brazen in design, the Indian Act intended no less than to sever Natives from the substance of their humanity. The Act, as law, condemned Native religion and, through its proscription of political, social, religious, and economic functions, reformatted their culture. As the foundation for the new status quo with Native people, it offered the rationale for an attack on Native language and their traditional educational system in an attempt to infuse Natives with the White ideals of civility. The passage of this repressive and comprehensive legislation was justified on the basis that it would turn Indians into 'civilized' and productive citizens of Canada.

Thereafter the matter of most concern to the government bureaucracy was the implementation of the agenda as outlined in the Act. As part of that plan, Indians were given some responsibility for their own local affairs as the act made provision for the election of chiefs and councillors. The powers of intrusion reserved to the Department, reserve inspectors, and the agent, however, were so extensive as to make the decision-making authority of the band and council, in the view of one contemporary official, practically a legal fiction.[67] An amendment to the Act in 1895 allowed the minister to depose chiefs, necessary, according to Tobias, "because the band leaders in the West were found to be resisting the innovations of the reserve system."[68]

The Act, a dynamic and evolving piece of legislation, was a weapon deftly wielded by politicians and bureaucrats to respond to all manner of circumstance. Amendments to the Act, in conjunction with officially accepted illegal repression, especially in times of perceived crisis and emergency, permitted the government to pursue its own agenda of 'protection, civilization, assimilation,' and domination. An examination of the government's treatment of the Indians subsequent to the 1885 Rebellion and during World War I will be illustrative.

SYSTEMS OF CONTROL: THE RESERVE

Though not based in the Indian Act, the pass system, implemented to control Indian movement, was made possible by the empowerment of Indian agents and government officials through the Act. Agents and police could pressure Indians into compliance because the pass system did not have to stand on its own merits but could be reinforced through a myriad of other supportive legislation which legalized dominance, and in which a culture of control was systemic and systematized. Sarah Carter says that the pass system "became an established institution" in the wake of the 1885 troubles and turned the West into "a virtually segregated society." Its intent was to confine Natives to their reserves, a crass attempt to control their behaviour. Without legal justification and mostly on his individual initiative, Assistant Commissioner Hayter Reed began imposing pass restrictions on Indians. Soon after the 1885 Rebellion, the government, responding to his enthusiasm, issued books of passes to Indian agencies across the West in 1886.[69]

Though initially intended to keep Indians under surveillance during the Rebellion, passes soon evolved into general application in attempts to control Indian movement for all manner of purpose, including food-gathering activities, off-reserve work, excursions, social activities, and the curtailing of parental access to children at the various residential schools. In this latter case, compliance in sending their children to school was coerced when families were threatened with removal from the reserve's rations list, the loss of an important and valued means of sustenance during difficult times. The intent changed from one of monitoring movement during a military crisis to coercion, the objective being to force Natives into following government-desired social patterns and economic behaviours.

The Indians quickly condemned this pass policy as a betrayal of treaty. Some historians condemn the policy as unduly repressive and stifling. Blair Stonechild has noted what he considers to be long-lasting repercussions of the pass system. "What little influence Indian people had over their own lives was removed," Stonechild observes, "and Indian people became vulnerable to government whim, manipulation and mismanagement."[70] Clearly the Indians became vulnerable, but the extent to which that vulnerability was taxed is less easy to quantify, given the lack of a full-scale study of the use of the pass system. Indeed some historians question the effectiveness of the pass system. Harring points out that the pass system was "extra-legal" and makes the point that department and government circulars "indicate that official lawlessness was structured and institutionalized, but they do not reveal the extent of the actual use of the pass system."[71] J.R. Miller supports this assessment.[72]

Although the pass system lacked legal foundation, it was in keeping with the repressive spirit of the Indian Act. The permit system, however, implemented to control and restrict Native and non-Native business transactions and interactions, was securely grounded in the Indian Act and the government and its agents could act secure in that knowledge. An Act to amend the Indian Act, 1880, permitted the government to restrict "the sale, barter, exchange or gift, by any band or irregular band of Indians … of any grain or root crops, or other produce grown upon any Indian Reserve in the North-West Territories" and all such transactions were null and void unless conducted in accordance of the provisions of the Act. To make such business transactions extremely risky for recipients, any produce or materials acquired from Indians could be seized.[73]

From the southern Alberta Indian perspective, and certainly from that of the Bloods, the permit system was used to stop them from taking advantage of local market demands for resources and labour. For some, the permit and pass systems were an abuse of power that made the Indians lose faith in the intentions of Whites regarding their dealing with the Indians. The fact that some Indians regard the permit and pass systems as one and the same may speak volumes about the government's duplicitous attempts to use the legality of the permit system to shore up the repressive and 'extra-legal' authority of the pass system.[74]

The Indian Act also regulated the leasing of Indian reserve land. Section 36 of the Amended Indian Act of 1880 stated: "no reserve or portion of a reserve shall be sold, alienated or leased until it has been released or surrender to the Crown for the purposes of this Act." Section 48 of the Act permitted the government to enforce payment for lease in case of arrears. The rules governing leases were clearly in the hands of the government, which had the power to act irrespective of Indian wishes. This was very clear when the government introduced the Greater Production program during World War I. The effect of this program on the Bloods will be discussed below, but it should be pointed out that the government felt no obligation to consult the Bloods before granting leases on their land to non-Natives. Strangely, one of the powers granted to chiefs under Section 74 of the act was that of the "prevention of trespass by cattle, – also for protection of sheep, horses, mules and cattle."[75] As will be discussed, the Bloods themselves were not without the ability to determine who got leases and under what conditions. It will also be clear that the Bloods took seriously the heavy demands placed on the reserve's grazing capacity through illegal incursion by non-Native-owned cattle and horses.

This official legal and extra-legal position, however, does not truly reflect the status of the Bloods and their chiefs and band council. The chiefs and council wielded a great deal of authority with regard to band and reserve matters. Though some agents were repressive, the Bloods and their leaders were determined not to surrender total control of their affairs to officials, they believed, ought to advance their cause and protect their rights. In such cases, the Bloods appealed to other authorities. When Agent James Wilson attempted to prohibit the holding of a Sun Dance in 1898, Red Crow appealed to the North West Mounted Police at Fort Macleod to use their influence to permit the holding of the event.[76] One notable attempt to coerce the Bloods into a surrender of a portion of their reserve failed in the face of the determined opposition of Chief Crop Eared Wolf. Crop Eared Wolf both cultivated and mustered his people's resistance to the alienation of the land.[77] Agents often sided with the Bloods against DIA policies regarding reserve land leasing and considered both the wishes and needs of the Bloods in their decisions and petitions to reserve inspectors and headquarters. It is clear that the Bloods were aggressive on behalf of their own interests.

Once the reserve was established, defending its integrity from the encroachment of neighbours determined on achieving access to its resources was a constant concern of both the Bloods and the Department of Indian Affairs.[78] After some initial growing pains, the boundaries of the reserve

image not available

Figure 1.1.
"Crop Eared Wolf, Head Chief of Bloods, Blood Reserve, Alberta, [ca. 1900-1913]."
Glenbow Archives, NB-3-9. Crop Eared Wolf, Chief of the Bloods, was a staunch
defender of his people's rights and land.

were established and its integrity was, in the main, successfully defended, though defending its resources was considerably more difficult.

THE RURAL COMMUNITY

As the Blood reserve was being occupied, the surrounding area was quickly coming under the dominance of the large cattle-ranching interests. Scattered settlers, such as Dave Akers and D.J. Cochrane, were harbingers of the formal occupation of the land that was to follow as the large ranches gave way to smaller ranches.[79] Eventually cereal farm and mixed farm agriculture predominated.

It can be assumed, but not without qualification, that the region experienced much the same cycle of growth as described by Paul Voisey for the Vulcan area. Here there occurred quick settlement, followed by continual growth and the realization that a quarter section of land was inadequate for prosperity. Subsequently, there was a forced exodus of surplus population and the redistribution of the land among those left.[80] During the various phases of settlement and growth, the rancher and farmer/settlers worked out an accommodation with the Bloods and their reserve as required. The demands most often placed on the Bloods were for direct use of the reserve land, subscription of labour, and supplies such as coal and hay.

FORT MACLEOD

Though the erection of the North West Mounted Police post at Fort Macleod predated the establishment of the Blood Reserve by a decade, the relationship between Fort Macleod and the Blood Indians began with the arrival of the police in 1874. The forces of integration were at play even before the reserve land base was established and the incidence of conflict was never severe enough to significantly impede this process. Fort Macleod, situated northwest of the chosen reserve site, was a focal point for an economy based on the import of consumer goods and export of raw materials along the Whoop-Up Trail (Map 3). Its selection as a NWMP post, and the later establishment of the town, were largely determined by the presence of the Blackfoot Indians among whom the Bloods figured prominently. The supply of the Indians with food and other goods following Treaty 7 in 1877, in large part, drove the economy of the region, creating wealth and attracting permanent non-Native settlement.[81]

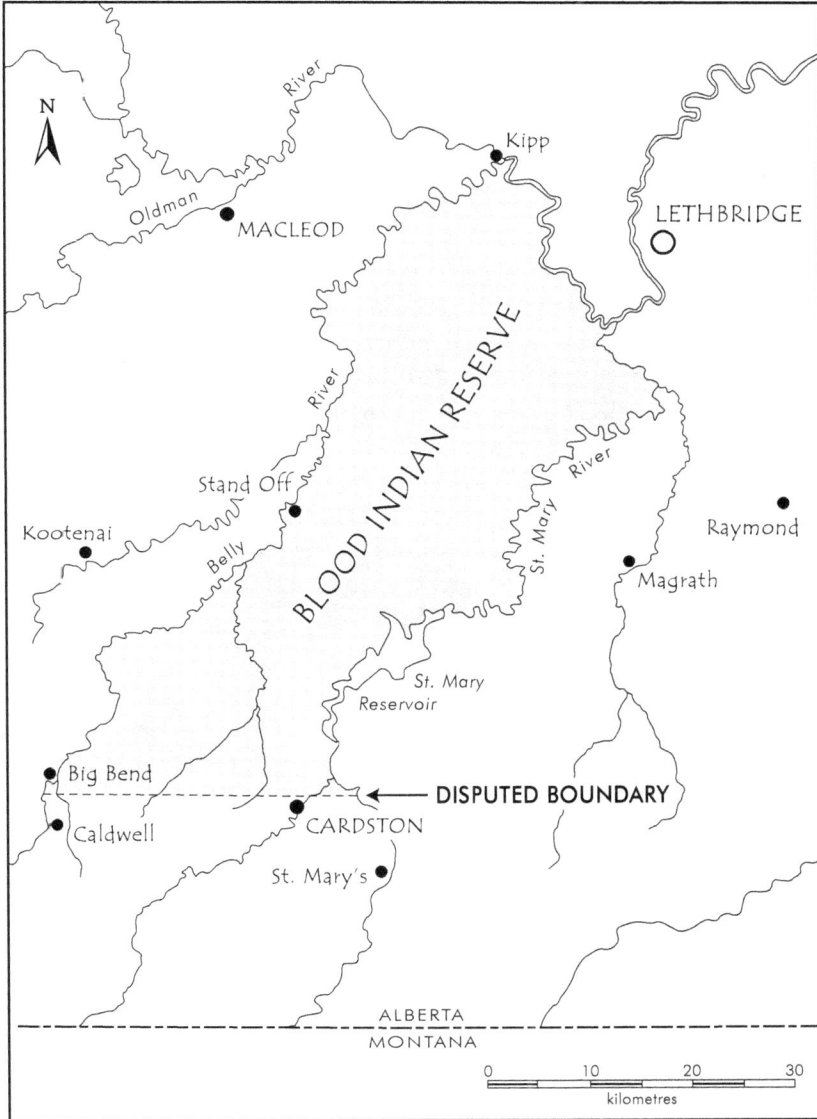

Map 3.
Map of Indian Reserve (Blood) No. 148, showing communications links. Adapted by
Marilyn Croot from a map in the *Lethbridge Herald*, February 24, 1976.

Although Paul Sharp correctly emphasizes Fort Macleod's commercial dependence on American trading companies out of Fort Benton, Montana, he sees this history as exclusive, with Fort Macleod as the meeting of "the two great streams of Anglo-Saxon pioneering."[82] The Natives are, therefore, relegated to the position of displaced hangers-on, reminders of a once-'noble' primordial past. This perception is common to the historiography of the formation of non-Native communities in Aboriginal territory, and the subsequent associations of Natives with non-Native communities is generally viewed by historians as negative. David Hamer has argued that the establishment of towns "involved the obliteration of, attractive aspects of the natural landscape … of all indications of the original, 'primitive' condition of the site. Included in this were the indigenous peoples of the territories being settled." The result was banishment to the hinterland and "their presence in towns became more and more marginal and ghostly."[83] But this view was/is more ideal than real and the banishment, no matter how much desired, never became totally effective or complete. In fact, the Bloods were drawn to the area reassured by the Mounties' presence.[84] The selection of the reserve with Macleod located to the northwest, therefore, only cemented an already established tie.

CARDSTON

Refugee Mormons from Utah led by Charles Ora Card founded the town of Cardston in 1887 near the St. Mary's River. Card and his followers chose to settle at Lee Creek, close to the Blood Reserve's southern border. From the very beginning relations between the Bloods and the Mormon settlers were based on mutual mistrust and disagreement. Initially the ill will stemmed from the belief that deception had been used to gain Blood acquiescence to Mormon settlement in the area. Blood Elder Camoose Bottle claimed that the Mormons acquired the land at Lee Creek by getting Red Crow drunk. This, and the fact that the subsequent agreement between the Bloods and Mormons was not sanctioned by the tribe, led to some Bloods questioning, and continuing to question, its legitimacy.[85]

It was clear from the beginning that the Mormons at Cardston saw themselves as a people apart, sharing little with their Native neighbours except the land which both claimed as their own. A clear indication of that separateness was the manner in which the *Cardston Record* chose to locate the community within the western setting. In 1898 the paper described Cardston's location in relation to the broader western region, as "nearly

800 miles due west of Winnipeg, forty-eight miles south-west from Lethbridge, and twenty miles north of the international boundary or the 49th parallel. A semi-weekly stage plies between Cardston and Lethbridge our most convenient railway station." The same article also noted that Cardston had more than one thousand residents and was close to the settlements of Aetna, Leavitt, and Mountain View.[86] Interestingly, no mention was made of the Blood reserve, which in 1897 had a population of 1,300, making it the largest community in the vicinity next to Lethbridge.[87]

Unlike Fort Macleod, the town of Cardston did increase its commercial influence in southern Alberta and became the dominant trading centre in the area around the Blood Reserve. The Blood and Peigan reserves to the north and west of Cardston separated the town from Euro-Canadian settlement to the west creating a 'sub-region' that Cardston dominated. Spared from competition and stimulated by railways, irrigation, and sugar beet growing and chosen as the religious centre of Mormonism, Cardston grew apace.[88]

RAYMOND

Unlike Fort Macleod and Cardston, Raymond, to the west of the Blood reserve, was, from the very beginning, planned as a one-industry town. It was the centre of a sugar beet industry that would be the mainstay of the community and provide an export commodity to supply the sugar needs of the immediate area and beyond.[89] The industry, however, held its brightest promise only in its planning stages; sustaining it proved to be a frustrating and in the end bitter experience.[90]

Initially, however, sugar beet cultivation brought Raymond stable and sustained growth. By 1906 it was the largest Mormon town in southern Alberta with a population of 1,500, and it soon began to rival Cardston as the centre of the Mormon religion in Canada.[91] But lacking Cardston's history, it also lacked its influence, and when Cardston was chosen as the site of the Mormon temple, Raymond's secondary status was confirmed.[92]

Interaction between Raymond and the Blood reserve revolved primarily around the need of the sugar beet industry for a stable labour supply to work the beet fields, especially during the fall harvest. Large groups of Bloods made the trip to Raymond to engage in wage labour during the period of 1903–15. It is reasonable to assume that there was commercial interaction between the Bloods and Raymond businesses during times of

Blood presence in the town. Little evidence appears in either the local press or government documents to shed much light on the subject.

CONCLUSION

Using the Blood reserve and its immediate geographic area this book argues against prevailing views that the post-buffalo period for the Blood People of southern Alberta was singularly unattractive. It promotes a view that the Bloods, through energy, foresight, and, above all, economic adaptation, both promoted their own integration and were encouraged to integrate into the regional economy. They were an important factor in fulfilling the economic visions of neighbours while also intent on realizing their own individual and collective ambitions. This approach examines the role of the reserve land and its resources, the Bloods' personal and individual wealth, and the Blood peoples' skills and labour in promoting local economic enterprise. This is in essence a case study, which, perhaps, may suggest approaches to considering the part played by other reserves and their people in regional area economies.

There is great benefit in doing a study such as this. Little has been done to evaluate Native initiatives during the post-buffalo period and what has been done generalizes a sorry state of affairs. Detailed site-specific studies are few and during the latter years this field has been largely abandoned, especially as regards western Canada's prairies. Consequently, much of the literature is dated, with the most significant ground-breaking studies, such as Fisher's and Samek's, now needing a broadened contextual environment. There are recent studies such as Brownville and Shewell, but these generalize and are focused on administrative generated and directed policy rather than on Native responses to immediate life issues. Brown's and Peer's recent study is specific to the Bloods but is an investigation into the methodology of inquiry and its interpretative implications.[93] Elofson and Evans have crafted significant studies of western prairie ranching history but these deal with Native issues only peripherally.[94] Subjugation of Natives when they encounter non-Natives may be but a temporary condition rather than inevitable and permanent and the assumed economic displacement may be limited. The relationship forged from the encounter is likely much more complex and varied than formerly allowed.

The belief in the sustained detrimental effect of the loss of the buffalo on the Plains Natives is a natural extension of the fallacy that the Blood and Blackfoot dependence on the buffalo was absolute and hence both their economy and culture were determined by that animal's abundance and utility. To say that the devastating impact of the destruction of the buffalo is a myth is not to argue that it was negligible. Indeed, it was severe in its impact and absolutely devastating in the short term. However, when historians have emphasized the dire consequences of the collapse of the buffalo as an exploitable resource, the focus has usually been on the attendant starvation and the miseries of reserve existence to the neglect of evidence of a tradition of ready economic and cultural accommodation.

There is ample evidence that economic and cultural reorientation was not new to the Bloods or other First Nations of the Treaty 7 area. Blackfoot scholar Betty Bastien considers the propensity for change as entirely natural and observes, "environmental and other natural changes were incorporated within the context of creation." Change and adaptation were rooted in Blackfoot being and should not be considered as surprising and unexpected.[95] Indeed, Blackfoot peoples in general reacted to "cosmological validation of adaptation and change."[96]

The acquisition of the horse and firearms clearly pointed out the adaptive economic strategies of the Blackfoot in general. Once the 'whites' and their trade wares arrived, the buffalo transcended its use as what Shepherd Krech III referred to as "a tribal department store."[97] Elizabeth Vibert has pointed out that from the mid-eighteenth to the mid-nineteenth centuries, the Blood were involved in contests over "territory in the mounting struggle for horses, firearms, hides and furs." The Blackfoot, in a determined effort to protect their good economic fortune, achieved ascendancy on the western Plains by the 1780s and 1790s. Blackfoot fortunes, however, fluctuated as rival groups also acquired guns and horses.[98]

It was keen adaptation to the horse in particular that changed Blood and Blackfoot trading strategy. Ray points out that during the early eighteenth century the Blackfoot made the long trip to York Factory on Hudson's Bay, an arduous thousand-mile journey that lasted three months, to trade.[99] Bloody confrontations between the Blackfoot and Cree centred on horses, and the ebb and flow of control was based on a continuous supply of both horses and guns.[100] As historian Olive Dickason has perceptively pointed out: "Apart from its usefulness for hunting and transport, the horse both extended and altered trade routes. Consequently, it became a symbol of wealth in its own right and, as always with the growth of affluence, polarized economic status both between individuals and between tribes."[101] It was the horse that occasioned the last great adaptive economic, social, and spiritual change in Blackfoot Indian culture until the collapse of the buffalo in the late nineteenth century.[102]

The Bloods, as did other Plains groups, made economic adjustments in response to the increased commodity value of buffalo robes and engaged in increased raiding and warfare to maintain their enhanced economic status. Buffalo robes became the focus of the Blackfoot hunt, producing up to 100,000 per year for the HBC and Fort Benton trade. Kennedy argues that when Plains Natives fully grasped the importance of the buffalo to the fur trade, it truly became an exploitable resource. Through trade it could be turned into other desired commodities.[103] Fur trade historian John Foster argues that as a consequence of the buffalo robe trade "consumerism had become institutionalized in their [Native] cultures ... inextricably linked with cultural ways which identified individuals and families of social and political consequence."[104] It has been pointed out that, aside from buffalo, antelope, deer, and elk hides, wolf pelts were "an important element of the furs exchanged to whiskey traders," and according to one census wolves amounted to one tenth of the number of buffalo killed by Blood, Blackfoot, Peigan, and Sarsi.[105] The southern Alberta and southwestern Saskatchewan trading network was composed of over fifty posts, and no fewer than seventeen of these were in the area where the Bloods later located their reserve.[106] All of these posts did not exist concurrently but do highlight sustained economic activity in the area over time. It seems likely that the Bloods' choice for a reserve was, in part, based on varied economic activities occurring immediately before the Treaty 7 period.

Evidently the Bloods possessed great ability for economic accommodation in the face of dramatic change, and had successfully done so, well before being faced with the altered circumstances caused by the demise of the buffalo as an exploitable species. Raiding fur trade posts and theft and resale of the goods were at times important economic activities. Dickason observes that war too became an economic measure, a means to wealth and its attendant status.[107] Clearly the buffalo were not the sum total of Blackfoot and Blood economic or cultural activities. Just as they successfully adjusted to the arrival of Europeans, to the acquisition of the horse and gun, to the ascendancy and decline of rival nations and to continually altering trade routes and patterns, so they altered their economic behaviours in the face of the loss of the buffalo. Their economy and culture had been profoundly transformed by earlier events, as it would be by the latter. True, the 'golden years' of Plains culture disappeared with the destruction of the buffalo and in the short term a great deal of dislocation was evident.[108] In the long term, however, a certain resilience came to the fore. The collapse of the buffalo did not just have an economic dimension and as with other aspects of culture the possibility existed for adaptation to relieve the stress of that loss. Jill St. Germain has pointed out that during the negotiations for Treaty 7 the Blackfoot were as much concerned about their land and the protective presence of the North West Mounted Police as they were about the preservation of the few remaining buffalo.[109] It is difficult to believe that the Bloods were not well aware that in the future great adjustment on their part would be required. In the words of Chief Earl Old Person of the Blackfeet, "'Our ability to adapt to the environment and to changes is infinite and assures our survival.'"[110]

Adaptation in the face of tremendous and traumatic change was broadly based and more complex than has been previously realized. Macleod and Rollason argue, "there is quite a lot of evidence that the Natives adopted an instrumental approach to the law; experimenting with it and using it where it seemed useful" even for resolving "inter-band and familial conflicts," which in earlier times would have been settled more traditionally.[111] Spindler and Spindler have observed that the Bloods have been able to "retain traditional cultural features ... and at the same time make a viable adaptation to white culture and society."[112] Brown and Peers sustain the argument for successful adaptation "from a nomadic to a settle lifestyle" because of the tenacity and adaptability of the population and strength of its leadership.[113]

The predisposition to shift economic strategies was evident in the terms of Treaty 7 and revealed in the subsequent relatively hasty selection of reserves and calculated move to a sedentary existence. Clearly the treaty clauses regarding education, cattle, farming, and implements, to name but a few, reinforces the fact that the Bloods had accepted reality and determined to move on. They most assuredly lamented that the buffalo were gone but looked to a post-buffalo period in which the beneficence of the government and the money economy offered different prospects for wealth and well-being. The fact that they had the intention of sharing and not selling the land and that elders claim that surface rights were never surrendered lends some credence to claims that they were in time, if not immediately, prepared to creatively meet new challenges.[114]

Maureen Lux, in her study *Medicine That Walks*, has pointed to the non-buffalo economy in which the Blackfoot traded for foods in order to maintain a balanced diet. Among the sought-after foods were onion bulbs, blue camas, and cow parsnip or 'Indian celery,' and prairie turnip. Besides these roots, wild fruits and berries comprised an important element of the diet as the Blackfoot are reported to have used some forty plant species in all.[115] Binnema observes of both the pre-equestrian and equestrian periods that gathering activities, as well as the exploitation of alternate species such as elk, deer, and bighorn sheep, occurred in conjunction with the pursuit of buffalo.[116] The severe food crisis following Treaty 7 likely prompted hasty attempts at modifying approaches to satisfying dietary needs that harkened back to earlier food-gathering traditions. Both John C. Ewers and Binnema point out that trade on the northern Plains was more than just a fur trade and was likely carried on for centuries before the arrival of Whites. Accordingly, Ewers suggests that there is no evidence that the purpose of Blackfoot warlike behaviour was to expand hunting territory, and that indeed the reasons for inter-tribal warfare were varied. Binnema suggests war was a reaction to stress and was undertaken reluctantly because of the few tangible rewards to be gained.[117]

Ranchers, and later settlers, entered this region with preconceived notions about its climate and about how the environment could best be made to serve their various interests. The Bloods too were forced to rethink their strategies regarding the utility of the land and the bounty it offered as "part of an internally validated process of adaptation to new circumstances."[118] Precipitation, temperatures, water resources, and soil ultimately determined that without artificial assistance such as irrigation, the area was best suited to ranching. How many cattle to how much land, however, remained problematic even while providing the Bloods with employment and income opportunities. The abundant resource of coal did much to determine the economy of the region and the Bloods' place in it. Reserve, ranch and farm, town and village were adaptations to a common environment that required and encouraged co-operation. Beneath the veneer of the frequent expressions of Natives as a race in the process of extinction, there was subtle recognition of Native persistence accompanied by the realization of the need for neighbourly accommodation. The subsequent relationship between the Bloods and their neighbours was not without its tribulations, but it endured despite fracture and fissure because its benefits were necessary to the well-being of both. The glue for this paradigm was the need to adapt and the desire to acquire a modicum of economic security, however limited in its realization.

A matter requiring some attention is the problem for the modern reader to appreciate dollar values for the period under study. How does one, for example, translate turn of twentieth-century dollars into a meaningful value? Although it is not possible to be exact in this regard, it is possible, fortunately, to achieve some appreciation for changes in the currency values over time. James Powell's *History of the Canadian Dollar* is a fitting place to start. Powell states, for example, that one dollar in 1914 (the first year for which consumer price data are available) had the purchasing power of $17.75 in 2005 dollars. He notes that even with a modest inflation rate of 2 per cent "a dollar will lose half of its purchasing power in approximately 35 years." However, by using the gross domestic product deflator and the Consumer Price Index, which "tend to move together over time" Powell calculates that one dollar in 1870 is roughly equivalent to $26.70 in today's money.[119]

Powell offers a glimpse of purchasing power for the Canadian dollar during much of the period of this study, illustrating that the purchasing power of the dollar decreased from 1900 to 1929 but increased in 1933 and had declined again by the mid-1940s. The cost of a dozen eggs, for example, increased from twenty-six cents in 1900, to forty-five cents in 1914 and to sixty-five cents in 1929. In 1933, however, the cost of a dozen eggs had declined again to forty-five cents. There were similar changes in prices for other basic foods such as meat, bread, butter, and milk.[120] This brief elucidation should provide the reader with some sense of the cost of items and the value of money and wages for the period under discussion. Those wishing a more sophisticated economic analysis should consult the *Historical Statistics of Canada*, edited by Urquhart and Buckley.[121]

This book is arranged thematically rather than chronologically, although each separate chapter is generally chronological within itself. This seemed the most sensible approach as each chapter's topics is best dealt with as a self-contained unit. It was also the most effective and least confusing way to deal with the transitions from one topic to another given the lengthy timeframe of the study and the diverse topics dealt with, for example, the lease of reserve land and the Bloods' initiatives regarding commodity sales such as hay and coal and their relations with local businesses.

2: 'Free Range or Private Property': Integrating Blood Reserve Land into the non-Native Economy

INTRODUCTION

Once the Blood reserve was established and occupied, there was considerable pressure on the Bloods to lease their reserve land to non-Native neighbours. This pressure was tied to the often-expressed opinion that the Bloods possessed land in excess of their needs and more than they were entitled to hold. Such belief was encouraged by the influx of land-hungry settlers in the southern Alberta region. The Bloods and their leaders, however, refused to recognize the legitimacy of these views. They were also reluctant to recognize arbitrary attempts by the Department of Indian Affairs to unilaterally determine the disposition of Blood property. The Bloods, and often their agents, were determined to guide the reserve's economic development in tandem with the DIA's course of *civilization* for the Bloods. However, one fact remains clear, during the development of the economy of the region between 1880 and 1939, there was little, if any, decline in demands by non-Natives for access to the reserve and its resources. Under such circumstances, the Bloods' perseverance, and the guardianship responsibility of the DIA for the Bloods and their property, was put to the test.

This chapter has two interrelated themes. The first is a discussion of changing perceptions of the economic value and utility of land in southern Alberta.[1] Integral to this analysis is a recognition that increased demands for more land resulted from these changes. Consequently, the Blood reserve was integrated into the non-Natives' land-use schemes. Although the focus here is on a small region of southern Alberta, these changes were but a microcosm of larger trends in land use affecting the Great Plains region of the continent.[2] The second theme is centred on the decision-making procedures employed by the Bloods and the DIA to determine the role the reserve played in local land-use plans.

An important and largely unexplored aspect of this economic agenda for Native reserves is the management of land and resources. The reserves were central to the overall policy of having Natives pay their own way. However, this raises the question why the use of the Bloods' land was so often manipulated to suit the needs or demands of non-Native neighbours, despite Blood protests. The Blood people clearly understood their neighbours' desires and the government's intentions and only their staunch defence of their rights prevented more interference in reserve affairs. The Bloods were not reluctant to enlist the aid of their agents in attempts to repeal or soften the DIA's determination to adhere to its set *civilization* and assimilation agenda. In conjunction with their agents, the Blood chiefs, headmen, and concerned individuals achieved some success in influencing the policies that were to affect them. Their efforts ensured that their will could not be entirely ignored.

Pressures resulting from competition for space, initially among ranchers, and subsequently by increasing population and environmental factors, brought about the first attempts to gain access to the resources of the Blood reserve. The onset of farming and mixed farming in turn increased the demand for the land of the reserve, while competition from settlers and towns near the reserve placed additional pressures on the reserve's borders. By the first decade of the twentieth century, the Blood reserve faced demands not only from non-Natives but also from the Bloods' own economic development objectives. The Bloods' awareness of the reserve's economic value also influenced the development of access policies. These contending forces, in one form or another, carried through to the end of the Great Depression.

The Bloods may properly be seen as important players in the local economic activities into which their land base was integrated. The non-Native view of the Bloods and their reserve was as resources that could be used either to relieve the growing need for more land or, alternatively, exploited for the benefits of the neighbouring non-Native community. The Bloods' decisions, and those of the Department of Indian Affairs on their behalf, to a large degree determined the character of the ranching industry and later the mixed farming enterprise in the southern Alberta locale surrounding the Blood reserve. Eventually the Blood tribe, by leasing their land to those in need of extra grazing or hay range and through attempts to forestall illegal access, helped determine the nature of the resultant economic association.

The second theme regards decision making by the Bloods. Such decisions, often communicated through their reserve agent and the DIA, also determined the role the reserve played in unfolding local circumstances. The main economic objective for administering Natives was to make them economically self-sufficient or at least 'self-supporting' to the extent of reducing costs to the DIA.[3] The government believed that the best way to achieve this end was to encourage the Indians to become 'peasant farmers' on forty-acre lots and thus to make more appropriate 'civilized' use of their land.[4] The DIA imposed paternalistic regulations on the Bloods and their land, necessitating calculated and determined responses from the Bloods. Clearly, with competing interests vying for access to Blood reserve land much antagonism developed. However, it was never sufficient to deter a melding and mutuality of economic interests and endeavours. In the face of change required by the loss of the buffalo and non-Native incursions into traditional Blood lands, the Bloods worked out patterns of accommodation.

INITIAL ARRANGEMENTS: THE RANCHING ERA

Indians, and in the case of the Bloods, their extensive land holdings, have not been credited with any positive formative or lasting influences on ranching commerce. Shelagh Jameson remarked that the Blood Indians were, because of their poverty following the decimation of the Plains bison, "probably the greatest potential danger" to early cattle interests.[5] Kelly opined, for example, that Natives "stole cattle when they willed."[6] It is important to recognize that this danger was never truly realized, and historians have generally rescued the Natives from the negative impression left by often groundless complaints of a small minority of ranching interests regarding the part played by Natives in the destruction of range cattle.[7] Indeed Macleod and Rallason have proven that such views of Native peoples cannot be sustained. Natives' rates of crime, including livestock theft, "were lower than for the rest of the population."[8]

The incursion of large- and small-scale ranching interests, their operational needs and environmental suitability have been analyzed and detailed by Elofson and Evans. Elofson's view that the uncertainty of the environmental demands of business, especially that of showing a profit, leads to the conclusion that the Blood reserve could remain neither detached nor immune to environmental and economic processes ranching interests brought into play.[9]

Among the first of the large Canadian ranching concerns in the vicinity of the Blood reserve was the Cochrane Ranche Company, headed by Senator Matthew H. Cochrane. Cochrane had been instrumental in encouraging Sir John A. Macdonald's Conservative government to formulate legislation favouring ranching ventures. The resulting land lease arrangements of twenty-one years to a maximum of 100,00 acres per lease reflected the mid-1880s belief, based on previous Plains exploration, that the region was fit only for a grazing economy.[10]

As significant parcels of public land in the North West Territories were taken in, leasehold demand for grazing space grew. The *Macleod Gazette*, April 28, 1893, revealed that 1,680,964 acres were given over to grazing on the prairies. The numbers of stock on these lands were given at 139,283 cattle, 20,579 horses, and 86,087 sheep.[11] In fact, during their peak the four largest ranching enterprises leased nearly one-third of land in the southwestern prairies, practically all the foothills region from Cochrane south being held in lease or homestead.[12]

Encouraged by initial favourable Canadian government legislation Cochrane cattle were on the Bow River in late 1881.[13] This heralded the arrival of large cattle interests, businesses that leased tens of thousands of acres of land and ran herds of cattle numbering in the tens of thousands. These large concerns directly competed with the small stock holders, many of whom engaged in mixed farming and ran small herds of up to forty cattle, which now found their positions considerably weakened.[14] The large Blood Reserve bordering the Cochrane lease grant on the east, and separated only by the Belly River, must certainly have looked inviting in the face of competitive pressure. As a result, the reserve soon figured prominently in the Cochrane Company's operational planning.

Cochrane Ranche cattle, driven by the need for more land, were already grazing the Blood Reserve in 1885 after an informal contract was initiated with the Bloods.[15] As early as 1884 grazing land was at a premium, and by 1885 all land bordering the reserve on the north and west was leased.[16] By 1886 significant blocks to the east of the reserve were taken and by this time there were an estimated 100,000 range cattle grazing four million acres of leased land. The Cochrane Ranche, the only large company with unimpeded access to the Bloods' land, regarded the reserve as a natural extension of their own grazing lease, an approach later taken by many settlers bordering the reserve.[17] The company was also driven to extend its competitive edge in the face of stock losses in the thousands in the first years of operation brought on by poor management decisions worsened by bad weather.[18] Similar future experiences continued to stimulate demands for hay.[19]

It soon became brutally clear that, contrary to ranchers' first impressions, the apparently limitless land was indeed limited and so was its cattle-sustaining capacity. The same range could not be used for summer and winter foraging, and it could not be used at all during extended dry periods or if ravaged by fire as during the winter of 1884–85. Evans has commented on the very complex relationship that exists between 'carrying capacity,' the number of animals, relative "timing and intensity" of grazing as well as precipitation and the fact that "biomass of a particular plant community is fine-tuned to climate." Early ranching interests were aware of this relationship and tried to accommodate environmental cycles to conserve grass supplies.[20]

It was this immediate circumstance that necessitated the initial arrangement with the Blood tribe, namely the need to graze Cochrane cattle on the south end of the reserve because of the burned ground on the north end of the Cochrane lease. From the Bloods' perspective, the agreement was essential because their attempts to keep Cochrane cattle from invading the unfenced reserve had been futile. After some difficulty caused by the absence of the influential Chief Red Crow from the initial negotiations, a deal was struck. The benefits were soon apparent, Cochrane later reporting that the cattle were doing well on the reserve's good feed.[21]

Subsequent arrangements followed when, in February, 1890, Blood Agent William Pocklington, initiated a meeting between Red Crow and W.F. Cochrane regarding a further accommodation for Cochrane cattle. Red Crow voiced no opposition to grazing Cochrane cattle on reserve land, and even expressed a willingness to forgo payment. He cited as his reason the fact that Cochrane cattle were used to supply the Blood beef rations.[22] Red Crow's understanding of the relationship between his people and the Cochrane Ranche Company, *vis-à-vis* the Department of Indian Affairs, is unclear. It is possible that Red Crow incorrectly felt that the source of the Bloods' rations came with obligations to the company. A similar arrangement for the placement of two hundred cattle on the reserve was concluded in August of 1890, but this time the company agreed to purchase all the hay Blood farmers and harvesters could provide. By December, however, Cochrane Ranche relations with the Bloods had soured. Agent

image not available

Figure 2.1.
"Men on Blood Reserve putting up hay for Cochrane Ranche, Alberta, [ca. 1892]." Glenbow Archives, NA-4461-1. Blood farmers and labourers meeting some of the demand for hay from the Cochrane Ranche, one of the Blood reserve's neighbours.

image not available

James Wilson, likely with the Bloods' encouragement, requested that the company remove its cattle from the reserve or face "less agreeable" means of encouragement to do so.[23]

The value of the Blood Reserve's significant open spaces were, by 1891, recognized by other ranchers and illegal incursions onto the reserve land became frequent. When Indian Commissioner Hayter Reed visited the reserve, Blood representatives complained about cattle illegally placed on their land and demanded their removal. Agent Pocklington duly wrote the Maunsell Brothers, Macleod, requesting removal of their stock, and similar requests were made of at least eleven others who the agent believed to be the offenders including the Cochrane Ranche Company. Agent Pocklington reported that responses were favourable.[24]

Such incursions were not easily prevented despite the assurances of the offending parties to remedy the problem. In the case of small stock-men and homesteaders these offences, at least in the view of the offenders, were necessary. David H. Breen points out that, after the advent of the commercial ranching ventures with their large areas of leases, small ranchers with little capital were left with no option except speculative ranging on increasingly limited free space.[25] Homesteaders and townsfolk, in the search of subsistence and profits therefore lacked adequate 'free space' to increase the scale of their operations. Sitting on the borders of and, in their view, the underutilized Blood reserve, it was natural for settlers to regard the area as part of their sphere of exploitation. After a complaint by Blood Indian Day Chief about the unauthorized grazing of stock in the area around Boundary Creek, Agent James Wilson detected some prevarication on the part of the settler/owners, believing that despite their protested need of right of way "there is not the slightest doubt that these men mean to hold their stock on the Reserve."[26]

Little wonder that, by 1893, Agent Wilson believed the area in the vicinity of the reserve was "over[run] with cattle."[27] Trespass, and apparently the DIA's reduced rations policy, frustrated many of the Blood Reserve's residents, and they angrily resorted to expelling cattle from the reserve, straining relations with ranchers and settlers still further and inevitably receiving the blame for cattle losses that could be ascribed to other factors.[28] As Elofson points out, the fact of open range and easy access likely coloured perceptions against the Indians.[29] In March 1893, as Macleod and Rollason point out, the *Gazette* ignoring its own evidence and exaggerating Native complicity railed against Indians roaming the countryside killing cattle and called for the enforcement of the pass system. The

Gazette was willing to see the establishment of a punitive system that restricted Native rights and liberties and opined that "any Indian found off his reserve without a pass, should be promptly arrested."[30] Needless to say, such restrictive laws were not intended to be applied to settlers trespassing the Blood reserve.

At times adverse environmental conditions affected the reserve, as in a severe dry spell in the fall of 1894, and heightened Blood ranchers' concern for their substantial horse herds and their rudimentary cattle interests begun when three "influential men" exchanged horses for twenty-three head of cattle.[31] Not only could the Bloods not offer relief to others but they were themselves forced to seek off-reserve grazing, thereby bringing them into direct competition with settlers and ranchers looking for assistance through grazing their stock on Dominion lands. The non-Native community's reluctance to accept that Native ranchers had equal access to non-leased Dominion lands between the Belly and Kootenai rivers brought Agent Wilson to their defence. Wilson cited hardship and expected loss of stock if Dominion lands were denied the Bloods. He reminded critics that in similar circumstances in previous years, the Blood tribe had generously permitted stricken non-Natives access to the reserve. Consequently, the Bloods could not be expected to forsake the only conveniently available free range in their own hour of need. In conclusion, he summed up the Bloods' view: "the Indians all very truly say it will be time enough for the white people to kick after they have taken their cattle off the reserve."[32]

Within the area around the Blood reserve, both co-operation and competition forged an economic relationship based on land use and need. From its inception, the Bloods had seen their reserve drawn into the pool of grazing land to which ranchers and settlers expected access. The treaty rights of the Bloods to sole utilization had been largely ignored, even under strenuous protest, as circumstances beyond the reserve required. Contractual arrangements, when resorted to, were of a nature deemed by ranchers as informal, and in many cases no such arrangements were attempted. The Bloods complained and the agents, within the limits of their capacity, or will, acted. Attitudes and exigencies, however, militated against easy or permanent solutions. No man-made physical structure set the Blood reserve apart. Furthermore, non-Natives did not regard the Belly and St. Mary's Rivers as borders delineating absolute separation of the reserve from grazing leases and the commons or land that was an open exploitable resource. It would take the Bloods' own strategies and persistence to make the border more recognizable and impermeable.

THE BLOODS TAKE CONTROL

During the first decade and a half after the reserve was established, it offered limited accommodation to the grazing needs of neighbouring ranchers. The results were, however, far from satisfactory, and resulted, in June 1895, in a shift in policy. The pressure exerted on reserve lands by its location in a "grazing district" and the inability to stop livestock trespass dictated that a readjustment in the relationship between the Bloods and their neighbours be attempted.[33] At the limits of their endurance, and likely concerned about the well-being of their own small cattle herd, Blood leaders were determined to forge a more formal and financially rewarding relationship with those companies or individuals wishing to use reserve land and resources.[34]

Consequently, Agent Wilson identified two classes of trespass and trespassers needing to be addressed: 1. those invading the reserve in search of feed; 2. those unable to confine their stock to their own lands. The former posed the greatest threat, and chief among the villains, in Wilson's opinion, were the Mormon settlers of Cardston. To counter the problems, Wilson intended charging grazing dues for summer and winter grazing. The levying of dues would, he anticipated, make owners more cautious about the whereabouts of their stock and substantially reduce the first kind of trespass. Wilson assumed, with good reason, that as the Bloods acquired more cattle of their own they would take more interest in keeping the stock of others at bay.[35] Wilson had little trouble convincing Red Crow and his followers of the soundness of his plan.[36]

The negative response from potential trespassers to the proposed change was much as Wilson had anticipated and indicated a determined reluctance among ranchers and settlers to pay for that which they had previously often acquired for free. Chief Red Crow denied any knowledge of an arrangement with one settler, and Wilson asserted: "Red Crow says ... he never gave you any authority to put your cattle on [the reserve] and does not see why payment should be refused."[37] However, Cardston's residents proved to be most difficult. In January 1897, Charles O. Card, the leader of the Cardston settlers, wrote Wilson requesting an exemption from grazing dues of fifty cents per head per annum for the previous season.[38] This attempt to achieve a better deal was based on the argument that the Cardston settlers owned mostly dairy cattle, which grazed only during the day and therefore consumed less feed than range cattle. To further complicate matters, Wilson, believing that some of the settlers were poor, recommended to the Commissioner of Indian Affairs that those who could afford it be charged at fifteen cents per head for half a year, while the others would be given free grazing.[39] How the Bloods responded to this proposal can only be imagined. However, Wilson's caution to Cardston residents against putting cattle on the reserve without a licence to do so probably sheds some light on the Bloods' response.[40]

There was also other potential for loss of grazing revenue. The files reveal that seventeen individuals had placed fifty-one cattle for which dues had been paid, but there were 130 cattle still to be collected on for a total of 181.[41] This accounting did not include those owned by larger concerns such as the Oxley Ranche that brought the total to 968 head.[42] The easily breached reserve boundaries, the termination by the federal government of the no settlement leases and the election of Wilfrid Laurier's Liberal government with its settler-friendly policies in 1896 gave added impetus to the assault on the reserve's integrity.[43]

The Bloods, however, were battling more than reluctant pocket books in their attempt to collect grazing dues. They often fell victim to the bottom line and to the attitudes many Anglo-Canadian settlers held towards Native peoples at this time. In July 1897, Wilson successfully collected dues from A.R. Springett, New Oxley Ranche Company "under protest." In Agent Wilson's opinion, Springett believed that because the reserve was unfenced the Bloods could not legally claim grazing dues for cattle wandering onto it or placed within its borders. Despite several conversations, Agent Wilson was unable to convince Springett of the legitimacy of the Bloods' request.[44] While he conceded that the lack of reserve fence contributed to the problem, Wilson argued that Indians, unlike other settlers, were under no obligation to fence their land. Why he took this view is unclear, but he was likely referring to the logistics and cost of fencing over five hundred square miles of land. He also pointed out that the Indian Act contained a section that protected reserves against trespass. Wilson further realized that if such attitudes from ranchers were countenanced to any degree "our Reserve would soon be over run." He refuted the argument, from ranchers, that living in stock range country brought special privileges with regard to the Blood reserve. Wilson, in argument, expressed his view that "the Indians['] Reserve is not free range but private property" for which use payment was required or alternatively ranchers would be threatened with having their cattle dispersed.[45]

The frequency with which the Bloods had difficulty collecting legitimate grazing dues suggests forces at work other than the mere inability to pay.[46] Attempts to collect monies owed resulted in evasion and denial of obligation. One possible explanation is that ranchers faced with the sod-buster invasion, and the attendant shrinkage of accessible Dominion lands, were driven to seek out alternate space and to protect grazing land through the setting aside of stock water reserves; that is, land with accessible water reserved for the use of cattle. There is little doubt that such reserves were increasingly necessary to ranchers for, as Jones points out, at one place along the Belly River, homesteaders' fences "blocked access to water for thirty continuous miles, rendering useless 30,000 acres of grazing land."[47]

The western Plains, however, eventually became a lure to many others who saw their economic salvation and prosperity in the vast open spaces. Thus by the 1890s ranchers needed no convincing that the increased settler demand for land threatened the survival of their operations. The hostility of farmer settlers, and the public alike, to the cattle ranchers had resulted in the federal government announcement in 1891 of the planned termination of all closed leases by the end of 1896.[48] Land grants to the Calgary and Edmonton Railway, in 1892, both reduced and disrupted the leases driving the tenants to seek other outlets.[49]

The election of the Liberals in 1896 saw the formation of a government sympathetic to both the wishes of farmers and the ideals of agrarian life. The Minister of the Interior, Clifford Sifton, actively supported the establishment of irrigation projects to increase settlement and prairie agricultural potential.[50] Only the creation of stock water reserves around crucial bodies of water and the prohibition of settlement ensured the continued viability of ranching enterprises in many areas. Nevertheless, the heady optimism and security of lease tenure that had initially attracted large-scale ranching to the southern Alberta area in particular, and to the west in general, was not sustained.

Ultimately, however, the security promised by such reserves proved transitory. Immigration was a driving force that threatened to displace ranchers. Little wonder that hard-pressed ranchers neighbouring the Bloods looked to the reserve to alleviate some of their growing concerns over inadequate pasture. The combination of irrigation technology and the science of dry-land farming, notes Andy den Otter, brought a "consensus among politicians, businessmen, and settlers ... that the rangelands were suitable for cultivation."[51] Government policies reinforcing this belief had been put into place and when dry-land techniques failed to meet expectations in years of drought, mixed farming, Paul Voisey points out, came to be touted, though erroneously, as an even better way to successfully cultivate the prairie.[52]

The rapidly growing population and surging economy in the period 1896–1913 were, in part, due to Clifford Sifton.[53] Sifton, as Liberal Minister of the Interior between 1896 and 1905, envisioned western agricultural development based on an expanding immigrant population that would eventually people the prairies with fifteen to twenty million new citizens.[54] The trickle that began in the 1890s became a deluge by the first decade of the twentieth century.[55] Two or more persons per square mile, for example, occupied all townships bordering the Blood reserve, by 1906.[56] By way of illustration, the Annual Royal North West Mounted Police for Fort Macleod for 1904 reported 329 entries for homesteads at the Fort Macleod land office from January 1 to November 30 and further observed that "In the Pincher Creek district, within a radius of twenty miles from the town, there is no land available for homesteading, some 200 settlers having taken up land there during the year."[57] Although the numbers envisioned by Sifton never materialized, government advertising that promised "fat black land, cheap or even free, in the region of sufficient rainfall" lured hundreds of thousands.[58]

Under pressure of expanding population demands, the Blood reserve came to be regarded, by many, as open territory to which settlers had a right without obligation. The view that the open expanse of the reserve was thus available reduced some of the anxiety and pressure caused by increasing settlement and reinforced the notion of boundless space.[59] This position was possible, however, only with the denial of the Bloods' equality as people, and their equality in possession of property. In this the settlers were buoyed by their own sense of superiority, and the Indian Act, which had established the legal wardship status of the Indians. Clearly some ranchers and settlers were determined to frustrate the Bloods' decision to set the agenda for reserve grazing privileges. They believed that the Blood tribe's claim to the land was not inviolate, that they were underutilizing it, and therefore stood in the way of progress and the settlers' own pressing needs.

The ranchers' fear and loathing of the newly developing agrarian frontier and its farmers illustrated the absolute necessity of the Blood reserve for grazing land. The *Cardston Record*, which observed in August, 1898, that over a hundred homestead entries had been made at the Cardston land office during the summer, highlighted this desire. The result was that once-abundant grazing land was "converted into prosperous farms and ranches.

Hundreds of miles of fence have been erected; hundreds of houses have been built and thousands of head of cattle and horses now subsist upon grass."[60] It was this process that had, by the turn of the twentieth century, compromised intuitive ranching practices so that alternating grazing land as a conservation measure was largely terminated.[61]

Now the cattle and horses of the homesteader, as well as the rancher, became a matter of concern for the Blood ranchers, farmers, haymakers, and reserve residents in general. Wilson warned local cattle owners that they would be forced to keep their stock off reserve land.[62] There were, of course, occasions when horses or cattle strayed onto the reserve, but the numbers that were continually brought to Wilson's attention could not simply be attributed to accidental straying.[63] Likely the expansive size of the reserve led some to believe that they could acquire free grazing either without being discovered or before being eventually discovered. Homesteaders, while making the agrarian ethos as much a reality as possible and engaging in land speculation ventures when opportunities existed, themselves demanded land use beyond the boundaries of their inadequate 160-acre quarter sections.[64]

By 1899 the pressure on public land caused by the declining acreage of open range was clear, as was the belief among non-Natives of their preeminent right to what little remained.[65] The attitude of one rancher/settler named Hillier put the issue in sharp relief. Hillier complained that Indians grazed their horses off the reserve, consuming grass essential to ranchers while keeping the reserve closed to non-Native-owned cattle. In Hillier's view the Indians' stock should be confined to the limits of the reserve or "ranchers should have equal privileges on the Reserve, that the Indians have off it." Not surprisingly Hillier did not see any reciprocal obligation for non-Natives to also keep their cattle on their own land. Amazingly, DIA Secretary J.D. McLean agreed with Hillier instructing Agent James Wilson to restrict Blood stock to the reserve.[66] In the interests of the non-Natives, the Bloods were to be denied the use of the commons.

Much to his credit, however, Wilson believed that the Blood right to equal use of public domain was protected by treaty. In a letter to McLean, he indignantly questioned the settlers' claim to preferential treatment. Wilson's query struck a sensitive nerve and eventually legal opinion bore out Wilson's observation that Indians had the same rights as others and that both Indians and ranchers required a permit if they wished to graze their stock on government lands. "Though the practice of using Dominion lands be prevalent with white men in the Territories," Law Clerk Reginald

Rimmer observed, "they can have no ground of complaint against the Indians while they themselves are wrong doers."[67]

Implementing a dues structure proved to be no panacea for controlling the use or abuse of the reserve. In a further effort to reduce conflict between the Bloods and their neighbours and to curb illegal cattle trespass, a barbed wire fence was constructed along the reserve's southern boundary with Cardston in 1899. The easy destruction of the fence, along with the difficulty in getting the Cardston settlers to pay their grazing dues, led to Wilson's advice, no doubt prompted by the Bloods, to discontinue the settlers' grazing privileges.[68] The fence, in Wilson's view, had been deliberately cut to permit "stock to pass of[f] and on the reserve at pleasure."[69]

The records for 1902 reveal that numerous people or groups had legitimate reserve grazing privileges at this time. A report on the leases for 1903 shows that some 6,750 cattle inhabited the reserve under lease arrangements, of one sort or another, with the Bloods. Agent Wilson noted of these lessees that Wallace and Hauks had not paid dues, Sergeant Hilliard had no grazing permit, and although Wilson allowed Hilliard's cattle on the reserve, he could not convince him to pay his dues.[70] Considering Wilson's concern over the lessees' "habit" of removing stock from the reserve in contravention of the Indian Act, and their continued evasion of the understandings contained in grazing agreements and permits, the outcome could be predicted.[71]

CIRCUMSTANCE AND CHANGE

In response to growing problems with grazing leases, the Blood leadership again changed their reserve lease policies. In 1903 the tribe cancelled the grazing permits of local homesteaders and ranchers, preferring instead to lease excess reserve grazing capacity to one or two large companies. The easier supervision of the land and prevention of illegal trespass and theft were necessary given the Bloods' own substantial cattle and horse interests of around 5,000 animals in total.[72] Although clearly warranted, the new policy was bound to receive a poor reception from homesteaders bordering the reserve.

Such encouragement of large leaseholders was in fact a return to the practices of the pre-homestead days. The Bloods were deliberately flying in the face of the agrarian development that had already taken place and were attempting to reverse the trend that helped bring about the end of the large lease era. A.A. Lupton argues that ranching on the range in the Fort

Macleod area finished in 1903 and Lethbridge followed suit in 1905.[73] The result of the Bloods' action was inevitably to threaten, or stifle, the ambitions of settlers with small holdings who desired to engage in mixed farming and to expand their cattle operations. The Bloods, for their part, simply wished to halt the plundering of their property.[74]

The first agreement under the new leasing arrangement was with the Donald McEwan Company of Brandon, Manitoba. The lease restricted the company cattle to the east and south areas of the reserve and committed the company to graze a maximum of 7,000 cattle for ten years for $5,000 a year. Importantly, the lease also contracted the company to purchase seven hundred tons of hay from Blood farmers, should they decide to supply it, and required that fences be kept in good repair to keep company and Blood stock apart. Blood cattle owners were free to graze their own stock as desired. The arrangement was exclusive to the company under the condition that it could not sublet.[75]

This contract, if effectively enforced, would, in effect, legally and practically sever the reserve from the surrounding ranching/mixed-farming environment for a ten-year period. The only possible avenue open to those settlers and ranchers still demanding grazing access to the reserve was an illegal invasion, which may account for the destruction of some reserve fencing during 1903.[76] The new arrangement was also eminently more profitable for the Bloods than the old arrangements, if for no other reason than there was unlikely to be a default on lease payments. Hugh Dempsey points out that the going rate for an Indian Department lease at this time was two cents per acre while the Blood lease was closer to one and one quarter cents per acre.[77]

The impact on other potential users of the exclusive arrangement with the McEwan Co. was immediately evident, and it drove some Cardston residents to attempt an alternate lease acquisition of three thousand acres through an appeal to the Honourable Clifford Sifton. The Blood tribe, however, "absolutely opposed" approval of this effort.[78] Despite the Bloods' clearly expressed wishes to the contrary, the Department's intention was to grant the Cardston settlers grazing privileges without further reference to the Bloods.[79] The Bloods were not pleased, believing that Cardston's residents had enjoyed years of free grazing despite Agent Wilson's repeated efforts to collect moneys owed. Even though not paying lease dues, the Mormons' latest effort intended to establish a closed lease "excluding Indians as well as others from making use of the land," and they were even looking to the possibility of acquiring some reserve land through purchase.[80]

Dissenting voices among the Bloods "complained of being annoyed by white men seeking to secure possession or the use of the land." Indeed, the "self-supporting squad," as the financially independent residents of the reserve were called, questioned the legitimacy of the McEwan lease.[81] These individuals saw their own interests compromised by the influx of 7,000 lease cattle that would further tax the reserve's resources. Their fears were substantiated. The McEwan company was soon interpreting its lease agreement liberally and with callous disregard permitted its cattle to roam the reservation and threaten the Bloods' much-needed hay supplies.[82]

In 1903 the Blood reserve sustained cattle in numbers that met or exceeded Agent Wilson's estimate of capacity at eight to ten thousand head. The Blood cattle owners themselves grazed 3,000 head of horses and 3,000 head of cattle. Others grazed 6,750 head. Of this total, the Co-chrane Ranche had 3,000 head and the Mormons 250. Wilson's estimate was put to the test when on May 5, 1904, Donald McEwan & Company began placing cattle from Mexico on the reserve.[83] Taking Wilson's upper estimate as a reasonable number, the reserve was, even before the arrival of the McEwan herd, overstocked by 22.5 per cent or 2,750 animals. When one considers that illegal trespass was constant and sometimes consider-able, it is almost certain that, except for short periods around roundup and sale, the reserve was continually overstocked.[84] Grazing regulations for the West, issued by the Department of the Interior in 1905, stipulated a ratio of one cow or five sheep per twenty acres.[85] Should McEwan stock the lease to the 7,000 allowable limit, the approximate acreage required to hold all the stock was 395,000 acres, more than the reserve's total of approximately 350,000 acres.

The Bloods' move to consolidate their grazing leases coincided with public recognition of a shift in land use to mixed farming. However, the Bloods' views of the part they would play in this shift collided with the public's wishes. This trend placed added pressure on declining grazing space and signified that the ranching era had peaked.[86] Touted by govern-ment, business, press and public alike, conventional wisdom at this time held that the diversification in the use of a homestead's limited acreage, offered by mixed farming, was the key to farmer prosperity and the cure for the dangerous reliance on a one-crop system. Interestingly W.M. Elof-son has argued that, except for the initial period of ranching in the West, ranchers engaged in mixed farming to maximize benefits and to fulfill their needs.[87]

MIXED FARMING INTERLUDE

Despite the Bloods' lease to the McEwan Company in the view of the press, the 'dark years' for ranching were imminent.[88] The prediction proved all too credible as commercial agriculture and the disastrous winter of 1906/07 devastated large-scale ranching across the prairies.[89] The farms and fences that dotted the stockmen's former grazing range were a clear indication of the ranchers' declining importance. Helpless in the face of the advance of the fence, ranchers offered an unheeded note of caution about the suitability of the region for farming, warning that "If this land is homesteaded and farming is not a success, there is not only the one industry crippled, but two."[90] Historian Gerald Friesen, in echoing the ranchers' sentiments, calls the opening of this region to farming settlement "a great error in Canadian domestic policy."[91] The environmental limitations that were to restrict the agricultural potential of southwestern Alberta, however, were in the future. No amount of warning, especially from ranching interests, could dampen the heady expectation that agricultural diversification could bring the unlimited prosperity that wheat growing had so far denied.[92]

In November 1912, the *Macleod Spectator* expressed its view of the local situation. As far as the paper was concerned, single-crop agriculture such as wheat was now passé. Large-scale ranching, according to the *Spectator*, was at an end and at any rate both mixed farming and ranching were dependent on access to the Blood reserve. This eventuality the *Spectator* both promoted and anticipated.[93] The *Macleod Advertiser* reported that farmers of Cardston, Magrath, Raymond, Spring Coulee, and Lethbridge districts wanted big cattle leases stopped and the reserve land made available to all other interested parties through lease. This agitation was driven by the belief that the 350,000 acres of reserve was a suitable inducement to the expansion of local mixed farming enterprises.[94] For the *Spectator* mixed farming was the answer to the conundrum of ever-elusive prosperity in 'next year country,' especially now that the big ranches were "being cut up."[95] The hope for future prosperity lay in a "few cows and chickens," and the alienation of Blood land.[96]

It was, therefore, with considerable shock and apprehension that the *Macleod Advertiser* greeted the news in June 1912, that the Winnipeg-based company of Gordon, Ironsides & Fares was to take a ten-year lease on the available Blood reserve land and stock it with 17,000 cattle. The company was a major western beef producer and packing company that ran tens of thousands of cattle in Alberta and Saskatchewan on hundreds of thousands of acres of leased Crown land. Simultaneously Knight and Watson, a local company, was also given a lease.[97] Responding to the arrangement with Gordon, Ironsides & Fares, the *Macleod Advertiser* predicted a serious challenge to Fort Macleod's potential for growth as the lease pre-empted, for at least a decade, any possibility of acquiring the reserve through a surrender. Hence the town would remain hemmed in from the east by the Blood reserve and by the Peigan reserve to the southwest.[98]

Ignoring any benefits accruing to the Bloods from the lease, the *Advertiser* denigrated the cattle trade, which they saw as serving eastern markets and not western needs, while the *Spectator* trumpeted both the 'need' for mixed farming and for the "many thousands of [wasted] fat acres" of the Blood reserve.[99] Admitting entrenched and hostile Blood opposition to the proposed surrender, and expressing the mistaken but prevalent attitude that Indians were doomed to extinction, the *Spectator* speculated on the benefits of a ninety-nine-year lease. In the interim, disease would destroy the Bloods as a people and thus the most substantial stumbling block to Fort Macleod's growth would be resolved.[100] However, opposition to large leases developed not only in response to the lease policy on the Blood reserve. It was also a backlash against cattle barons like Pat Burns who had cornered the Alberta beef market and whose large leases, the paper believed, restricted the ability of mixed farming operations.[101]

There appears to have been great local demand for leased portions of the Blood reserve with the *Macleod Advertiser* reporting applications for 126,000 acres of reserve land.[102] One farmer in Magrath, for example, wanted 15,000 acres of reserve land, just two miles west of his farm, to go with the 320 acres of his homestead. If granted a twenty-year lease, he planned to stock it with cattle, horses, and sheep. Ever hopeful, the *Advertiser* reported that government officials, including Dr. W. Roche, Minister of the Interior, were in favour of leases being granted to local farmers, a contention not borne out by subsequent debate in the House of Commons.[103]

The agitation was, however, out of step with the desires of Blood leadership and band members. By 1913 they had accepted the fact that the large leases were preferable to general subletting, both for animal control and income, and so they rejected local bids to lease reserve land.[104] The tribe voted unanimously "to give *all* the grazing privileges possible" to Gordon Ironsides and Fares with a guarantee in place that the rental due the Bloods would never be less than $10,000 per year[105]

Though the *Cardston Globe* hoped that preaching would bring converts to the support of mixed farming, denial of reality and castigation of ranching were no sure means of expelling the cattle barons from the Blood Reserve.[106] On May 30, 1913, the *Globe* demanded that the lease held by Gordon, Ironsides & Fares be cancelled and the land be made available for general leasing. Resolutions to this effect came from farmers in the communities of Cardston, Magrath, Raymond, Spring Coulee, Lethbridge, and Orton, and the Bloods were said to be in favour.[107] This was wishful thinking given the Bloods' past experience with rent collection and illegal trespass and the recent election of Shot Both Sides, a staunch defender of the Bloods' rights, as chief. Ignored and thwarted, the locals eventually blamed their failure on the power of mammon: "The chiefs have been having a lot of long green bills of late and their attitude in opposition to the leasing of their lands to the small mixed farming may be explained thereby." In desperation, the *Globe* predicted that the lessees, because of their corruption, would not carry the day.[108]

Despite the predictions the Bloods renewed the Gordon, Ironsides and Fares lease in 1913. Dismayed, the *Spectator* reported that "not a single member of the tribe was in favor of the policy" of granting leases to small ranchers.[109] Given the previous coverage of this matter, one might expect the press to announce the death knell of mixed farming and small-scale ranching. Glen Campbell, Superintendent of Indian Agencies, told the *Spectator* that the Bloods opposed leases to small interests because it led to endless confusion. The tribe also appreciated the increasing value of their grazing and in the future, Campbell predicted, the rental would rise.[110]

The local press, however, continued to promote a different reality from that encouraged by the Bloods through their insistence on large lease grants. The impression now reinforced was that the West was full and space was at a premium.[111] The bounds of the homestead no longer sufficed to sustain a settler's financial ambitions and thus caused a movement towards expansion. Settlers on the Blood reserve's boundaries cast a covetous eye on its seemingly open and neglected spaces. Just as the reserve had alleviated pressure on overextended cattle herds in the past, it could now relieve the pressure on homesteads that were too small. The solution was for the government to open the Blood reserve to lease and rescue stockmen "forced to sell their cows and cut down their herds on account of the diminishing of the range."[112] To expect such a solution, however, was a denial of the history of relations with the Bloods and their intention not to surrender but instead to defend their own considerable interests. The Bloods' decision, in

March 1915, to renew the Gordon Ironsides and Fares lease, "if they meet our terms," of $10,000.00 per year for not more than 5,000 head of cattle on the reserve subject to a $2.00 per head penalty, reminded the locals of their inability to change the *status quo*.[113]

THE BLOODS' CONTINUED RESISTANCE

The full impact of the closure of the reserve to the surrounding community through restricted lease policies only became apparent as settlers determined to get through stealth what had been denied them by decision. By far the largest illegal breach of the reserve's integrity was the constant invasion of stray animals, especially horses. Serious problems with strays dated back to the early reserve years and had gotten progressively worse. Agent Dilworth reported in December 1914, that "With the coming of winter those ranchers living adjacent to the reserve on the north and east ... as has been their custom for 10 years past, have turned their horses onto the reserve for winter grazing." The practice had gone on unchecked for years and in 1913 Dilworth found strays sufficient to compromise the Bloods' interests.[114] Again in 1914, 234 strays were rounded up with between forty and fifty being eventually claimed by owners.[115] The Cardston *Globe*'s report, May 1916, of numbers of strays bearing the same brand suggests that some individuals were intentionally and illegally running their stock on the reserve. On this occasion the roundup netted ninety-four horses.[116] In January 1918, 195 horses were captured with at least seventeen bearing the same brand.[117] Agent Dilworth caused a momentary outcry when he impounded both stray horses and cattle and claimed a grazing fee of three dollars per head. On this occasion the numbers posed no apparent threat to the reserve's resources so Dilworth proposed accepting the animals for a grazing fee.[118] The offenders, meanwhile, had managed to acquire free grazing for their animals from the Bloods. The costs to the tribe and savings to the owners are difficult to evaluate, as there is no way to accurately determine how long some animals were on the reserve being fattened on free grass.[119]

In August, 1920, 102 animals found on the reserve were impounded.[120] The Alberta Provincial Police constable W.W. Henderson, Cardston, reported that some individuals went to great lengths to surreptitiously graze their cattle on the Bloods' land. As this was an offence under the Indian Act, some wrongdoers attempted to evade detection by resorting to the use of a hair brand.[121] Henderson declared that this tactic so incensed the

Bloods that they killed the strays in retaliation. He reported that three Indians were awaiting trial charged with this offence.[122] Meanwhile, the belief that reserve access was "essential to successful stock-raising in this district" continued, even though continually thwarted by the Bloods.[123]

A 1922 report to R.H. Campbell, Director of Forestry, Department of the Interior, suggests that grazing land continued to be at a premium and that large blocks of land, such as the Blood Reserve, could be critical in determining success or failure for ventures in mixed farming and stock ranching. Though the report focused on the use of forest ranges for grazing, the conclusions were equally applicable to the area around the Blood Reserve. In his report Campbell discussed several classes of 'ranchers': those with large economically viable acreages purchased when land was cheap, 'local' ranchers who mostly leased Dominion lands and who therefore had to live with the spectre of cancellation, those who farmed and ranched with about two hundred head of stock and limited pasture, and finally farmers who kept a few head of stock for home consumption. The general conclusion reached was that they all needed grazing land in addition to their holdings. The depressed markets, in conjunction with acute grazing shortages, led to intense pressure on forest reserves and other government lease lands.[124]

Substituting the term "Blood reserve" for "forest reserve" one immediately realizes that the same arguments had been made by all manner of ranchers and homesteaders living next to the Blood reserve since its inception. Though the report blamed the current depressed state of the industry on the drought beginning in 1917 and peaking in the winter of 1919–20 and the expense of feed requirements, these were problems produced by nature, not by a perceived need or a claim to the right to utilization.[125] Agent J.T. Faunt aptly summed up the apparent attitude of one homesteader, McGovern, charged with the abuse of reserve land: "He has some land just across the river from the Reserve & is running a herd of horses & cattle away out of proportion to his land holdings," Faunt wrote, "with the result that for years his stock have been running on the Reserve & in fact they were practically all raised on the Reserve & won't stay off."[126]

According to Indian Commissioner W.M. Graham, in 1922 there were sixteen leases on the Blood reserve, not counting the grazing leases and three other farming leases "of which you are aware." Because of Graham's wording, only six of these can be determined to have been paid up, four did not respond to inquiries and three had rent deferred or some owing. Some lessees, such as J.E. Neilson, sought longer leases but Agent Faunt suspected that they wanted to graze until the feed was gone and then abandon the lease, a fear not supported by Graham.[127] Most of these leases were likely holdovers granted without Blood consent as a consequence of the amendment to Section 90 of the Indian Act in 1918. This amendment permitted the government to implement its Greater Production Campaign, during World War I, by conscripting 'idle' land and resources on Native reserves. The Bloods were involuntarily conscripted into this program.[128] Hugh Dempsey suggests that the amendment was partly precipitated by the Blood refusal of a land surrender.[129] Locally, however, the *Macleod Times* still viewed securing grazing as "one of the vital problems of our farmers."[130]

WORLD WAR I AND GREATER PRODUCTION

For a brief interlude during and after World War I, the government imposed a land-use policy on some western Native tribes, including the Bloods. At best the government's agenda was a serious inconvenience to the Bloods; at worst, according to some accounts, there was a serious negative impact on the Bloods' economic well-being for decades to come. This Greater Production Program, introduced in 1918, was the brainchild of Inspector of Indian Agencies William Graham and grew out of the erroneous belief that some Native tribes had excess and unused lands that could be pressed into national service during the wartime emergency. The plan was aimed at the increased production of food to meet wartime needs. Graham pointed out to the government that his western inspectorate alone contained 340,000 acres of pasturage most of which, in his view, was unused. To facilitate the development of the program, Graham also noted that many Indian bands had "idle" money that could be conscripted in aid of implementing the Greater Production Plan. Consequently the Meighen Government amended the Indian Act, it being noted that the consent of the Natives with regard to their land and resources could be dispensed with. Graham was duly authorized to establish Greater Production farms on Indian reserves in the West. Included with the plan was the leasing of Indian lands to non-Indians for farming and grazing. Any proceeds from the program would accrue to the band after expenses were deducted.[131] At least one member of the House of Commons, however, noted that farmers with lands adjoining the reserves stood to benefit and that "there is something in connection with this enactment which does not seem square to the Indians."[132] Although of questionable necessity, the program was in keeping with the broad scope of power the government had appropriated to itself under the War Measures Act.

Under Greater Production surrender of 1918, the Bloods granted the government "the free use of whatever land on the Blood Indian reserve it may require for the greater production of food producing grains." Consequently 4,800 acres of Blood land was organized into a Greater Production farm and another 6,000 acres were granted to Whites as well as 90,000 acres given to grazing leases.[133] Ultimately the grazing leases were touted as the most profitable aspect of the entire greater production scheme.[134]

Although the government claimed much success with the program, there was little, if any, positive impact on the Bloods. All indications are that the Bloods were doing well agriculturally, and especially with their cattle and horse herds, before the implementation of the program and suffered considerable loss while the program remained in force. The problem arises in separating losses directly attributable to the Greater Production Plan from those caused by environmental factors. Regardless, the negative fallout during the period of Greater Production scheme was dramatic. With regard to cattle, for example, the Bloods had 4,406, 3,742, 2,074, 1,230, and 1,481 for the years 1918, 1919, 1920, 1921, and 1922, respectively. Clearly, cattle losses by 1921 and 1922 were tremendous. There was a similar dramatic decline in bushels of grain harvested with a high of 92,130 bushels harvested in 1917 and a low of 992 bushels in 1920, despite an increase in acres sown with 3,374 in 1917, while that for 1920 was 4,709. The horse herd experienced smaller fluctuating declines. Interestingly, a DIA statement of cost per acre to run five Greater Production farms has only the Blood farm showing a no-cost expenditure for "Compensation to Indians."[135] The Bloods had reason to be unhappy with their forced conscription into the Greater Production scheme.

The government offered, in its own defence, the mitigating factor of a weather disaster and pointed out that Blood losses in cattle and horses were typical of the southern Alberta area during this time.[136] The research of David Jones suggests that there may be some legitimacy to the government's claim. The Lethbridge area, for example, experienced generally drier conditions, and 1918 was "the driest year ever, before or since, totalling only 7.63 inches of moisture." Consequently total crop yields were down for 1917, 1918, and 1919, and this calamity was followed by a severe grasshopper infestation for 1919–21.[137]

Although some historians are skeptical, the Bloods accept the veracity of former Indian Agent R.N. Wilson's charges against the government delivered in his self-published "Our Betrayed Wards" in 1921. Wilson recognized the part played by the weather but unreservedly states that there was a deliberate effort by the government and ranchers to sabotage the Bloods' developing cattle and agricultural business in an effort to sustain the profitable rations system.[138] This deliberate act, Wilson charges, was compounded by the general neglect of the Bloods' interests. To support his claim, he listed a litany of offences; cattle and horses had been permitted to destroy an unfenced wheat crop, deliberate overgrazing of the range was ignored, and a herd of cattle had been sold at a substantial loss. In this latter case the agent, not the government, took the blame and he was fired.[139]

It has been argued that the emphasis on Greater Production and the siphoning off of resources and machinery for that program deprived the Bloods of their use when needed and therefore negatively affected the Bloods' own agricultural and ranching efforts. The result was an economic decline that set the Bloods back decades and brought about destitution.[140] One is left to speculate, however, whether the Bloods' losses would have been so acute if Greater Production had not been, among others, an additional complicating factor, a fact mooted by Graham when he admitted that the DIA might not emerge unscathed from an investigation.[141]

As Taylor points out, however, Greater Production declined in importance after the war and resulted in no permanent alienation of reserve land.[142] The major problem with Greater Production for this study is the difficulty in assessing its impact on the Bloods due to the absence of hard data. Unlike other aspects of Blood reserve integration; involvement in Greater Production was totally involuntary. Greater Production was forced on the Bloods as on other Natives, by the perceived wartime emergency and they appear to have had no part to play in determining its course or in mitigating the worst of its consequences.

In the end the government was not totally convinced of the practicality of the Greater Production program. Superintendent General D.C. Scott informed Graham on February 22, 1922, that with the war emergency past there was little need to continue Greater Production. It was realized that the rationale of the scheme's farms and leases was beyond the scope of the department and hampered its main aim of securing the advancement of the Natives. Farming leases should be discontinued on expiration, as they were contrary to the development of an appropriate work ethic. Scott wanted the Bloods, and other Natives, to earn rewards from the sweat of their own brows rather than "sit by and derive an unearned income from the work of others." Grazing leases could continue but so should efforts at securing surrenders of 'idle lands.'[143]

Ultimately Greater Production did not succeed in assimilating the Bloods as willing and wholehearted participants in efforts to force greater economic rewards from them and their land. Unfortunately for the government's plan, the dictatorial way in which the scheme was forced on the Bloods and its administration by the most rigid of bureaucrats in the person of William Graham increased their resolve to be the masters of their own fate once the regime of Greater Production ceased to exist.[144] By the end of the program, the Bloods were certainly in no mood to contemplate any alienation of their land.

THE CHALLENGES OF LEASE

A First Nations convention held at Macleod, in November 1924, brought the matter of grazing leases to a head. The Indians themselves had decided, according to the *Lethbridge Herald*, that some leasing policies were an infringement of Treaty 7, a view upheld by both Chief Shot Both Sides and local M.P. George Coote.[145] The troublesome flash point was a Blood reserve lease to the Hon. A.J. McLean. McLean had trouble stocking the lease to the maximum allowable 5,000 head of cattle and wanted the cost adjusted accordingly, a proposal rejected by Agent Faunt, who demanded the full $10,000 payment. McLean also wanted to fence his lease, which Blood ranchers objected to because their own cattle tended to drift along the fence and over the riverbanks to their destruction.[146] These concerns, communicated to Minister of the Interior and Superintendent General of Indian Affairs Charles Stewart, were dismissed as possibly "imaginary," rather than legitimate grievances resulting from the still unrepealed Section 90 of the Indian Act.[147]

While the records are generally mute on the issue of grazing in the mid- to late 1920s, Dempsey points to the general prosperity of farmers on the reserve in 1927.[148] This suggests that reserve grazing remained good and so demand remained high. The reserve could accommodate some export demand because many of the reserve residents were employed outside of the reserve and only some of the reserve land was suitable for farming.[149] The year 1927, however, was an "abnormally wet year," an anomaly in the climatic pattern for the region that experienced, Marchildon observes, practically continual drought conditions from 1917 through the 1930s.[150] Jones points out that "the three Alberta dry belt census divisions had more

Table 2.1. Lease Monies Due Bloods for use of their land.

CLIENT	LOCATION	YEAR	RATE / $1.25
Blackmore, H.J.	Cardston	1934	194.60
		1935	194.60
		1935	32.00
Penney, W.T.	McGrath	1935	570.54
Patterson Ranching Co.	Lethbridge	1935	600.00
Parker, R.	Orton	1935	112.15
?, B.G.	Lethbridge	1935	11.00
Horn, F.	Lethbridge	1935	70.68
Stringham, G.L.	Glenwood	1935	1100.18
Crest, C.S.	Lethbridge	1935	869.09
Jensen, L.	Lethbridge	1935	916.06
Meldrum, J.	Mcgrath	1935	322.41
Pitcher, WFM	Cardston	1935	824.59
Smith, J. / Kearl, S.	Cardston	1935	248.80
		1935	.60
Whitney, A., et al.	Kipp	1935	429.28
McNab, W.H., et al.	Macleod	1935	153.60

Above statistics taken from LAC, RG 10, vol. 1538.

[farm] abandonments in 1926 than the *five* most heavily vacated Saskatchewan census divisions in 1936."[151] By 1933, in the midst of the Depression, the reserve was deemed, by a Department of Agriculture Report, to be "without a doubt, the best stock raising land in Western Canada" and supported more sheep per acre than any other part of Alberta. Still lessees tried to force a fee reduction from ten to eight cents an acre by submitting payments based on the reduced rate. Though Blood leadership and the DIA determined not to give in, eight different leaseholders were in arrears by August 1933. As the leaseholders changed, or encountered economic difficulty, the problem with collecting rents was increasingly difficult (Table 2.1).[152] Max Foran describes the 1920s as an increasingly burdensome period for ranchers because of accumulating debt from leasing tax arrears. This problem was compounded by the collapse of beef prices during the 1930s, which left Alberta ranchers in "dire straits."[153] These national economic problems likely were reflected in the dealings locals had with the Bloods and in their attempts to force down lease rates.

Historical experience, reserve politics, and environmental conditions combined, in 1933, causing official hesitation to accommodate the needs of the non-Native community. In November the DIA was approached by the Jenkins Brothers, Fishburn, Alberta, for a lease of ten years on a southern portion of the reserve in order to ensure winter range: "it makes it very hard for us to carry on with our cattle if we are not sure of winter range for them." To this point, the Jenkins Brothers indicated, their arrangement with the Bloods had been both cordial and satisfactory.[154] Inspector of Indian Agencies M. Christianson's response regarding the 6,000-acre lease was not encouraging. Although several ranchers had been given leases to winter cattle on the reserve in 1932, environmental conditions on the reserve had deteriorated in the interim. Agent J.E. Pugh thus reported that the chief and headmen were "absolutely opposed" to further leases in the southern portion of the reserve, which was the tribe's essential grazing range and hay land.[155] Although the reserve was a significant factor in determining the stock policy of off-reserve individuals, or groups, the Bloods were unwilling to compromise their own anticipated future grass reserves.

Agent Pugh summed up his view of the basic economic conflict that existed in the demands placed on the reserve by the non-Native community. "Are we as a reserve," queried Pugh, "to be more or less tentatively responsible for the carrying of outside ranchers, who wish to protect their range in winter for summer, at the expense of the Indians" while he, as agent, was obliged to protect the Bloods' similar interests.[156] It was clear that local stock raisers regarded reserve land as critical to their success. Stock raising in the area adjoining the reserve could not thrive without access to more grazing land than was available outside the reserve's borders.

Beginning in 1933, there was an apparent attempt by some Bloods and cattle owners to circumvent the power of the agent and the DIA. Becoming entrepreneurs in their own right, they engaged in leasing contracts with non-Native stockowners to graze outside stock on individually fenced land. Christianson thought this policy wrong as it would encourage others to follow suit. He predicted that such actions would result in a reserve overrun with stock "and the whole management of the agency will simply 'go up in smoke.'" Despite such reservations twelve such agreements were eventually concluded.[157]

Christianson was aware that the survivability of the reserve was at stake if overgrazing occurred. He was equally aware that this new direction in managing grazing on an individual contract basis posed a severe challenge to DIA authority. Certainly there was potential for serious management confusion but Christianson was going in the face of reserve and regional economic history when he speculated: "The only system that we can adopt is to keep the Indians from trucking and trading with outsiders."[158] In attempting to stifle such commercial exchange, Christianson advocated an impractical policy that existed only in the overzealous minds of Department bureaucrats. Although official government policy had at least ideally been aimed in this direction, the history of grazing contracts, and the demands and expectations of the Bloods' neighbours, had mitigated against such a policy ever becoming reality.

DEPRESSION AND DROUGHT

Through deliberate arrangements and enforcement of their policy in the past, the Bloods and their agents had managed, with difficulty, to practically keep control over the reserve's grazing land and hay. The onset of the Depression, however, along with the devastating environmental crisis, increased both the settlers' need for land and their determination to have it. As a result, the DIA became more responsive to the needs of non-Natives living in the area of the reserve and attempted to improve the crisis at hand. Ultimately what control the Bloods had been able to gain during the previous decades was slowly eroded away.[159]

Economic and financial conditions in the Great Depression played a significant part in the desire for the use of Blood reserve land and determined the attitudes lessees exhibited once the land was made available to them. A bone of contention was whether or not the lease terms granted the lessee right of exclusive use. The case of W.T. McCaugherty, Lethbridge, illustrates this point. In November 1935, he complained to Agent Pugh about certain Indians camped on his lease. In an effort at encouraging McCaugherty to be more conciliatory, Pugh reminded him that a clause in the lease provided for removal of land from a lease if desired by "those Indians living on the lands leased." This McCaugherty could not, or would not, accept and he threatened the Indians with "criminal action … for trespassing."[160]

The McCaugherty problem came to a head in January 1936, with his assault on a reserve resident and resulted in Agent Pugh raising serious questions about leasing technicalities and procedures. Despite the fact that a lease was a "conditional surrender," Pugh recognized that ejecting the Indians from leased land in favour of the lessee would result in much bitterness and disaffection among them.[161] McCaugherty, however, was unmoved and furthermore believed that the lease legally permitted him to treat the Bloods as "trespassers" on his leased land.[162] Pugh's attempts at mediation failed, leading the Department to conclude that McCaugherty was "unreasonable" in his assumptions.[163] Tribal members, of course, did not accept Pugh's explanation that by not being resident on the leased portion of the reserve prior to the granting of the lease they had "forfeited all rights to the lease lands."[164]

The abuse of individual Blood property and individual rights, at times, went to such provocative extremes as permitting sheep to invade Indian homes during their absence. In another case, a Blood was lassoed and dragged around by a lessee. Such incidents, Christianson said, were "too numerous to mention."[165] The attitudes engendered by such behaviour magnified the already negative aspects of the leasing system. The behaviour of lessees such as McCaugherty dictated that such leasing arrangements should have properly been discontinued.[166]

By 1935 conditions on the reserve suggested an environmental catastrophe of major proportions in the making, and sound management practices dictated that leasing be ended, or at least temporarily curtailed. According to Pugh, 145,000 acres of range (approximately 41 per cent of the reserve) on the north end of the reserve was in serious condition from soil erosion due to drought and overgrazing. Land to a depth of four miles from the rivers was 'beyond restoration' unless grazing was halted. The effects of stress on the land are indicated by the fact that one lease of 4,627 acres, with a stocking capacity of 250, had in excess of 500 cattle. The inevitable consequence of such conditions was intense competition for grass with the result that lessees had resorted to the illegal and chaotic practice of invading each other's ranges.[167]

This inevitably resulted in a great deal of dissatisfaction among both the Bloods and the lessees. Blood ranchers and farmers found their movement and access to their own land continually restricted as lessees, driven by harsh environmental conditions, neglected the spirit of their leases and interpreted the letter of the lease to their own benefit. The Bloods, at the end of their patience, wanted the leases ended. Pugh supported that sentiment when he recommended that, based on grass conditions, the leases be cancelled.[168]

Despite the informed opposition of the Bloods and Agent Pugh, the Department chose to ignore the weight of evidence and opinion and proceeded to implement its own agenda. The Bloods' cancellation of the

Town of Cardston lease, in 1936, for example, was based on environmental concerns and "economics," while locals needed the land to expand their operations. The DIA, however, decided to renew Cardston's lease for another year. The rationale for the renewal, as explained to Pugh, was that in the Department's estimation "the Town of Cardston will continue to require these pasturage privileges." The only remedial action taken by the Department was to remind the town to be more appreciative of the use of the Bloods' property.[169]

The Bloods, however, saw nothing magnanimous in the Department's gesture. This became abundantly clear when, in a vote taken on May 26, 1936, "on the question of renewal of Grazing lease granted by the Blood Band of Indians in 1924," they voted 186 to 4 for cancellation.[170]

Environmental conditions continued to deteriorate and, although the DIA often ignored the wishes of the Bloods, it could not ignore the condition of the land. In June Agent Pugh estimated that drought and grasshoppers affected 60,000 acres of the reserve, threatening both current lease use and winter grazing prospects.[171] Lessees, of course, did not want to pay for land ravaged by grasshoppers. As a consequence, some lessees were both unwilling and unable to carry on with their agreements. In September, for example, Agent Pugh reported that Christian Jensen and W.T. Passey, Magrath, holders of leases Nos. 133 and 131, respectively, wished to relinquish their holdings. "The reason for vacating in the Jensen case," Pugh wrote, "is because of shortage of grazing, due to drouth and this lease being very heavily hit by locusts. In the case of Passey, I think it is a matter of inability to carry such a large acreage." It is highly likely that Passey's ability to carry his "large acreage" was adversely affected by climatic conditions. At least one lessee, the Pitcher Sheep Co., went out of business.[172]

When Pugh received petitions for the continuation of leases in August, he advised the Department against it because conditions had worsened to such an extent that the reserve could not sustain the stock. In fairness, and because of the Indians' decision in the recent vote, Pugh recommended that the leases be ended and that lessees be given final notification.[173] Christianson was noncommittal, agreeing only to cancel one troublesome lease which had no grass and from which the owner drove his cattle onto Indian pasture and succeeded in ruining it.[174] That Pugh was "very nearly run of[f] his feet at times trying to adjust disputes between lessees and Indians," is a clear indication that the Bloods were not passive observers with regard to the economic well-being of their reserve.[175]

The problems faced by the local homesteaders, and their impressions of how to best gain relief, were well illustrated by M.E. Ririe, Magrath, and his accomplices, who sent an inquiry about lease land in August 1935 to Lethbridge MP J.S. Stewart. They told Stewart that the lessees were in dire straits and they resented having to purchase hay outside of their leases from the Indians. Ririe was set straight when told that the money from haying was practically the only income for some Bloods and that hay land could therefore not be leased.[176] It is hard to escape the conclusion, however, that Ririe felt that he had a right to the wealth and convenience of the reserve as if it were public domain. He was likely encouraged in this view by the increasingly difficult circumstances, which, historian James Gray says, would have driven ranchers out of southern Alberta, had they been able to extricate themselves.[177]

At the end of 1935 the Department acknowledged the Indians' frustration with the leases and their desire to cancel the lease agreements about to expire in 1936 and 1937. The matter was urgent in that the lessees had to be given proper notification. The existing arrangements meant that some 145,000 acres of the north end of the reserve were alienated in lease contracts. Admittedly the income from the leases had been uncertain and now there was the issue of environmental damage that further reduced the value and use of the land to the Bloods.[178]

Despite this, in December 1936, the Department contemplated leasing 70,000 acres of Blood reserve land.[179] The only consideration given to the Bloods' feelings was to stipulate ten basic provisions for the lease. Among the most important were that the land could be used only for grazing, wood or timber could not be cut, and that the lease could not be sublet. The lease further stipulated a stock limit of one sheep to ten acres, one cow to twenty-four acres, and one horse to twenty acres. Lessees were also prohibited from concluding private business deals with individual Natives without the express permission of the Bloods. Given previous experiences, the most important provision was likely number ten: "That if in the lessee's area Indians reside thereon, their property shall at all times be protected from the lessee's stock, and that the Indians shall be permitted to retain their live stock holdings on the undefined reservation within his lease."[180]

The Department's determination to lease was probably triggered by the desire to reduce growing relief bills. The problem of relief expenditures bolstered the perception that the Bloods, among other tribes, had large unproductive land holdings that should be more aggressively used in the furtherance of self-support. Inspector of Agencies C. Schmidt believed that the benefit of an increase in cattle and grain production accrued only to the small minority who had cattle or who farmed, while at the same time relief costs increased. The Department's response was to encourage the Inspector to convince the Indians to lease their 'idle' lands.[181]

By late 1938, however, it appears that leases were being closed out and related issues were being wound up.[182] Despite new requests for leasing, the DIA determined that, given the condition of the land, and considering the needs of "our Special Welfare I[ndian] D[epartment] Herd," the granting of new leases was inadvisable. The Department's perception of the well-being of the Bloods and their land and increasing DIA expectations, if not the Bloods' wishes, now appeared to be uppermost in determining the new policy.[183]

CONCLUSION

One can only conclude that the absolute defining motivation for the leasing system, from the perspective of both the lessee and the DIA, was the general view that unleased Indian land was wasted land. Clearly, however, this view far from completes the picture of the reserve's incorporation into local ranching market structures characterized mainly through lease and hay sales. The true picture is much more complicated. For the Bloods, their reserve land was a resource on which to draw, though they had to balance their own and others' usage with its market disposition. As well, its long-term sustainability had to be factored in. Agents often approached the issue from an economic and legal perspective, concerned about both the Bloods' income and their legitimate rights. Many agents took the fiduciary responsibilities inherited with their positions more serious, or at least interpreted it more favourable to Native wishes, than did the DIA's upper bureaucracy. The Bloods' neighbours wanted access to enhance their economic wellbeing. Time and changed circumstances and the Bloods' refusal to be cowed, however, did not permit the uniform generalizations that often propelled the DIA's approach and rancher/settler views.

Perhaps there was no uniform approach that could cater to the variety of conflicting agendas that emerged over time. The Bloods acted on their perceived needs for use of their land, their desire to control their own affairs and for the income. The agent, caught in a difficult situation, had to take into account the Bloods' desires, his duty to protect their interests and the application of the Department's dictums. The Department, an arm of the government of White Canada, held the Bloods in legal and paternalistic wardship and was generally responsible to the direction of the non-Native population. Angry ranchers and homesteaders petitioning Frank Oliver, circa 1902, summed up the enduring economic and political reality of the West: that the Indians were wards of the government and the government "servant of the people" and the Indians were, therefore, in a position to be coerced according to the will of the White man.[184]

The unpredictable environment and the demands of local ranchers and homesteaders further militated against the smooth functioning of the bureaucratic machine. Little wonder that the Bloods' needs were often placed last on the agenda. It was generally the case that those in charge of administering the Bloods' affairs felt that they knew best what the Bloods wanted and needed. Allan G. Harper has stated that protecting the integrity of Indian land "is perhaps the principal purpose of the Indian Act."[185] In the case of the Blood reserve and the lease system, both the Act and the government often failed to fulfill that mandate.

Many agents, however, took their guardianship of the Bloods seriously and did their utmost to protect Native interests, even to the point of disagreeing with bureaucratic bosses in Ottawa. This behaviour is very much at odds with the stereotype of corrupt and dictatorial Indian agents lording it over their wards. The Bloods, in conjunction with the agents were, at times, able to set and control the reserve land agenda. They deliberately chose to integrate their reserve into a larger community land base even if in a limited way. It was not, however, always easy to enforce the limits of this integration as they defined them or wished them to be. Too often the clients of the Bloods sought to evade their legitimate responsibilities.

The Department of Indian Affairs brokered the relationship between the Bloods and their neighbours and in the end satisfied neither. But business carried on driven by the need for a scarce commodity of much value and in great demand, accessible grazing and hay land. By an ironic twist, the Bloods, though dispossessed of their vast traditional land holdings by treaty in 1877, now possessed a large area of reserve land that had become a most valued commodity in the agrarian-based culture of southern Alberta. Beal notes that it was the intention of the DIA that reserve lands not be regarded as 'commodities'; in reality, however, during the reserve period land and labour were not "fictitious commodities" as markets existed for both.[186] It was this reality that both encouraged and determined the nature of the economic dynamic between them and their neighbours. The Bloods possessed land for which their neighbours had a real and imagined need. However, because the Bloods' powers to protect the reserve's integrity were limited, an economic co-operation developed between the Bloods and their neighbours. For those individuals driven to, or inclined to, the use of the Blood reserve, for which no suitable alternative existed, its availability was a critical factor in their future planning. Treaty 7, by taking Indian land surrenders, had laid the basis for the establishment of the ranching and agricultural frontiers. But by setting out the principles for institutionalizing the Blood reserve, the treaty had determined there would be economic interplay betwee Native and non-Native in the locale surrounding that reserve.

3: 'Selling to Outsiders': Marketing Coal, Hay, and Freighting Services

INTRODUCTION

The belief that Native Canadians have participated little in the national economy is not uncommon. Thus the activities of Native peoples in local economic environments have been largely ignored as an area of study. Historian Walter Hildebrandt observed, "for Native people, inclusion in the national and international economy has not been carefully planned at all."[1] Hanna Samek, in her *The Blackfoot Confederacy 1880–1920*, paid scant attention to Canadian Blackfoot economic interaction with the communities surrounding the various reserves generally viewing the reserves in isolation.[2] Where attention has been given to the inclusion of Natives in the workplace, the conclusion has been that, hamstrung by bureaucratic indifference to their needs and proscriptive interference in their plans, Natives have not been able to overcome Anglo-Canadian competition for available resources.[3] Indeed the focus has been on the planned exclusion of Aboriginal people from integrative activities with non-Native neighbours through the pass and permit systems. These policies are believed so successful that some historians conclude that generally Natives entered an era of 'irrelevance' in the mid-nineteenth century and did not emerge for approximately a hundred years.

There is, however, an emerging consensus among social scientists that Native peoples were participants in, and contributors to, the capitalist market-driven economy, even during the era of supposed 'irrelevance.' John Lutz, for example, argues that Natives "were the main labour force of the early settlement era, essential to the capitalist development of British Columbia."[4] Noted earlier was the work of Rolf Knight. The work of Carl Beal on Saskatchewan Indian reserves, however, is of particular note in refuting standard interpretations that reserve economies failed and there-fore exerted no market influences. Indeed, Beal concludes, "Between 1870 and 1885, the Indian population was pivotal for the initial development of monetized markets in western Canada."[5] Similarly, Innes, Macdougall, and Tough illustrate the diversity of Saskatchewan reserve economies be-tween 1897 and 1915 and note: "The growth experienced by band econo-mies corresponds to a general economic recovery and expansion of prairie settlement."[6] It may take some time, however, before these revisionist trends become accepted consensus, with more general applicability, among scholars of western Canadian and Native economic history.

In southern Alberta the close proximity of Native groups to Anglo-Canadian settlements and the altering or destruction of the environment occurred to such an extent that traditional Native economic behaviours were largely rendered obsolete. The Bloods, like their non-Native neigh-bours, faced basic problems of survival. The search for solutions dictated participation in the local economies to which the Bloods and various other Native groups found themselves attached. The only practical means of ac-quiring credit, currency, and merchandise was through providing a market commodity in the form of goods or services, the latter often in the form of seasonally determined labour. Beginning in the 1890s, the Bloods im-mersed themselves in various economic activities both in response to local market demands and their subsistence needs in keeping with Beal's obser-vation that money "fosters a calculating rationality one moreover which tends to reduce qualities of things to their measure in money."[7]

The western Canadian economy was laid on a foundation of agriculture and basic extractive industries, such as coal mining, driven by the market in that price determined production. These production activities were la-bour-intensive, mining requiring a continual supply of labour and agricul-ture requiring seasonal workers especially during the fall harvests. From the beginning, the West was plagued by labour shortages, which drew immigrants to work the coalfields and harvest crops in southern Alberta and British Columbia. Harvest excursions, as Cherwinski has pointed out, encouraged by the government and railways witnessed yearly migrations of predominantly male workers from eastern Canada, the United States, and Europe to labour in the fields and were a response to perennial labour shortages.[8]

This situation increased market opportunities for Blood entrepreneurs and labourers. The growing population of immigrants determined to make their homes on the prairies combined with seasonal floods of itinerant workers created demand for the Bloods' products and labour. They became participants in the market economy, offering the commodities they produced and competing with others engaged in coal mining, haying, and freighting. At times the Bloods' productive proficiency created a demand for their products and services and earned them a market share. Their competitiveness also at times drew the wrath of their non-Native competitors.

By the early 1890s, most Bloods had come to grips with changed circumstance such as the loss of the buffalo and the restrictions imposed by reserve life and had adjusted accordingly. Realizing that their reserve could not immediately provide a livelihood for all, many Bloods adopted strategies suitable for survival in the new economic setting. Agents, responsive to the DIA's dual goals to economize and make Natives self-supporting citizens, actively tried to place Bloods in off-reserve occupations. Although the program was never fully realized, some 292 Bloods of approximately 1,200 reserve residents left the reserve for work in 1899–1900. The work opportunities were varied and often of limited duration: logging, freighting, mail cartage, scouting for the NWMP, day labour, and seasonal participation in fairs and exhibitions.[9] It is not clear who these individuals were or the length of their absence. If this is a reference only to working males, then a substantial percentage of the male working population of the reserve worked away during this brief period, and this is a clear indication of the Bloods' economic significance and their adaptive capability. Some of these men were certainly accompanied by family, which added to the percentage of reserve absentees. For those wishing to stay on the reserve, coal mining, haying, cattle ranching and agriculture, some in support of Euro-Canadian entrepreneurial initiatives, were the occupations of choice.[10]

The focus of this chapter will be on the economic interaction of the Bloods with the local community. Emphasis will be placed on their roles as coal and hay merchants and as freighters because these were significant points of interaction between the Bloods and their neighbours. These occupations or activities offered the Bloods the greatest opportunities for both employment and the sale of reserve resources. The agents encouraged such work as training in the ways of 'civilization' and, it was hoped, it would ultimately lead to the Bloods' economic independence. It will become clear, however, that as the area economy developed, the Bloods' attachment to and participation in local economic activities was deliberate and considerable and changed with time and circumstance.

MARKET ACTIVITIES

Coal

One of the first commodities the Bloods offered for sale was coal, which they began mining in 1890. The first coal mine was small. The coal was dug initially with pick and shovel from a coal seam, likely of a non-coking bituminous or sub-bituminous variety, located in a cutbank about twenty miles from the agency.[11] Afterwards the assistance of two or three men was all that was required to work the seam. However, the operator, Heavy Gun, was ambitious and opened a tunnel with rails for a car to bring coal to the surface. Eventually two rooms were opened with an air course, shoot and screen for cleaning the coal and a loading bank.[12]

As a commercial venture, this mining was hampered by lack of quality and inconsistency of output. Though limited, the operation was in part driven by the prospect of "selling to outsiders," that is "marketed by the Indians themselves."[13] Agent James Wilson, however, believed that opportunities for off-reserve sales were limited by low quality and competition. The coal seam, he reported, was divided into three layers with slate between each. Mixed with the coal was also a large amount of white mineral "which causes a large accumulation of ashes and keeps the coal from burning." This condition made it both expensive to mine and reduced its value. However, Wilson did believe that the mine could supply reserve needs for the hospital, mission, and agency.[14]

Though experiencing some initial success, the mine operated with difficulty, and Wilson felt that some of the problems were due to the absence of 'white' expertise. The work remained generally unsupervised, except for the involvement of the agent, until the accidental death of Mistaken Chief at the mine in 1930, and "a coal mining expert" more closely supervised operations thereafter.[15] Generally while it operated, however, the Blood reserve coal mine was solely a Native operation, jealously guarded by the Bloods, and the only non-Native participation was in an advisory capacity.

Despite its limitations the mine intermittently produced marketable coal, though in small quantities. Having their own transportation and being closely situated to Fort Macleod and the surrounding area made the Blood coal mine, at times, competitive. In February 1894, the *Macleod Gazette* announced the arrival of Blood reserve coal in the town but dismissed the rumour that the coal was superior to that produced by the Galt mines at Lethbridge.[16] Regardless of the *Gazette's* disclaimer, the mine produced

200 tons of coal in 1894, 130 for use of the agency, fifty for the boarding school, and twenty tons for settlers in Macleod and district.[17] Hugh Dempsey reports that an additional 100 tons of reserve coal were sold to the Galt mining company.[18] Though, perhaps, not significant enough to affect the supply or price of coal on the local market, there was at least a market presence. Black Horse, who had taken over the mine operations by 1894, approached the business with enthusiasm, producing approximately 260 tons in the following year, for both reserve and public needs.[19]

Though production from the reserve mine was spotty, its significance is perhaps suggested by the fact that local entrepreneurs expressed occasional interest in acquiring the mine operations or commercial mining rights on the reserve. However, periodic inquiries about coal rights evinced no interest from the Bloods or the DIA.[20] One inquiry made in 1911 was based on a predicted increased need likely tied to an ongoing coal strike in southern Alberta since April of that year.[21] By January 1913, this prediction had come to pass and the *Raymond Leader* reported shortages in Raymond because Lethbridge's Galt mine could not keep up with local demand.[22] Agent S. Swinford recognized the potential for Blood coal sales in light of the rapidly expanding local economy when he reported, "To have coal there would be worth a lot and be a tremendous advantage not only to those on the Reserve but it could be sold to all the settlers across the Belly River and would give those Indians who cares [sic] to work a chance to make a good living all winter long."[23] However, with too many 'domestic' coal producers and with the seasonal nature of the demand for fuel, such expressions of hope were misplaced.[24]

Fuel shortages occurred intermittently during the next several years, increasing the value of potentially productive coal seams on the Blood reserve. This was particularly so during World War I when demand was high and labour was in short supply. For example, the desire by local individuals to open and operate coal seams led to a minor squabble in 1917 when Frank Bruce and N.X. Hansen, Hill Spring, "entered into a contract with some Indian residing in the Blood Reserve." They subsequently opened a vein with the intention of supplying their own community and Glenwoodville (Glenwood) with coal. When the small mine became productive, however, the Bloods refused permission to mine, causing the men to seek legal advice. Their attorney, Z.W. Jacobs, Cardston, attempted to persuade the Honourable C.A. Magrath, Fuel Controller, Ottawa, that as a result of the thwarted coal production "the people in that locality are experiencing considerable difficulty in obtaining fuel." The Fuel Controller's Office pointed out that as the greatest possible coal production was important in wartime the matter should be looked into with a view to allowing mining to resume. Permission was granted only "on the distinct understanding, however, that this is not to form a precedent," the Department in this instance considering only "the existing exceptional circumstances."[25]

Although some elected politicians, such as Frank Oliver, Independent member from Alberta, might express regret that Natives competed with non-Native commercial enterprise, senior DIA officials were faced with the agent's plans for the Indians and the need to balance the books.[26] As a result, the desire to have Natives pay their own way overcame reservations about market place competition. Agent J.T. Faunt, for example, in the face of complaints from local producers, affirmed his belief in the Bloods' right to market coal and indicated that they were certainly competitive locally. He estimated that the Bloods sold at least 200 tons in December 1920. Faunt further observed that the mine had been in operation for over three decades and that in 1921 "more coal has been taken out than usual, as I have been encouraging the Indians in this work, as on account of the crop failure at the North end of the Reserve, this appeared to me as a means of putting some of them through the winter with no expense to the Department." D.C. Scott supported Faunt's policy and stressed that Blood coal producers were not to be interfered with in their usual practice of selling their coal on the open market.[27]

In this case the DIA justified Blood competition in the market place because of the savings it produced for the Department. This was certainly the case in 1934 when Inspector M. Christianson reported:

> ... as long as the Indians of this band had nothing to work at during the winter we would be called on from time to time to issue rations to them.... In 1919 we had a total crop failure on this reserve: everything was burned off – even the grass. We lost about 40% of our cattle herds during the winter of 1919–1920 ... on the Blood Reserve, if we have not grain or livestock to sell the Indians are not able to make a living and we simply have to call upon the Department for assistance. That is why I have been so anxious to get a coal mine going as that seems to be the only natural resource on this reserve that there is any chance of developing.[28]

On at least one occasion, however, when the Bloods were not able to supply sufficient product to meet local demands, permission was given to Whites to enter and remove resources from the reserve. Despite the fact that Blood miners were already working a coal area, in 1934 Agent Pugh issued over 200 passes for farmers from Glenwoodville and Hill Spring to enter the reserve and take coal from the river bottom. There is no indication what charge, if any, was made for this coal. Christianson did believe that demand was such that a new Blood mining operation could be profitable during the winter as farmers, temporarily idle, had the resources and time to purchase and haul coal provided they could acquire the fuel at a reasonable price.[29] Clearly, there were times when the official policy and the aims it envisioned were not applicable to local circumstances. The policy was then modified to suit the situation.

The coal venture on the reserve, though having occasional market influence, never established a definitive market presence. Operations continued sporadically during the 1920s and 1930s. In November 1933, Blood miners and freighters were hauling coal to the Raymond sugar beet factory and the factory had been given permission to haul from the reserve. Prospecting for coal on the reserve also continued. It is likely that Blood reserve coal mining became unprofitable over time due to poor quality, inadequate capacity, competition, and shifts in market demand.[30]

Hay

Like coal mining, the cutting, sale, and hauling of hay afforded Blood hay producers opportunities to compete in the local market. Production, as with other crops, was determined both by climatic conditions, especially rainfall, and natural disasters such as fire, and the number of acres given to hay. Yield per acre, therefore, varied. In 1876 one settler in the Red River area estimated that each acre of prairie could yield three to four tons of hay.[31] The yields on the Blood reserve varied from year to year and such variations were caused by changes in the number of acres given to hay as well as the impact of climatic conditions.

Haying was done in summer and employed both men and machinery. Initially the haying crews utilized basic tools such as scythes, mowers, and forks. From about 1900 the introduction of hay loaders eased the toil of loading wagons and the development of overhead horse forks and slings simplified stacking. Eventually mechanical mowers, side delivery rakes, and hay tedders increased both capacity and efficiency, but these

Figure 3.1.
"Caravan of loaded hay-racks on the Blood reserve, [ca. 1905]." Glenbow Archives, NA-451-6. The caravan depicted here, and Figure 3.2 below, illustrates the Blood' organization and capacity to produce hay for reserve consumption and sale.

NEIGHBOURS AND NETWORKS

image not available

also required more expert personnel. When machinery was used, a crew was required to run and maintain the equipment through to the end of the haying.[32]

With hay production, just as with coal, the Bloods' own needs took priority over market sales. In 1890, for example, although Agent Pocklington encouraged Blood producers to supply the North West Mounted Police (NWMP) detachments of Big Bend and Stand Off, he declined to contract 250 tons, at fifteen dollars per ton, for Lethbridge, claiming a shortage of hay on the reserve and in the district.[33] In seasons of scarcity, considerable effort was required to fill contracts. Chief Moon, for example, had to haul hay twenty miles to fill the terms of his contract with the NWMP.[34] When the season was over, Agent Pocklington concluded that, in future, such contracts should be declined unless the Indians received more transport and more machines with which to do the work.[35] Pocklington was likely aware that his sentiment was expressly contrary to DIA wishes to turn Natives into peasant farmers tied to the soil through their own exertions of physical labour and not in any way liberated through the employ of mechanical devices. As the man on the spot, however, he was keenly aware of the difficulties of fulfilling contractual obligations without recourse to labour-saving devices.

In July 1891, Pocklington succeeded in securing the contract to supply forty tons of hay to the Stand Off NWMP Detachment and, despite the poor season, fulfilled the contract in October. Other reserve residents entered into other arrangements such as cutting hay on a share basis with local White settlers adjacent to the reserve. These agreements, as described by Agent Pocklington, had Whites supplying the machinery and horses and the Bloods the labour. The Bloods then sold their share of the hay to the Whites. An added bonus with this arrangement, in the eyes of the agent, was that Blood farmers became familiar with the operation of agricultural machinery that the Department was so anxious to deny them.[36]

At the same time, Heavy Gun, who had overcome departmental resistance and acquired his own machinery, was cutting for two others as well as for himself and was putting up hay for a beef contractor, likely the Cochrane Ranche. According to Pocklington, the Indians put up sixty-eight tons of hay for the contractor for which they were paid $3.00 per ton. The agricultural tabular statement of December 1891 shows that the Bloods harvested 168 tons of hay both individually and on share agreements with Whites. It is likely that the Indians' sale of their portion of the harvest was an agreed-upon part of the share arrangement. It is not clear whether or not they could withhold their hay for their own needs in the event of hay shortages. There was, for example, a hay shortage in July 1892, and on this occasion the agent, on behalf of Blood farmers, declined a contract to supply the NWMP.[37]

In another case during the 1893 season Agent James Wilson thought it advisable not to attempt to fill a hay contract for the St. Mary's NWMP Detachment, citing the difficulty in securing the quality and quantity desired by the police because of a very poor growing season. Wilson did feel that he could supply fifteen tons to the Big Bend NWMP Detachment and the same for the Kootenai NWMP Detachment, "as hay in the neighbourhood of these places is good and plentiful." Wilson wanted six dollars per ton, though he eventually agreed on $5.50 per ton of 600 cubic feet for Big Bend and Kootenai detachments, and he pointed out to Inspector Sam Steele that a White man would oversee the work to ensure that the quality of the hay was satisfactory. Eventually Wilson agreed to provide 135 tons of hay to all the various detachments.[38] At the same time other Bloods were contracting with neighbouring settlers. Wilson also actively sought a contract to supply hay to the New Oxley Ranche Company.[39]

Agent Wilson, however, did not always calculate the needs of the reserve correctly and in his enthusiasm to find employment for some Bloods may have, in 1893, oversold the reserve's hay. When approached by Father Legal for ten tons of hay to see the two hospital cows through the winter, Wilson refused and confessed to the likelihood of a winter shortage. He requested departmental permission to purchase hay from any Natives who had extra for sale.[40]

During times of shortage the agent's permission to sell reserve hay to outsiders was refused and unauthorized sales were discouraged through the rigid enforcement of the permit system. In 1899, for example, Agent Wilson requested police assistance in stopping hay sales in Lethbridge. In cases where individuals were caught attempting such sales, the police were requested to seize the Indians' hay and sell it, remitting the proceeds to Wilson, an action not calculated to improve reserve supply shortages unless in its salutary effect. But with reserve farmers complaining that much needed hay was being spirited away at night, Wilson's concern was for winter shortage.[41]

There were some legitimate hay sales to locals, however, as Wilson, guided by circumstances, continued his efforts to gain market advantage for Blood farmers in securing contracts to supply the NWMP with their fodder needs.[42] In June 1899, he inquired as to whether his tender to deliver

image not available

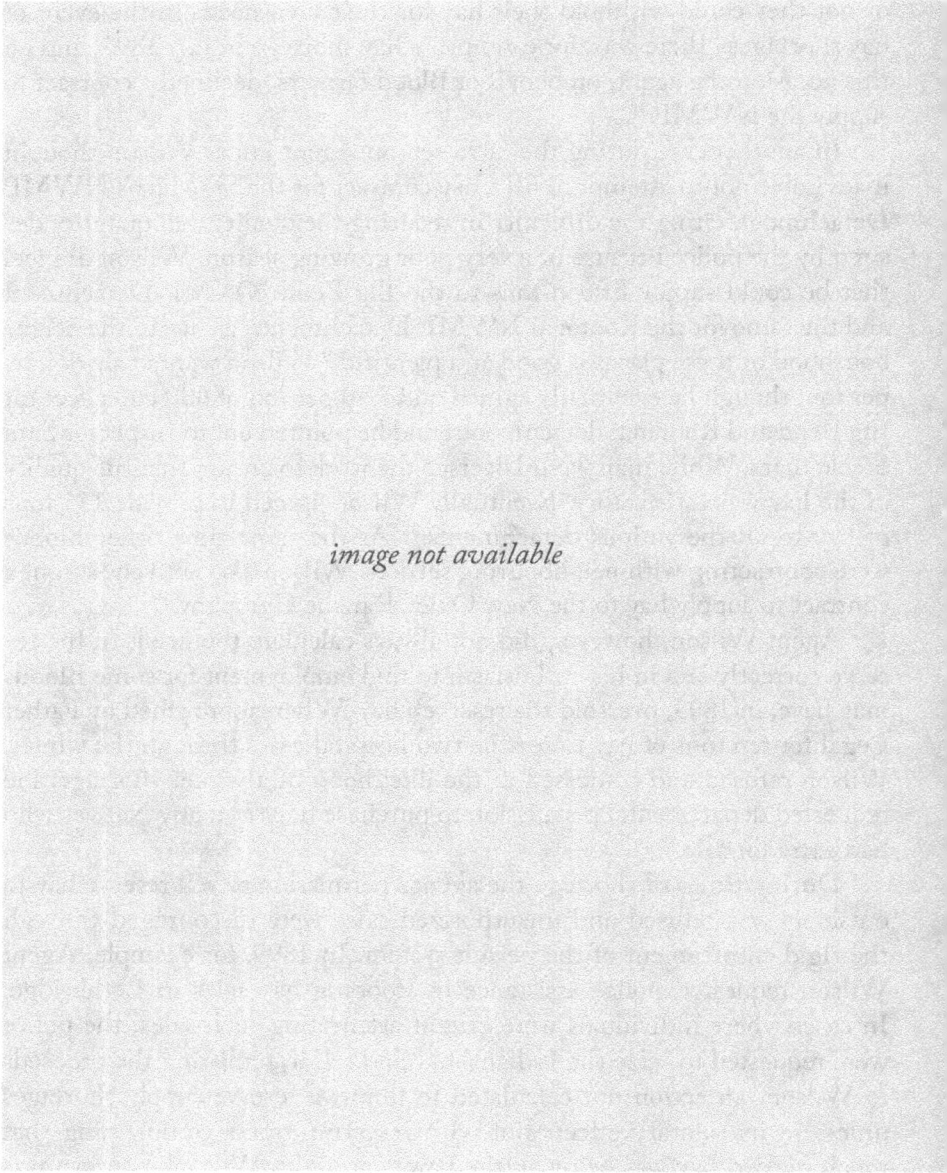

Figure 3.2.
"Hay making on the Blood Reserve, [ca. 1905]." Glenbow Archives, NA-451-5.

NEIGHBOURS AND NETWORKS

image not available

Figure 3.3.
"Rumely steam engine and plough owned by the Blood, probably Blood reserve, southern Alberta, 1915." Glenbow Archives, NA-4429-4. The use of such technology indicates a progressive approach to agriculture and resistance to any intention to make the Bloods 'peasant farmers.'

hay for the police would be accepted without a deposit as in the past, even though others were required to do so. The tender that Wilson eventually submitted was for hay delivered to the police detachments at Kootenai, Stand Off, and Kipp. Wilson also secured a contract for the delivery of oats to the Stand Off, St. Mary's, Kootenai, Big Bend, and Cardston Detachments. For 1899 the Bloods put up 2,269 tons of hay of which 1,186 tons were sold to the NWMP, Cochrane Ranche, and settlers for sales approximating $5,900.00.[43] What special consideration, if any, was given to Wilson to secure this contract is unclear but special favours from one government Department to another is a likely explanation. It is also possible that Wilson managed to underbid others because Blood producers were willing to contract their produce and services for less.

Whatever the circumstances, the Bloods' presence in this market did affect supply and price. In 1901 the *Lethbridge News* reported that the reserve sold over 1,000 tons of hay "in filling police and ranchers' contracts, to livery stables and citizens of Macleod and Lethbridge." The agent's report for 1901 notes that "Situated as the reserve is, near to Macleod, Lethbridge, and Cardston, a good demand is always had for hay in these places, and at fairly remunerative prices, while the larger ranches along the rivers and boundary lines also look to the Indians to put up their supply."[44] PCH Primrose, Mounted Police, reported from Macleod that hay was very expensive in 1903 because the Indians were not selling as much as before.[45] The agent's report for 1903 states that the Bloods put up a total of 3,500 tons of hay and sold 1,200 tons to the police and local settlers for prices ranging from $4.50 and $7.50 per ton. This range in prices suggests that the Bloods may have been withholding hay from the market or from the police because of unhappiness with the price. The Bloods harvested approximately the same amount of hay in 1901, at 3,451 tons. By 1906 Blood producers were so prominent with their hay sales that the *Macleod Gazette* called them the "hay maker[s] of southern Alberta." The *Gazette* reported the Bloods were taking large contracts to supply livery stables and local ranchers "usually filling the contracts in short order."[46]

The making and harvesting of hay continued to be an important source of income for Blood farmers. Agent W.J. Dilworth reported in 1914: "nearly every adult puts up every year a large quantity of hay for sale."[47] During August 1914, the Bloods put up more hay than ever before, providing 1,353 tons for agency consumption plus 4,000 tons for their own use. They had also provided 300 of a 1,500-ton lessee contract as well as contracts to provide 242 tons to various Mounted Police posts, and additional contracts for

500 tons. The agent commenting on the Bloods' willingness reported, "No difficulty has been experienced in getting them to do this work."[48] Agent Dilworth's report for 1914–15 stipulates that the Bloods harvested 10,000 tons of hay for which they realized $30,000.00, not an inconsiderable sum and indicative of a serious and effective approach to this work.[49]

Blood haymakers were certainly a market presence, and it is only sensible to conclude that besides being competitive in pricing labour, they did good work and delivered a high quality product, which helped them to sustain their market share. A copy of a 1915 hay contract between the NWMP and Agent Dilworth indicates that the police were exacting in their specifications. The contract called for 108 tons of hay delivered to Barracks at Macleod between October 1914 and June 1915 with the specification being "That the hay shall be Upland Bunch Grass Hay No. 1 quality of this year's crop, well cured, free from weeds, dirt and old bottom that it shall be subject to inspection and rejection as delivered." The Bloods were to be paid $12.00 per ton. Interestingly, section four of the contract requiring the bidder to deposit 5 per cent of the value of the contract was deleted, likely as one government department's accommodation of another. Should the Bloods fail in their contract with regard to quality or quantity, the contract stipulated that other sources would be sought to make up the remainder, with the Bloods liable for the difference in price.[50] When it became clear in May that they would default on their contract, for reasons not given, seventy-four tons of more expensive hay had to be purchased elsewhere at a loss to the government of $131.10. The NWMP comptroller deducted this from the amount due the Bloods.[51]

The Bloods themselves, however, could also be demanding in their contract specifications. Their 1915 hay contract with Gordon Ironsides and Fares, under the terms of the company's lease, stipulated that the company purchase from the Bloods not less than 700 tons at the rate of $5.00 per ton. The Bloods, however, were under no obligation to supply that amount. When the company wanted to break or alter the terms of this agreement, the agent responded that he was determined to "see that these Indians get a square deal."[52]

There is little detailed comment on the haying activities of the Bloods in later years, but hay sales continued, much as they did for the Blackfoot, for example, in subsequent decades.[53] Kainai elders Eva Hind Bull (born 1928), Jim Shot Both Sides (born 1912), and Mabel Beebe (born 1915) recall haying activities to supplement their incomes.[54] Leasing to large ranching interests continued on the reserve well beyond the period of study, and it is likely that the Bloods continued to supply hay on at least an occasional basis, if not more often. Grazing lands also continued to be leased, offering a different approach to the sale of hay.

Freighting

Freighting also brought lucrative market involvement for the Bloods. This activity provided opportunities for employment off the reserve and was required to transport the reserve's resources to market. Such work likely appealed to the Bloods because of their involvement with horses, which many of them owned. Freighting also offered some flexibility as one could accept work when needed or desired. The basic requirements were simple; a man needed a wagon and horses, usually consisting of two or four horse teams, the latter appearing to have been most common. During the appropriate seasons, the haulage teams could be very busy with as many as fifty-three freighters operating at any one time.[55] This was a substantial commitment of men, wagons, and horses.

Freighting, for the Bloods, took place along well-travelled routes. Generally they were engaged in hauling reserve coal to the various locations needed on the reserve as well as into Fort Macleod, Cardston, and Lethbridge. Among the more travelled routes were those connecting the various mines, especially at Lethbridge, with the NWMP posts in southern Alberta. (See Figure 2.5.) Also important were the routes connecting the reserve and area hay lands with the local farmers and the ranches, such as the Cochrane Ranche. There were also lesser routes taken when Blood freighters engaged in incidental freighting for businesses or worked on construction projects such as the irrigation works around Cardston. Freighting services offered significant opportunity for the utilization of the Bloods' labour resources in the local economy.

In the case of freighting, the Blood freighters' invasion of the marketplace was based on two simple strategies, competitive pricing and influence. They were often willing to freight commodities from the various mines to the customer at the cheapest rate. Under these circumstances they were self-employed with Agent Wilson arranging contracts for their services. In 1893 Wilson reported that the Galt Coal Company would provide him coal for the NWMP contract, at the mine for $3.25 per ton. It was Wilson's opinion that the district market would support a price of $7.50 a ton and he was hoping for a 100-ton delivery at that price to the various

Mounted Police posts. The $3.25 per ton difference was calculated to clear expenses and provide attractive profit for the individuals engaged.[56]

October of that year proved to be a very busy time for coal hauling as preparations were made for getting in a winter supply. Agent Wilson reported twenty four-horse teams and one two-horse team hauling coal to the various NWMP posts. The 100-ton contract for the Mounted Police was completed inside of two weeks. Wilson anticipated that this prompt delivery would result in a larger share of future police contracts.[57] Clearly Wilson counted on Blood freighters winning contracts away from local non-Native haulage contractors.

In February 1898 the Bloods were busy filling their coal contract with the NWMP having delivered 280 tons of a 600-ton contract. Wilson also reported: "A number of Indians were also engaged [in] purchasing coal on their own account and taking it to Macleod for sale" for eleven dollars per load.[58] He noted in January 1897 that forty-nine Bloods earned $1,895.96 freighting coal, which compares favourably with the $7,510.11 of total earnings declared for 1896.[59] The Bloods delivered 115 tons of coal to the NWMP at Macleod in late 1898 and earned $650.00. In requesting speedy payment, Wilson pointed out that the "Indians are hard up for money at present to purchase winter clothing, extra food, etc."[60]

By 1898 Wilson had abandoned any prospect of the Blood coalmine being able to produce commercial quality or quantities of coal but he continued to obtain delivery contracts. In September he gave the police quotations for coal delivered to the various southern Alberta detachments. His plan was to purchase the coal from other companies and resell it, adding a delivery charge. Although police Inspector R. Burton Deane tried to drive a hard bargain, Wilson was inflexible and pointed out to Deane that, besides increased coal prices, a shortage of labour in the freighting business placed upward pressure on value.[61] Wilson, as the Bloods' representative, was intent on exploiting prevailing market conditions and maximizing returns to Blood freighters for the services they provided.

The fact that the Mounted Police were the Blood reserve's biggest non-agency customer came to the attention of the *Lethbridge News*, which reported, in March 1901, that the Bloods, in an obviously efficient operation, had delivered 120 tons of coal to the police in just three days. As well, "a large quantity of coal" was delivered to the Cochrane Ranche, and to a variety of Agency institutions.[62]

The *News* observed that Blood freighters were significant players in the freighter-for-hire marketplace:

image not available

Figure 3.4.
"Blood men, freighters, west of Macleod, Alberta, [1894]." Glenbow Archives, NA-2459-1. Figure 3.4, and Figure 3.5 below, provide a good indication of the men, horses, and equipment the Bloods could muster to engage in the freighting business for income.

NEIGHBOURS AND NETWORKS

The Indians are very eager to get freighting, but although the agent never misses a chance to procure it, either in single loads or in large contracts, he [the agent] cannot keep them regularly employed. This, however, is not surprising: they can turn out one hundred and thirty four-horse teams, instantly, upon receiving notice that they are wanted.[63]

Such communal effort was a significant factor in the Bloods' ability to secure freighting contracts and caused local non-Native freighters and suppliers some concern, anxiety, and aggravation over their own loss of work and income.

When shortages of freighting services occurred, the Bloods were sought out by businesses needing haulage teams. The agent noted in his yearly report for 1898 that freighting was a principal occupation of the Bloods, including freighting for the agency, the NWMP, local ranchers, local merchant houses, as well as on one occasion freighting lumber for the construction of an irrigation canal undertaken by the Mormons at Cardston.[64]

After 1901, little detail of the freighting activities of the Bloods is available. It is reasonable to assume, however, that the Bloods continued to take advantage of freighting opportunities offered by local farmers, businesses, and works projects. In 1914, for example, they were reported doing "a large amount of freighting" for local farmers, and during the 1916 harvest season "Some 150 teams and 200 men availed themselves of the labour at remunerative wages and with satisfaction to their employers."[65] It is likely that Blood freighters were involved in the large irrigation projects going on in southern Alberta at this time. As the Bloods acquired motor vehicles, they could take advantage of opportunities farther from the reserve.[66] Though treaty promises to protect the traditional economy were seldom honoured, and with the passage of time, it became impractical to remain tied to outmoded economic activities, the Bloods, through their own and their agents' initiatives, secured alternative sources of income.

THE SPECIAL EFFORTS OF AGENT WILSON

When Hayter Reed became Indian Commissioner in 1888, he took advantage of existing legislation, specifically the pass and permit systems, to attempt control of Native participation in local economies through isolating them on reserves in an effort to turn them into 'peasant farmers.' A pass gave an Indian the agent's official permission to be away from the reserve. The permit granted the legal right to dispose of goods or produce in the off-reserve marketplace. The pass system originated with the 1885 rebellion and was intended as a temporary measure to monitor the movement of Natives leaving their reserves. It was likely maintained following the rebellion because the DIA recognized it as an expedient method of control over many aspects of Native culture and life.[67] Evidence shows that some agents were very rigid in applying the policy in an attempt to restrict, as much as possible, Indian involvement in the marketplace on the one hand, and to encourage the husbanding of the reserve's resources on the other.[68] In the case of the Bloods, the pass and permit systems failed to meet the Department's expectations for two basic reasons. The first was the complicity of reserve and departmental officials in undermining the legislation by generally encouraging and permitting the Bloods to leave the reserve to work. The second was the obvious need and/or desire of the Bloods to circumvent the official regulations to their own benefit.

By the 1890s Blood farmers, in keeping with advancing trends in farm mechanization, had become acutely aware of the value of machines as labour-saving devices and sought to acquire them in order to be more productive.[69] Efforts in this direction were met with little sympathy from the Department as they ran counter to Commissioner Hayter Reed's desire to tie Canada's western Native 'peasant farmers' to the soil.[70] Reed determined that reserve farmers were "not to be assisted in the purchase of labour saving machines." At the same time, Agent William Pocklington noted that non-Natives were not to be permitted to cut hay on the reserve; instead, the Bloods were to be encouraged to cut and market the hay themselves.[71] The Department appeared to ignore the contradiction of wishing the Blood farmers to market a commodity in an increasingly mechanized agricultural setting without mechanical assistance.[72] With the Bloods desperate for both money and work, it is inconceivable that Pocklington would grant permits to outsiders to cut reserve hay, in any case.

But even during Reed's tenure, local circumstance and cost considerations sometimes took precedence over "official" policy. Before 1894, for example, the Blood hay producers had enjoyed special consideration with regard to the granting of government contracts in that the usual 10 per cent deposit was dispensed with in favour of the Indians. The rules for government contracts, however, were altered in that year, and not in favour of the Bloods.[73] In June, Agent James Wilson wrote Superintendent Sam

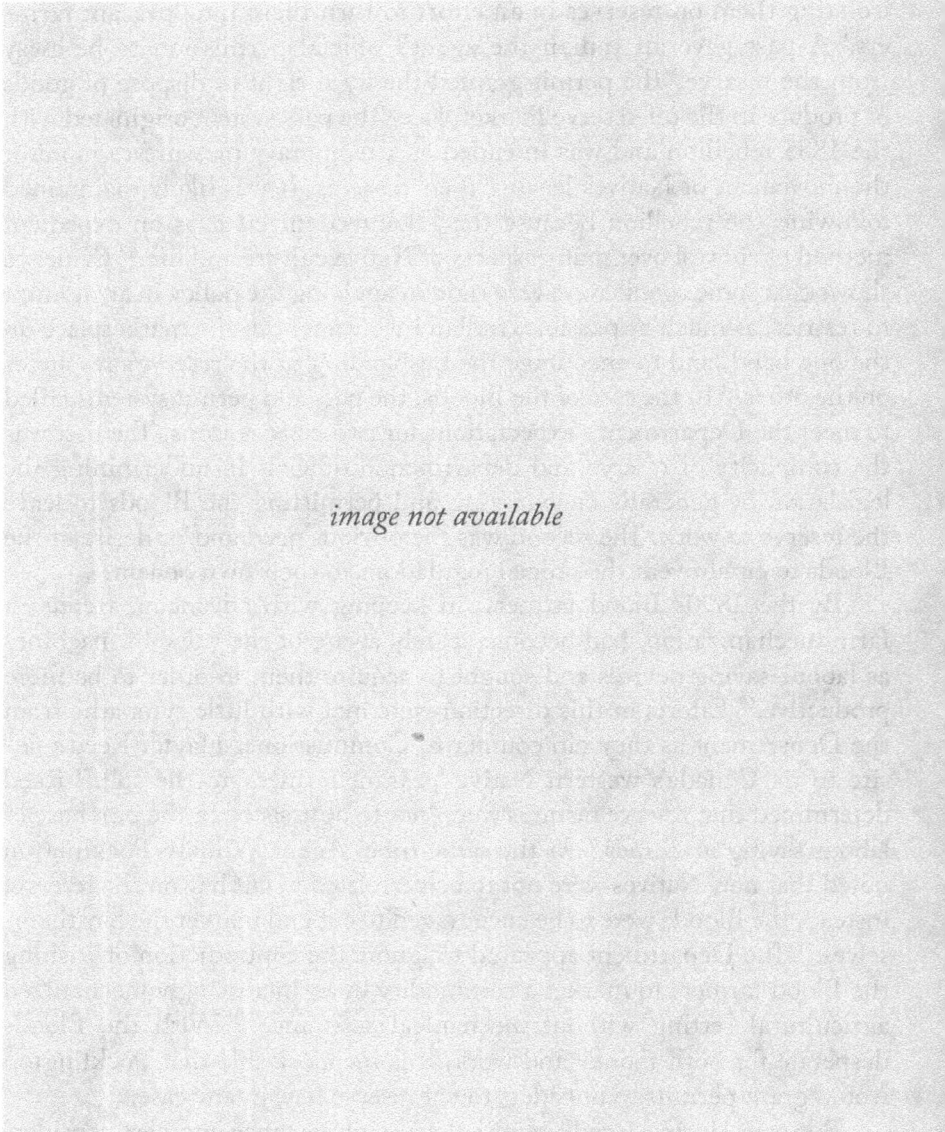

image not available

Figure 3.5. "Blood people hauling grain, [ca. 1900-1903]." Glenbow Archives, NA-1437-8.

NEIGHBOURS AND NETWORKS

Steele, NWMP, that he could put up the hay at the Stand Off Detachment for eight dollars per ton instead of the earlier agreed nine.[74] The reason for this reduction he made clear in a subsequent letter. The granting of DIA contracts to Indians was to be placed on the same footing as others: to be awarded to the contractors with the lowest bids. Wilson petitioned the Indian Commissioner to intercede with the Police Commissioner to secure an agreement that 25 per cent of the police contracts be held for the Indians as was previously the custom. In the meantime he was forced to lower his bid to secure work for the Bloods.[75]

The Bloods' impact on market conditions often depended on the agent working on their behalf. In this respect Agent James Wilson stood out for his unceasing and untiring efforts. In July 1894, for example, the ever-aggressive Wilson agreed to have the Bloods deliver coal to NWMP detachments at Macleod, Kipp, and Stand Off from any of the Galt, Sharon, or Hauk's mines for $7.00, $6.50, and $6.00 per ton, respectively.[76] On this occasion, however, Wilson's bid to secure the NWMP contract for Macleod failed and so he approached W.D. Barclay, Lethbridge, who held the contract, with the idea of sub-contracting about 200 tons of the contracted amount. If this were not possible, he wished to have the Bloods hauling coal to Barclay's agents in Fort Macleod. Wilson was ostensibly driven by his desire to have "some work for these Indians to do during the next month or two."[77]

Success for the Bloods, as for the remainder of the community, also depended upon the vitality of the local economy. In January 1895, Wilson reported that during the previous month little outside work was done except for minimal freighting of hay and coal. With regard to the latter, "sales are hard to make at any price in Macleod at present."[78]

As a result of Wilson's efforts, however, and their willingness to accept whatever contracts were available, a number of Blood freighters remained busy. Wilson reported in October 1895:

> The freighting of lumber etc. is quite a serious affair at the present moment and I have just completed arrangements with Major Steele to haul other [sic] 75 tons of coal to Stand Off detachment before the middle of the next month and I have also made a contract with the Cochrane Ranche Company to deliver 40 tons of coal and 4000 bricks. All this coal and brick must be hauled from Lethbridge which is distant from Stand Off 35 miles and 47 from the Cochrane Ranche.[79]

Similarly, Wilson's request that departmental officials use their influence to secure work for the Bloods bore fruit. Indian Commissioner Hayter Reed wired Agent Wilson that "If you can freight six hundred tons coal police require at Macleod at five ninety five I shall get contract for you."[80] Reed also wanted the reserve mine to supply various other police outposts. The Bloods said they could deliver on the request. Although they secured the police contract, the arrangement collapsed.[81] The NWMP, complaining of the quality, refused to accept coal from the Indian mine. Local citizens at Fort Macleod exhibited a similar reluctance.[82] The Blood teamsters then turned to delivering coal from Lethbridge under contract. Although, in this case, contracting their haulage equipment to deliver a competitor's coal left the reserve mine without delivery capacity, it was a sensible alternative and secured both work and income.[83]

What is most interesting about Hayter Reed's involvement in acquiring off-reserve employment for the Bloods is that it was, as he knew, in direct contradiction to both the spirit and letter of "official" departmental policy, a policy devised by and driven by Reed himself.[84] Why then did he acquire work for the Bloods that was so likely to bring them to public notice? As a DIA official, Reed was certainly aware that the pass system had no legal basis and that the North West Mounted Police were reluctant to enforce it.[85] Making the pass system work, therefore, was both a difficult and legally dicey business. Also, with the experience of 1885 fading, the policy likely seemed less urgent. Another possible explanation is that the policy was, in part, a public relations ploy for the benefit of local settlers and never envisioned as absolute. One also suspects that the policy was very idealistic and thus easily forsaken in the face of financial considerations. It was, therefore, a way to pay lip service to those occasional complaints of unfair Native competition that were inevitably followed by public demands that the Indians have only restricted access to local economic opportunities. If the policy, however, could be circumvented without too much public notice and outcry, and such evasion presented the promise of reduced departmental expenditure, then Native involvement in the marketplace was encouraged.

THE MARKET RESPONDS

The Department's, and especially the agent's, aggressive activity on behalf of the Blood freighters and producers was bound to lead to resentment from locals intent on protecting their livelihoods. When Agent James

Wilson tendered for the delivery of 400 tons of coal to the NWMP barracks at Fort Macleod and other detachments, in August 1895, he warned the Commissioner:

> ... as there is a considerable amount of feeling among the white people in this district about Indians doing such work I would ask you to kindly see the Commissioner of the Police on this matter and do what you can to obtain a share of this work for the Indians. I am afraid a good deal of pressure may be put upon the Commissioner to try and prevent us getting any.[86]

Clearly Wilson expected a backlash against the Bloods' freighting activities and wished to pre-empt any attempt to cut them out of the lucrative work.

Wilson also wished to reduce the uncertainty of winning freighting contracts during the yearly bidding competition. He suggested to the Indian Commissioner that perhaps in future it could be "arranged that a certain part (say one half) of the coal supply should be held back for the Indians to deliver without putting it to open tenders.... If this was done it might tend to lessen the feeling that the Indians were taking away the living of the white men."[87] It is difficult to see how the removal of one half of the business opportunities afforded by these important contracts would lessen local entrepreneurial resentment against the Bloods, unless it was a case that half a loaf was considered better than none. Wilson's action not only reveals concern for the well-being of his charges but also suggests that, through the auspices of the agency, the Bloods had considerable influence in tendering on contracts.

Clearly the Bloods were not reluctant participants in the marketplace. Nor were the pass and permit systems, designed to prevent market access and the squandering of reserve resources, an unqualified success. Inevitably competition from the Bloods, and other Indians, led to complaints. A letter to the editor of the *Macleod Gazette* from "Freighter" bluntly stated the case against Indian competition. It criticized those perceived as "not only permitting, but assisting the Blood Reserve Indians to compete with the White settlers and laborers in the putting 'up' and sale of hay." The basis of the complaint was that the Bloods had secured large contracts through underbidding the Whites. "It is bad enough to allow these Indians to put up hay on outside contracts," the writer observed, "but when it comes to their bringing it into town for sale in large quantities, as they are doing now, it is carrying the thing a little too far." The crux of the matter, as this particular complainant saw it, was that the government, thus giving them a competitive edge, supplied all the material and resources placed at the Indians' disposal. "Because their machines, wagons, grub and every other thing necessary for the business are provided for them," the writer protested, "and because, in order that these things may be provided, the very men with whom they compete pay dollar for dollar the same money as others in Canada into the fund, out of which the machines, wagons, etc., used by these Indians are purchased," it was hardly fair.[88] Competition was no problem, as long as equity prevailed.

The *Gazette* supported this complaint and observed, "The only apparent argument that can be used in favor of the present system seems to be that the Indians have not been very successful in their other pursuits, and that putting up hay seems to be one of the very few things that they can do." The *Gazette* railed against the government's expensive and futile effort at making Indians self-sufficient. The paper also charged there was unfairness in that the peoples' wards were being financed in undercutting their beneficiaries:

> It is submitted that these Indians are earning a certain amount of money by putting up hay with implements supplied by the government; by hauling supplies with wagons obtained from the same source, and by getting out (under a white man) and hauling coal, in all of which occupations they compete with hard working white men, does not indicate any advance toward independent self-support.[89]

Blood producers, however, were simply availing themselves of market opportunities presented by local settlers and towns people looking for a bargain. There were bargains to be had as the Bloods, among other things, freighted supplies, hauled coal, hunted wolves cut logs, and did herding and other work for settlers.[90] They were especially successful with the production and sale of hay, and in 1896 exceeded the agent's "most sanguine expectations" and again in 1898 they sold a considerable amount of hay in Fort Macleod.[91] Indeed prices were so good, and the market so brisk, that Agent Wilson was concerned about the possibility of Blood farmers selling hay that they needed for their own cattle. In July he requested that the Lethbridge town police warn the public that the purchase of hay from Bloods not possessing a duly authorized permit to sell left the purchaser open to prosecution.[92] He did note that "A great deal of talk had been going on among the White men [freighters] in Macleod district about the Indians doing freighting work and if I am to put in tenders for police hay and coal then I will require to cut down low to secure them and that will cause them [freighters] to kick more than ever." Consequently Wilson did succeed in getting the contracts for the Stand Off and Big Bend Mounted Police detachments, because the Bloods had the competitive edge.[93]

Complaints against the Bloods fluctuated with time and economic conditions. The 'exceptional circumstances' created by World War I and a 1917 coal strike, for example, shut down most of the coalmines in western Canada.[94] By 1921, however, market conditions had returned to normal so complaints were received about Blood reserve coal competing in a restricted market environment. G. Finnie, the Chief Inspector of Mines for Alberta, notified the Department of Indian Affairs of complaints from operators in Magrath and Raymond in particular. Local producers expressed dissatisfaction because the Blood sales presented unfair competition because Blood miners did not have to pay leasing dues and royalties. Thus the right of the Bloods to sell coal on the open market was challenged but without effect. In an open market situation complaints from competitors who believed themselves at a disadvantage were bound to occur.[95]

CONCLUSIONS

The Bloods participated in the local marketplace with the assistance and encouragement of the local agent and often the Department of Indian Affairs. Coal mining occurred because some Bloods saw it as profitable and because the agents encouraged this activity despite, at times, some misgivings about its viability. Coal mining, sales, and freighting fitted nicely into the local economic infrastructure. There was a constant demand on the reserve for coal and often from those in the vicinity. Both the Bloods and the DIA were cautious with regard to the management of this resource and so it was never allowed to come under the control of non-Natives, outside of occasional advisory services.

Haying illustrates the interactive exploitation of a Blood reserve resource. The share-crop agreements regarding the harvesting and sale of hay is indicative of mutually beneficial resource use, the reserve provided a product for which there was much demand in the surrounding community. Farmers, ranchers, the Mounted Police, and the Bloods themselves placed great reliance on hay in this particular period when horses were a major source of agricultural power and transportation, and cattle were a chief source of food.

Freighting or shipping activities brought the Bloods into most direct conflict with non-Native economic agencies. This work was separated, in the public mind, from other activities that originated on the reserve. The perception was that, whereas the Bloods owned the coal and hay, they did not own the freighting and there was great concern that the livelihoods of non-Natives be protected through assured equal access. Non-Natives were well aware of the Bloods' special status as wards of the state and saw any advantages accruing as a result of that status as unfair competition. Despite public perceptions, however, there is no evidence that the government made any attempts to curb the Bloods' participation in freighting activities.

The willingness to exploit on- and off-reserve opportunities likely made the difference between marginal survival and abject poverty, a fate that faced many of the Bloods' contemporaries, both Native and non-Native. The *Macleod Times* of July 21, 1920 reported that both Bloods and Peigans were digging bones from the south bank of the Oldman River and selling them for fertilizer, one endeavour that the *Times* estimated earned the Indians several thousand dollars.[96] In his memoir, amateur historian Bud Spencer reported Blood teams engaged in hauling wheat for local farmers some twenty miles to Cardston.[97] In 1927, the Bloods shipped over 2,000 "canner" horses to Great Falls, Montana, for forty to fifty cents per hundredweight.[98] By 1928 the Bloods were granting oil leases on the reserve.[99]

Some individuals like James Gladstone, the future senator, sought economic security for his family, wherever opportunity presented itself. Gladstone shared in the "general prosperity" of the 186 Blood reserve farmers during the latter years of the 1920s, and in the unexpected and devastating collapse of grain prices in 1929. Despite the economic hardships of the 1930s, he established a small trucking outfit on the reserve and secured contracts hauling wheat, coal, and cattle, eventually acquiring contracts from the Department of Indian Affairs. As business developed, the tiny company was able to expand and provide Gladstone and his family with some financial security.[100]

Despite the sometimes overwhelming management control of the agent and DIA, the Bloods' economic activities were self-motivated. They opened and worked the mines and sought out contracts. They instigated the share-crop arrangements with local farmers and ranchers, and they mustered their horses and wagons to ensure efficient delivery of coal, hay, and other commodities under contract. It was the Bloods who laboured to ensure their own livelihoods. Their evident motivation, perhaps, ensured the willingness of the DIA to, at times, adjust its policies to local circumstances. It also ensured the behind-the-scenes work of the various agents currying favour from one government agency or another. This was sufficient to secure for the Bloods a periodic, profitable, and sometimes influential market presence, especially in the supply of coal, hay, and freighting services. Criticism from the non-Native public seems to have had little impact on curbing the Bloods' desire to take positive action to secure economic independence. Clearly, and as will be illustrated below, the Bloods had a marvellous capacity for work and a ready willingness to engage competitively and energetically in the marketplace.

4: 'All the Indians have gone to the beet': Blood Labour in the Raymond Sugar Beet Fields

INTRODUCTION

The local industry that offered the Bloods the greatest opportunity for the sale of their labour was the sugar beet industry at Raymond. However one rationalizes the Bloods' presence, it is clear that in this case Blood labourers were vital to sustaining the industrial process during the first phase of its operations from 1903 to 1915. They appear to have played a minor part in the industry thereafter. Though studies of the Bloods have paid little or no attention to their participation in the sugar beet fields, this work was, in many ways, central to both the industry and the Bloods' livelihood for more than a decade.[1]

THE INDUSTRY: LOCAL EVOLUTION

During 1901, Jesse Knight, a Mormon from Provo, Utah, with some encouragement from Elliot Galt and John W. Taylor of the Latter Day Saints, chose a site east of the Blood reserve, at Raymond, to establish a sugar beet processing plant. Local settlers regarded the site as fit only for hay land, but Knight became convinced it had great potential for the cultivation of sugar beet.[2] The *Raymond Rustler* later defined the sugar beet business as: "an industry requiring a great amount of labor and the investment of a large sum of money." Interestingly, it pointed out that the two main requirements of money and manpower "were not obstacles but incentives." Incentives were so attractive that Knight hastily put down a $50,000 deposit as security in an agreement with the North West

Irrigation Company and the Alberta Railway and Coal Company to purchase the 200,000 acres of land needed for his enterprise.[3] Knight believed that, with suitable land and plenty of available labour, the outlook was exceedingly promising for an industry that could fill an insatiable consumer demand for a product at present entirely imported from outside the region.[4] The Raymond area stood to reap great benefits as an estimated 150 people would have continuous employment in the factory and others would be "employed continuously by the company in their own fields, as experts[,] managers and office hands," to say nothing of the farmers and workers who would be needed to grow beets.[5]

Initially the company hoped to cultivate enough of its beets to meet its own needs. This failed and by 1904 the company's production methods changed with the enlistment of local farmers to grow beets under contract, an arrangement that was to be continued in future years. The Cardston *Alberta Star* revealed that the company planned to have 4,000 acres in beets, 3,000 cultivated by the company directly, with local farmers cultivating the remaining acres. The new arrangements promised to pay farmers $5.00 per ton and a share of the government bounty on sugar, thus bringing the price paid to the farmer to $5.35 per ton.[6] Although it appeared lucrative, contract beet growing never solved the company's perennial shortages. Dawson says that the company "was never able to secure more than 22,000 tons of beets a year, and in some years the tonnage dropped as low as 8,000."[7]

Shortages became so severe that by 1913 J.W. Evans, Agricultural Superintendent of the Knight Sugar Co., tried to induce more local farmers to plant sugar beet by promoting both the agricultural and financial benefits of beet culture. Beet cultivation, he argued, brought a number of benefits, including the encouragement of crop rotation and an increased yield for other crops. The industry also created a demand for labour, thus making possible the employment of children who, otherwise, in his opinion, provided no economic benefit. Beet cultivation also offered price stability, since growers knew the price of their product before planting. The fact that farmers of small means could grow beets was also touted as an attraction. In 1914, for example, instructions were given in the *Leader* on how to prepare the land for planting.[8] In a last-ditch attempt at persuasion, Evans waxed poetic, "Then let us raise the SUGAR BEET, No question bout the pay 'Cause if we work the balance sheet[,] Will show a better day.'"[9]

In case there were still skeptics, Evans went on to argue: "A comparison of a ten ton crop of sugar beets with a forty bushel crop of wheat assumed to be grown on summer fallowed land" yielded a net profit per acre of $18.70 for beets compared to $14.05 for wheat or a difference of $4.65 in favour of beet growing. "In addition to this the beet tops are worth from $5.00 to $10.00 for feed." He also admonished the local population to support this Native industry: "If it is true, … that ten pounds of imported sugar are used in Lethbridge to one of Raymond, we as citizens ought to be heartily ashamed of ourselves.… Lethbridge coal is good enough for us. So is Raymond Sugar."[10] The reported payroll of over $10,000 during the plant production run was money kept in the community, and the employment of about three hundred men when other work was scarce was also calculated to tie the Knight Sugar Company fortunes to the general well-being of the community.[11]

By December 1914, it was evident that the appeals to local loyalty, and the highlighting of benefits for the local economy, were not enough. In December 1914 the *Leader* reported that the Knight Sugar factory was planning to move its operation closer to Great Falls, Montana. With relocation imminent, the locals marshalled their influence and enthusiasm with a public meeting on December 20, 1914, to protest the move and attempt to secure "a guarantee of 2,000 acres of beets next year," the minimum required to bring about a reconsideration of the proposed move.[12] It was too late, however, and by January 8, 1915, the *Leader* had to admit that, "Beets talk and 1,800 acres isn't very strong language."[13] Consequently, on January 15, the paper announced the loss of the sugar plant to Layton, Utah.[14] It was an ignominious, if temporary, end to an enterprise that had seemingly held out such promise.

THE BLOODS' SIGNIFICANCE

There is no direct evidence that Jesse Knight had the Bloods in mind when he chose the site for his sugar factory. However, they quickly became so important to the sugar company's operations that it is inconceivable that Knight was not aware of the benefits of tapping the potential labour pool of the Blood reserve and its 1,200 inhabitants directly to the west of the factory site.[15] In its early stages of development, sugar beet agriculture was labour-intensive, and a readily available source of dependable cheap labour was essential.

In southern Alberta the sugar beet season generally began in April with seeding, with the all-important thinning occurring in June. Throughout the growing season, hand-cultivating and weeding were essential.

Weather permitting, the beets were ready to harvest by the end of October. Harvesting required the pulling and topping of the beets, with sugar-making beginning when the beets were delivered to the factory. Thinning and harvesting both required back-breaking intensive labour. Thinning in particular forced the worker to crawl on hands and knees through the field. The weather, especially during the fall harvest season, was often cold and wet and this added to the physical discomfort of those working in the fields.

The Bloods, permanent residents in the area, were an ideal labour source and, perhaps, Knight had them in mind when he claimed that acquiring sufficient workforce would present no difficulties.[16] One fact is clear, there was no other identifiable body of potential labour in such close proximity to the factory. Where else could one hope to find hundreds of workers available at a moment's notice? When the opportunity was available and the conditions suitable, many Bloods left the reserve each fall to labour in the Raymond beet fields.

In anticipation of a smooth startup for the 1903 processing season, Knight began arranging for field hands and the first place he apparently turned to was the Blood Reserve. In November 1902, well before the first beet planting, company representative H.S. Allen wrote Blood Indian Agent James Wilson of the company's need for "A great number of hands ... to weed and thin beets." Allen hoped Blood labourers could be hired for this work. In an effort to get good value for the company's dollar, Allen attempted to give Wilson a lesson in Native work habits, pointing out that, in his opinion, women and children would do work as good as or better than the "bucks" and, should they prove willing, "large numbers" would be employed.[17]

In January 1903, company manager E.P. Ellison approached Wilson once again to arrange for the Bloods' assistance with the fall harvest. Although Wilson promised Ellison help in any way possible, he refused to guarantee any specific number of Bloods for the work because he feared that they might not be able to perform this new and specialized labour.[18] By March, however, Wilson again promised, keeping Allen's reservations about male labour in mind, to encourage the employment of women and children in the beet fields. By late October, however, any labour shortage had been resolved and Agent Wilson was unable to find haulage teams to deliver hay to Lethbridge owing to the fact that "all the Indians have gone to the Beet [sic] cutting and hauling at Raymond."[19] This arrangement with the Bloods was so rewarding that the company expressed a desire to contract Blood labourers, by the acre or on a daily basis, to thin, hoe, dig, and top six hundred acres of beets from May to October of the following year. However, still lacking confidence in the Bloods' abilities, Wilson advised that they be restricted to thinning activities and that Whites be employed for the other tasks.[20] The company, however, was so impressed with the Bloods' work that it hoped to use Blood labourers to also put up hay.[21]

Initially the use of Blood labour was beneficial for all concerned, and in the opinion of the new Blood Agent, R.N. Wilson, the business relationship of the Blood reserve with Knight Sugar and the Raymond citizenry was worth encouraging. The new agent was also more aggressive on the part of the Bloods, and more confident of their suitability for beet work. Responding to a Department of Indian Affairs inquiry about Indian labour in the beet fields Wilson wrote:

> ... there is nothing in connection with the growing of beets that may not be learned by our Indians, and as the work appears to be profitable enough I am of the opinion that we should encourage some of them to go to Raymond when required by the Sugar Company. Other points in favor of the scheme are the fact that women and children can materially assist in the occupation.

Wilson also noted that the nature and timing of the work in the beet fields did not interfere with the Bloods' yearly round of activities on the reserve.[22] In the one case where they conflicted with the issuance of treaty annuities, the DIA was willing to consider an adjustment of the payment schedule, so as not to interfere with the beet harvest or with the Bloods' opportunity to earn extra income. This was an important consideration in the Department's desire to turn Natives into self-supporting independent workers on the theoretical White model.[23]

Increased sugar beet acreage planted by Knight Sugar resulted in greater demand for Blood labour at various critical times during the growing season. A query from the Home-Seekers Association, Cardston District, wondered whether the organization was at liberty to hire Blood labour "as we wish."[24] The DIA officials, however, were not about to let the Bloods be hired on an individual basis, perhaps to ensure that fair hiring practices were followed and that pay equity prevailed. Indian Affairs official Frank Pedley stipulated that Native labour be paid at the same rate as

Figure 4.1.
"Robert Nathaniel Wilson, [ca. 1895]." Glenbow Archives, ND-34-17. Robert Wilson, as Blood Indian agent, often defended the tribe's interests against both government regulations and local business concerns.

Whites, in cash, and that accommodation be provided to workers if they were not expected to provide their own. Both Pedley and (earlier) Wilson expressed a preference that the Bloods be hired for certain tasks only, and these generally were outside activities: a reflection of the Darwinist belief that Natives needed the outdoor freedom. As for wages, "It is stated that from $1.00 to $1.75 per day can be made."[25] In the end, however, the 1904 season likely brought less opportunity for labour wages in the sugar beet fields when drought saw both grain and sugar beet harvests reduced.[26]

By the 1905 growing season, it was evident that Knight Sugar had come to rely on the Bloods as the main labour source for their beet production. That fall manager Ellison once again asked for Bloods at Raymond and reminded the agent that they would be paid "what it is worth."[27] Blood workers, in turn, began to count on the employment at Raymond as an important source of yearly income. Depending on the numbers employed, the sugar beet work was profitable. The Department reported that "Some of the Blood Indians ... earned over $2,000 in topping and hauling beets."[28] In fact this work became so profitable that the Bloods avoided less remunerative work. For example, the delivery of twenty-five tons of hay requested by George Skelding of Macleod was delayed because most of the Bloods and their teams were in the Raymond beet fields. In fact the exodus from the reserve was so complete that, on October 23, the agent was not even able to arrange delivery of a load of sawdust because of a lack of freighters and equipment.[29]

In 1906, the *Calgary Herald* recognized both the Bloods' capacity for work and the skill acquired after three years of experience with all aspects of sugar beet cultivation. The writer noted: "One likes best to watch the Indians at work; they make their long, rapid strokes with inimitable grace and the utmost nonchalance. When the whites are listlessly and laboriously getting in the last hours of a long, hot day, [the Indians] seem quite as unexhausted as in early dewy morning." This opinion does not support the contention that one of the main dissatisfactions with Indian labour was that they damaged beets during the thinning stage.[30] The acquired skill and dedicated labour did indeed bring its rewards. The company estimated that about $12,000 was paid to Natives in wages in 1905. Although the company had to estimate what was paid by local farmers and did not know if all the labourers were Bloods, it is fairly certain the vast majority of workers were indeed Bloods from the reserve.[31]

In the fall of 1906, with a fourth harvest imminent, the importance of the Bloods' contribution to the Raymond sugar beet industry was blatantly obvious. One local farmer using Blood labour wrote Agent Wilson in the hope that the coming annuity payments could be delayed so as not to interfere with the harvest. To impress upon Wilson the urgency of his request, he added: "If you can arrange this for them it will be a great favor to the Knight Sugar Co. and us as we are *depending* on them to harvest the crop."[32]

On October 24, E.P. Ellison made the case for Knight Sugar with the same urgency. He pointed out that Blood workers had employment until December 1 and requested a deferment of annuities for thirty days.[33] The request was accommodated but this was later found to be a mistake as the poor weather cut the harvest short. Wilson wrote, with some irritation and concern, that the delay in treaty payments had left many of the Bloods short of funds to purchase necessary winter clothing. But when weather or culture did not dictate otherwise, the Bloods were dedicated workers.

Agent Wilson's report for 1908 observed that during the previous spring "several hundreds" of the Bloods secured a month's employment thinning beets "and in the month of October practically the whole population of the reservation was busy harvesting beets in the same fields."[34]

An apparent exception to the general rule of Indians being designated field labourers occurred when a Blood by the name of Prairie Chicken grew beets for Knight Sugar on contract. The factory leased him ten acres, ploughed it for twenty dollars, disked and levelled it for ten, furnished seed and planted it for eighteen, supplied needed water for six, and charged him thirty-five dollars for rent, for a total investment of eighty-nine dollars. The company agreed to purchase his beets at five dollars a ton delivered to the factory (a distance of one and a half miles) and speculated that "with good care he should get from 8 to 10 tons per acre from the land." The ever-cautious Agent Wilson sanctioned this contract on the understanding that the payments were to be deducted from the sale of the beet crop and that the Department would in no way be responsible should the joint venture fail.[35] Prairie Chicken experienced some initial success as he was reported thinning his ten acres of beets in July.[36] The final results of his efforts remain a mystery.[37] Were he successful, however, Prairie Chicken, even with the minimum estimated harvest, stood to net $311.00 on the sale of his beets.

En masse or individually, the Bloods' contribution to the sugar beet industry was significant. Royal North West Mounted Police Commissioner A.B. Perry believed the Bloods' participation critical due to the large numbers involved and because of the scarcity of non-Native labour. Officer J.O. Wilson, Lethbridge, felt it was impossible to carry on the beet industry except for the Indians.[38] This 'stoop labor' was so difficult that it was considered "too tedious for the white man, the yellow labor was tried, but without success. The work was then given to the Indians, who, with their stolid natures, have proved to be the most successful."[39] Given prevailing attitudes about the nature of the work, and the belief that it was unsuited to Whites, Natives were especially desired for both the thinning and harvesting phases of the operation. Unappreciated in the above assessment was the willingness and determination of the Bloods to earn a living even at the cost of physically demanding labour in what generally would be considered the most uncomfortable of circumstances.

Sporadic attempts to import labour for the beet fields had no permanent impact on the industry, and in the fall of 1911 Knight Sugar once again anticipated the Bloods entering into their employ. Clearly, Blood labourers were needed, and Raymond Knight implored Agent Julius Hyde, "we would like if possible for you to let all the Indians come that you can spare, thinking that it will both benefit ourselves and the Indians also."[40] Almost a month later, Knight Sugar urgently requested a deferral of treaty payments so as not to hinder harvesting and immediately stated the crux of the company's problem. The Bloods' presence at Raymond was essential "as we are very short of help, and will likely lose a lot of our beets unless the Indians remain to help us."[41] By this time, company dependence on the Bloods' labour throughout the various phases of growing and harvesting sugar beets was all but complete. Missing, however, was the realization of this reality and so the Knight Sugar Company failed to appreciate precarious reduced margins for success, which were directly related to the treatment of the people in their labour pool.

INDUSTRY PROBLEMS

Although the Bloods were critical to the industry, an important fact not fully grasped by the company was that the Bloods did not view sugar beet harvest labour as essential to their own survival. Sometimes they had an aversion to the taxing work and found other income opportunities more appealing. On other occasions they were indifferent to the benefits of the income earned. These changing attitudes proved a source of great frustration to Knight Sugar. According to Agent James Wilson, in October 1903, approximately 150 Bloods were engaged in filling hay contracts and were thus not available for sugar beet labour. He sensibly enough concluded that the trip to Raymond was too difficult for the elderly who were available. It was only several weeks later, with their other work completed, that the harvest at Raymond received the attention of the larger work force.[42]

Many Bloods were willing to work in the beet fields, but only if the times they were required meshed with their own needs, in other words, when obligations and preference did not dictate their presence elsewhere. They considered themselves free and independent and unwilling to become part of a captive labour pool where others largely determined the value of their labour.

That the Bloods were unwilling to entirely adapt their routines to accommodate Knight Company's seasonal demands was a realization not easily grasped by the whole community. J.W. Woolf, a company manager, wrote Agent Wilson in apparent frustration, in September 1903, that the sugar factory was prepared to hire up to four hundred Bloods at the White labour rate of eight dollars per acre for topping and throwing the beets into collection wagons. There was a warning, however, that, should Wilson fail to convince the Bloods to appear at Raymond, he, Woolf, would be "compelled to bring in foreign labour."[43] Hartley reports that the company hired seventy-five Chinese labourers the previous spring but is silent on the success of this venture.[44] Here, perhaps, is an indication of the White attitude to the labour-intensive work. Woolf's promise to now pay at the White labour rate suggests that initially the Bloods had been paid less and this may well explain the source of his current frustration as well as his appeal.

In 1904 Knight Sugar wanted about fifty Bloods to work its fields but, in light of experience and expectation, stipulated that they needed a guarantee that their contracts would be fulfilled. This proviso grew out of an unhappy experience in the fall of 1903 when "a large number" of Blood workers, not unexpectedly, abandoned the beet harvest to receive their treaty payment. Aware of the problem, the Department expressed the desire that arrangements be made so that, in future, the one activity might not interfere with the other.[45]

That said, however, Agent Wilson was unwilling to offer the guarantees that Knight Sugar wanted: that the Bloods perform stated amounts of work. His argument was that the beet work was "new to them and they must acquire considerably more familiarity with it than they now possess before being in a position to sign contracts." Wilson added for good measure: "Our Indians are not Chinamen to be farmed out by bosess [sic]."[46]

Wilson also took the opportunity to comment on what he perceived as the double standard applied by the Company in the employment of Indian labour: "When harvesting beets in the fall the hauling in, one of the most profitable jobs, is done by White men, Mormons, and as our Indians have lots of wagons and horses we should insist upon the Indians being permitted to haul in all the roots 'lifted' by themselves."[47] Wilson's observation may in part explain the Bloods' willingness to abandon the backbreaking labour in the fields at treaty payment time. Treaty money, free for the taking, certainly had more allure, especially when one recognized, as Blood beet workers surely did, that the least physically demanding and best paying work was reserved for Whites.

It is also possible that the avoidance of work in the beet fields by some Bloods was an effort on their part to break the agent's control over their economic decisions. The agency's attempt, in 1904, to have Knight Sugar garnishee the wages of Bloods in debt to the Department succeeded in finding only one of those on the list working for the company. Manager E.P. Ellison speculated that the remainder worked for local farmers and at any rate he doubted if the agent's request would be granted.[48] He likely recognized that to accede to the Agent's wishes would compromise his future appeals to the Bloods for their labour.

The 1906 growing season strained relations between the Blood labourers and individual contractors at Raymond, the result of an apparent bid by contractors to force down the costs of Blood field labour. But the Bloods were having none of it and by late November the sugar beet crop remained unharvested. This situation brought an urgent request from one contractor, J.T. Smellie, to Agent Wilson for some two hundred Bloods to work his seventy acres, and three hundred acres belonging to Knight Sugar as soon as the weather proved favourable. Agent Wilson's response, however, contradicted Smellie's view that only inclement weather was responsible for the delay. Although the weather was, at the time, too cold and wet to allow for outside work, Wilson stated:

> Should such a thing occur as a warm spell I will be glad to send over any Indians who can be found that are *willing* to go but I have serious doubts of your being able to get any further material assistance from here this year. Those to whom I have mentioned the matter ridicule the idea of returning and blame the beet farmers for the present situation. They say that they were at Raymond quite long enough to lift the whole crop had they not been delayed by attempts to force down the price and other vexations. If a period of mild weather does come such as to encourage an attempt to dig beets you had better come over and see what you can do yourself with the Indians.[49]

It appears that Knight Sugar had adopted what Pentland terms a free market and commodification view of beet labour, intending to "hire labour freely for as short or long a time as it was wanted, at the lowest wages necessary to obtain it." The company, however, seems to have missed that it was not expedient for it to force the issue with the Bloods as there was no surplus pool of labour to manipulate and so the cost of labour would not default to its own low market price, determined by competition.[50] Essentially it was a seller's and not a buyer's market.

The Bloods' abandonment of the harvest was frustrating for the industry and there was likely some temptation to criticize their work habits. But there were none more interested than the Department and Agent Wilson in having the Bloods perform productive labour for which they received cold hard cash. Wilson's comments and concern leaves no doubt that, on this occasion, the beet harvest, with its exposure to the elements, was beyond sensible human endurance. Suitable and comfortable housing was needed for shelter and warmth and warm clothing were required against the chill of the fall damp and snow. It is difficult to blame the Bloods for abandoning the beet work when plain common sense dictated such a course of action.

The Bloods also brought with them to the beet fields particular habits that frustrated their employers. When J.T. Smellie was approached by two Bloods for work in February of 1907, he indicated a willingness to employ one, provided he "would consent to stay steady during the season ... but they [Indians] must make up their minds to stay with it and only go to town Saturday afternoons." For this they would be paid twenty cents an acre with the expectation of making three or four dollars a day if they were dedicated. Similarly Ellison wrote the reserve agent hoping to recruit fifteen teamsters willing to work, not for days, but for months, at forty dollars a month without board. Clearly the Bloods did not subscribe to non-Native contract labour expectation and work habits and so Ellison queried Wilson on "how we can best handle the Indian labor in the Beet fields."[51] The Bloods' own preferences and needs, the labour-intensive nature of the work, employee and employer relations, and the weather all contributed to produce a less than ideal experience for the Bloods. Few of them showed up in the fields for the thinning operations in June 1907 because Fourth of July celebrations in Montana proved more of an attraction than thinning beets at Raymond.[52] Regarding the Bloods' attitude towards the beet harvest, the agent observed: "the Indians will drop it and come home as soon as the weather gets too cold for such work no matter what quantity happens to be still in the ground."[53] This must have been particularly galling to the company that was, during 1906–7, experiencing its "high point in productivity."[54]

Some problems encountered with Blood labourers, however, were rooted in the nature of the industry and were more the making of the employer than the shortcomings of the employees. The Bloods were often affected by the restrictive and demanding agreements between contractors and Knight Sugar. A contract between Knight Sugar Company and Thomas Bennett, for example, indicates that Bennett tied himself to specific obligations that included the requirement that his beets test at 12 per cent saccharine and 80 per cent purity. Bennett also had to rent and keep in good repair the company boarding house. The contract further stipulated that Bennett produce a specified tonnage of beets, accept the expense for both the preparation and rental of the land at $1.00 per acre, and other per acre costs as follows: ploughing at $2.00, smoothing at $0.85, seed at a rate of $1.35, planting at $0.40, cultivating twice at $0.80, ploughing up the beets at $1.25, and haulage of the beets to the factory at $2.35.[55] Little wonder that contractors such as Bennett felt themselves squeezed between Knight Sugar and their hired labour. They had to agree initially to costs and wages based on a sugar beet whose quality and quantity they could not guarantee or predict.

The 1907 season brought the first public admission that the industry was not achieving its expected potential and that the whole venture was in trouble. The *Raymond Chronicle* reported in May that beet seeding had begun late and that beet acreage was down from the previous year because of fewer contracts. The paper attributed this shortfall to 'labour scarcity' and stated "although Indian labor will be available as far as it can be made to go, the drawback being that there is not enough of it" was likely an indication that contractors were not competitively remunerating labour in a market with expanding and competitive opportunities.[56] Adleman says that a period of increasing harvest wages began in 1907 and that "Wages rose by almost 60 percent between 1907 and 1912."[57]

The accuracy of the *Chronicle's* assumption about the shortage of labour is difficult to gauge. Farmers have always planted their crop without assurance of harvest labour and fluctuations in availability are common to the history of agriculture in the West.[58] One never knew how this situation would change from one season to the next. Perhaps in this period of increasing harvest costs contractors unwilling to accept the risks as being worth the effort turned their fields to crops that were less labour-intensive and therefore cheaper to harvest.[59]

There is no doubt, however, that Knight Sugar believed labour to be the main problem as later in the month the *Chronicle* reported that Manager Ellison had returned from a business trip east in which he had made arrangements to ensure adequate workers for the approaching season. According to the *Chronicle* "Labors [*sic*] agencies and emigration bureaus were brought into requisition and we are assured labor will be shot in here in such quantities that a scarcity will not again occur."[60] This new source of labour was likely calculated to arrive for the fall harvest as the *Chronicle* reported an "Indian Influx" completing the June thinning activity. "These

image not available

NEIGHBOURS AND NETWORKS

Figure 4.2.
"Field of sugar beets, Raymond, Alberta, July 1904." Glenbow Archives, PD-310-153. A picture of the expanse of sugar beet fields where many Bloods did backbreaking labour.

nimble fingered 'bloods' are hailed," the *Chronicle* said "as the salt of the situation who will save the crop."[61] Without the Bloods the beet industry would indeed have been in dire straits, its very survival doubtful.[62]

In 1908 another solution to the labour shortage appeared with the report that Knight Sugar had entered into contract to have its lands operated by a Japanese "syndicate." This new arrangement, along with the importation of labourers from British Columbia, was, the *Alberta Star* said, essential to the survival of the beet business at the present time.[63] Strangely this reported labour shortage is not in keeping with Agent Wilson's report that practically the whole Blood reservation was engaged in the beet fields during the 1907 season. On October 9, the *Star* reported that the Raymond beet harvest was on in earnest with the best crop in some years. The respite was brief. Although beet acreage reached its height during the 1908 season of 5,200 acres, it decreased annually thereafter. No report was made of Japanese or Indian labourers at work on the 1908 beet harvest.[64]

The continual preoccupation with the need to import labour was based on the view that the Blood labourers were undependable. What was not recognized, however, was that the Bloods refused to become a captive labour pool at the beck and call of Knight Sugar. The rhythms of their own lives and the potential offered by other opportunities determined how attractive sugar beet labour would be at any particular time or season. In the fall of 1911, for example, there was concern that looming treaty payments, an occasion for which the Indians were not willing to be absent from the reserve, would leave the beet fields short of essential labour. On October 12, Agent Hyde warned Raymond Knight to expect an exodus of Bloods from the area for treaty payment. Hyde agreed, however, even in the face of the Bloods' objections, to arrange treaty payments at an earlier date so as not to compromise the company's harvest interests.[65] Anticipating that the beet harvest would be finished by the end of October, Hyde set treaty days for November 7 and 8. A fall storm curtailed the harvest and left the company facing the prospect of having to leave half its beet crop in the ground as the planned dates loomed. Hyde was then asked to postpone the new treaty payment date to November 20.[66] Despite urgent appeals, Hyde's hands were tied and only a few Bloods worked the company's fields in the fall harvest of 1911. To make matters even more difficult for the company, there was a rumour that the agent wanted the Indians to demand "$8.00 per acre for pulling and topping beets" or else they should quit. If true, this would present a serious problem as the industry claimed that this work was only worth $5.00 an acre.[67] That there were problems with Knight Sugar operations is illustrated by the fact that the company acquired twenty-three men from Utah to help with sugar manufacturing in October.[68]

Labour shortages were again a problem in the fall of 1912 when the company requested "about fifty Indians ... at once" for beet field labour.[69] The difficulty with recruitment this time, however, was due to the fact that the Bloods had found more profitable employment elsewhere and thus the company faced stiff competition for hands. Although some of the Bloods agreed to go, Hyde advised that because of the demand for "Indian labor" many of the Bloods had already departed the reserve for Lethbridge and so Knight Sugar was directed there in its search for more field hands.[70] The company had earlier done a recruitment campaign for field labour in Europe and succeeded in acquiring fifty-eight labourers from Belgium – not enough, apparently, to satisfy its labour demands.[71]

Another aspect of the company's difficulty recruiting sufficient Blood labour may have been of its own doing: its willingness to surrender an individual's wages to the agent at his request. Thus in 1913 the company garnisheed the wages of one Hind Bull, sending Agent Hyde $14.55 for the ten and one half days worked.[72] The unfortunate Hind Bull had earned only $15.55 in total of which one dollar went for horse feed.[73] The end result was that Hind Bull pocketed nothing for his efforts. This behaviour was not likely to endear the company to him or to encourage his working in company fields if employment was available elsewhere.

RETROSPECTIVE AND CONCLUSIONS

Critics then, and scholars since, have attempted to explain the failure of the Knight Sugar Company in 1915. On April 26, 1917, in a retrospective, the *Cardston Globe* presented its version of this "most unfortunate chapter of Raymond's history," and correctly observed that acrimony between Knight Sugar and local farmers was the problem. "The latter could not understand the attitude of the company," the *Globe* observed, "while they in turn seemingly would not cater to the wishes of the man on the land. The result was ill feeling, non-cooperation and finally – no beets." The troubles, the *Globe* believed, began with minor grievances, the farmers wanting concessions – the nature of which the paper did not explain – which the company did not give, so farmers abandoned beet cultivation. The company then undertook beet growing on its own account, and "A certain class of outside labor was imported but it was not a success. Then another race [Japanese?] was brought in but they were unable to grow sufficient beets to make the running of the factory profitable." The *Globe* stated that the fault was not with the country, which was well suited to the growing of sugar beets, and "not in the ability of the farmers to grow beets but in his ability to overlook the shortcomings of the Sugar company."[74] Thus the failure of the industry was put to the failings of man, not the land.

John F. Sweeting, Industrial Commissioner for the C.P.R., had, in 1914, investigated the industry at Raymond. In a presentation before the Western Canada Irrigation Congress, which met in Kamloops, British Columbia, in July 1916, Sweeting argued that the history of sugar beet cultivation made its 'unlimited' potential self-evident, but it "remains a question of capital and labour to extend production up to market require-ments."[75] Sweeting did not give details about the labour but his contention was supported by another beet grower who stressed, "I cannot produce sugar beets at Agassiz [B.C.] and pay twenty cents an hour for ordinary labour and twenty-five cents an hour for a team, and pay interest on $150 an acre on land. That would be the quickest way for me to starve to death." He concluded that the biggest obstacle to success in the business was 'la-bour.'[76] An observer from the Lethbridge Experimental Farm presented the argument that the collapse of the Knight Sugar Co. operations was due to the failure of management to "bring in the proper labour" creating dependence "on local labour and Indian labour. There were other reasons, too, but that was the principal reason.... If the manager does not see to that question of labour; that is, thinning and topping, the factory cannot be operated successfully." Another observer unequivocally stated, "the la-bour *has* to be imported."[77] Raymond Knight also believed the latter to be true and reportedly said "the sugar industry failed because the *proper labor* was not available at the proper time."[78]

Unfortunately, because the critics did not elaborate on the problems with local or Indian labour, it is difficult to evaluate these criticisms. The company had imported labour and that too had failed. Despite evidence to the contrary, both critics and supporters of the sugar beet industry re-garded labour as the weakest link in the chain of factors that hampered the successful development of Knight Sugar. Considering the period in which this industry had its rise and fall, one should not find this conclu-sion surprising. This was a difficult time for labour/management relations in Canada as workers strove to share in the booming Canadian economy during the pre–World War I period. This was followed by depression and unemployment in 1913 and 1914.[79] Much of this unrest occurred in Al-berta and British Columbia, and it is inconceivable that this atmosphere of conflict, along with the employer's own attitudes, did not contaminate the view of labour's place in the failure of Knight Sugar.

Labour problems undoubtedly played a role in the operational difficulties experienced by Knight Sugar, but how significant a part is questionable. A major labour problem beyond anyone's control was *demand* and the resulting market-driven wage levels. It is hard to escape the conclusion that sugar beet culture was simply unprofitable in inflated wage circumstances and that the industry could not afford to meet market demands for labour.

There were other factors that compounded this industry's problems. According to sociologist C.A. Dawson, it was the combination of weather, supply, and labour that ultimately brought about the failure of Knight Sugar. The problems for the industry were rooted in the initial miscalculations about the Southern Alberta environment. The Mormons had settled in that part of Alberta during a cycle of 'wet years,' and so erroneously concluded the area suitable for sugar beet agriculture. The arrival of Chinooks that resulted in the thawing of beets, after they had been initially frozen, were, if not common, certainly more than rare occurrences. Consequently, according to Dawson, the company failed to secure sufficient beets, never more than 22,000 tons, sometimes as low as 8,000.[80] According to one estimate, once production began, the Raymond plant required 400 tons of beets for a twenty-four-hour run, and the season lasted for approximately two months.[81] Both Raymond Knight and J.E. Ellison had criticized the lack of support from local farmers as one of the problems.[82] In part this was explained by the farmers' preference for growing grain or raising livestock, likely because such activities were more traditional, familiar, and predictable.[83]

Industry boosters promoted beet cultivation, and indeed mixed farming in general, on the basis of a false economy. Far from being economically profitable, beets, requiring approximately 115 hours of hand labour to the acre, were "more than ten times the labour required for an acre of grain."[84] It was the cost of labour, not the supply that could alter this reality. Had the Bloods been willing to work for Knight Sugar for less than they could command for their labour elsewhere, they would have alleviated the pressure on the company thus allowing it to stagger on into oblivion. However, to expect the Bloods to subsidize the company with their labour was totally unrealistic.

The concerted efforts of the company in the latter phase of its existence to arrange for a more extensive beet cultivation supports the contention that it was a shortage of sugar beets, not labour, that was the main reason for the difficulties experienced by Knight Sugar. Production for 1907 fell below that of 1906 because contract growers were abandoning the enterprise or reducing their cultivated acreages.[85] Labour shortages were a frontier reality, but the sugar beet industry should have been no more affected by labour problems than other sectors of agriculture, perhaps less so.[86] Beet harvesting occurred in October and November, after the harvesting of wheat and other grains had generally finished, and when, therefore, one could anticipate a surplus of harvesters, or at least little competition from other sectors of the agricultural economy and when labour costs might conceivably be driven down. The fact that the plant closed when the government's twelve-year tax exemption ended is a good indication that sugar beet cultivation was not a profitable enterprise.[87]

Although more extensive investigation is required to confirm the part they played, other market factors were likely significant in the demise of Knight Sugar. One contract grower complained of being left with a "Hinky Dinky narrow track" when the rail line between Cardston and Raymond was upgraded to standard gauge and so he contemplated leaving his beets in the ground.[88]

There are also indications that Knight Sugar lacked a certain marketing savvy. The company cancelled a sales agreement it had with Nicholson & Bain, Calgary, apparently because of a lack of sales of its product. Nicholson & Bain protested that the problem was not of its making but could instead be attributed to Knight Sugar's failure to meet consumer demand for product in twenty-pound sacks. Furthermore, an Edmonton retailer complained that one of its competitors was receiving Knight Sugar at "jobbers" prices and threatened to "cut out Raymond sugar" unless this matter were rectified.[89] Indeed, only 20 per cent of the 46,229 bags of sugar produced in 1906 were sold.[90] Quality control (the company complained to one group of contractors about beets falling to the ground and not being properly cleaned before they were loaded), the importance of government subsidies, transportation costs, competition from non-regional producers, and government regulation are other factors worthy of detailed study.[91]

As indicated above, others agree with Dawson's assessment of the failure of the initial enterprise, and, although these various factors, compounded by labour difficulties, may explain the ultimate failure of the Knight Sugar Company, they do not explain its survival for more than a decade. Clearly Blood labourers were pivotal to sustaining the business. True, the relationship between the Bloods, on the one hand, and Knight

Sugar and its contractors, for whom the Bloods worked, on the other, was not without its irritants. And it may well be that the company and local farmers, acting on the expectation or perception of undependable Natives, wanted an alternate source of labour. But the simple fact was that no other was available locally, and importing labour proved to be no solution; indeed, it was as problematic as it was helpful. Cecilia Danysk has observed that 'hired hands' were notoriously unreliable since "Agricultural labourers operated within the framework of capitalism but they pursued their own aims, which were often antithetical to those of capital."[92] The Bloods, however, were locally situated, unlike migratory harvesters. Year after year they provided honest, and for the most part dependable, labour in the beet fields. Both Knight Sugar and the contractors readily admitted the Bloods were essential to all aspects of beet cultivation but particularly valuable at harvest.

Unfortunately for the industry, the Bloods, like the hired hands they were, refused to subvert their own interests for the sake of the sugar beet, even though the agent occasionally altered the tribal calendar for the benefit of the company. Blood workers were also aware of the value of their labour and, as any sensible group in a competitive market, sold it to the highest bidder. Had Knight Sugar and its contractors been less determined to drive a hard bargain, they would likely have gained a better appreciation for the Bloods' abilities in the sugar beet fields. When wage offers for sugar beet labour were too low, however, they simply withheld their services from the market or sold to a higher bidder.

But the Bloods, as producers of labour and consumers of goods in the capitalist economy of which they were clearly a part, were willing to work more often than not, and as a consequence Knight Sugar survived as long as it did. The industry had not by 1915–16 reached such a state of mechanization that it could do without significant amounts of manual labour. An opportunity to break the fetters of the agent's control and to gain additional income and economic independence lured the Bloods into the Raymond beet fields. No amount of chicanery or cajoling short of accommodating the Bloods' cultural and economic agenda, and their desire for adequate pay, could keep them there. Knight Sugar and local farmer contractors never mastered the art of dealing with a homogeneous and local labour pool such as the Bloods who generally responded in concert with their own cultural imperatives. Thus there were few strategies of divide and conquer that could be employed against them in efforts to tie some or all to the seasonal demands and ever-changing whims of the sugar beet industry and local contractors.

The closing of the Knight Sugar Company factory at Raymond ended the initial phase of the sugar beet industry in southern Alberta. The second phase began with the reopening of a factory, in 1925, by the Canadian Sugar Factory, Ltd., a subsidiary of the Utah-Idaho Sugar Company.[93] It appears that the Bloods played only a minor and sporadic role in the newly reconstituted industry, and why this is so is not entirely clear. A possible explanation remains the relative prosperity experienced on the reserve and the Bloods' pre-occupation with their own affairs. In the first year of production and harvest, 1925, the company imported Hungarians from British Columbia to do the contract labour of thinning and hoeing for eight dollars a day. With the crop ready to harvest, however, the local press again trumpeted the shortage of labour, a problem that also plagued the 1926 harvest season.[94] On this occasion, the labour problem was expected to be solved by settling immigrant families "right on the farms of the growers," thus ending the need to use "transient labour."[95]

The industry was by this time in transition. Hill Spring students were given a two-week leave from school to assist in the 1927 harvest, which was expected to produce 45,000 to 50,000 tons of beets.[96] There was also a new invention in the beet field, an automatic beet loader developed by Frank Leavitt of Glenwood, which could "easily load 400 or 500 lbs. of beets at a single operation." Drawn behind a beet wagon, it speeded up collection. The *News* predicted that this invention would change the nature of beet harvesting, giving "promise of eliminating one of the most backbreaking and disagreeable phases of beet-growing, for the loading of beets into the wagon has always been the bug-bear of the be[e]t field."[97]

When the sugar factory began its production run in October 1928, the nature of the work had changed such as to permit the employment of young high school girls for the lighter work but the identity of the remainder of the 200 employees is not clear.[98] At the close of the beet harvest in November, it was noted that "A number of foreign laborers left Hill Spring" while others found employment with the local farmers.[99] It was now obvious that the sugar beet industry had ceased to depend on local sources for the bulk of its labour needs.

The references to the Bloods' participation in the sugar beet industry during the 1930s and subsequently are sporadic. It is interesting to note, however, that, in a collection of reminiscence put together by Zaharia and Fox, no fewer than six Kainai elders born in the second and third decades of the twentieth century recall working the sugar beet fields. Elder Marga-ret Fox (born 1917) noted "In late spring and in the fall many people went to work on the sugar beet farms."[100] Esther Goldfrank makes reference to Blood sugar beet labour during the 1930s but offers no indication of the extent of this work. There is evidence to suggest that, although they may have participated on an individual family basis during the 1930s and 1940s, other groups, such as Hungarian immigrants and Japanese Cana-dians, dominated labour in the beet fields.[101] During the war, in particular, there was a captive labour pool of interned Japanese-Canadians, German prisoners of war, and Canadian conscientious objectors pressed into the service of the beet industry. Curiously, Ronald Laliberté noted that an attempt by the sugar beet industry to recruit Blood reserve labour in 1953 was unsuccessful but he does not explain why.[102]

What is uncertain at this point is whether the Bloods abandoned the sugar beet fields because they could not command fair remuneration for their labour or simply because more lucrative opportunities existed on the reserve or elsewhere. If the latter was the reason for the Bloods' behaviour, then clearly the Bloods suffered no marginalization by their failure to par-ticipate. Indeed, if anything, it was the industry that was marginalized and forced, with Government of Canada complicity, to import under coercion cheaper northern Alberta and Saskatchewan Native labour in efforts to sustain viability.[103]

Not much has emerged about the Bloods' integrative economic pursuits in the decade of the twenties and thirties, but there is no reason to suppose that their energies waned or that their desire to participate in local eco-nomic activities subsided. Kainai elder Harold Chief Moon (born 1918), for example, laboured on a variety of projects at Fort Macleod, Claresholm, Hill Spring, and Glenwood.[104] The changing economic fortunes of the twenties and the economic collapse of the thirties brought more pressing problems for the Bloods and their neighbours. This period saw the collapse of commodity prices in the post–World War I period and the devastation of the Blood cattle herd during the winter of 1919–20. Those individuals engaged in agriculture experienced some success during the 1920s, but their enterprise alone could not wholly sustain the tribe. Such conditions made the search for additional income even more pressing.[105]

5: 'A prospective citizen of no mean importance': The Bloods and the Business Community

INTRODUCTION

Credit arrangements and cash expenditures were but other aspects of the commercial interactions between the Bloods and the local Anglo-European entrepreneurial community. This business relationship in the post-buffalo period was largely determined by Treaty 7, which established an economic partnership between Native and non-Native in southern Alberta. That Natives saw a 'shared' partnership or reciprocal relationship as opposed to a surrender of their territory is little argued.[1] Sharon Venne, a Cree scholar, acknowledged the complexity regarding understanding the treaties and their intent. According to Venne, any applied interpretation of treaties that leans to a First Nations surrender of territory and sovereignty to the state on a 'once and for all basis' is in denial of the reality of treaty negotiation circumstances and First Nations' intent. Interpretations, Venne argues, must take into account Native epistemological views of 'Creation.'[2] Similarly, Patricia Seed has added another dimension to the debate by questioning language usage and meaning of words such as *treaty* and differences in written and oral accounts of treaties.[3]

Less accepted is the view that any sustained and beneficial result came from the formal treaty contract. Ovide Mercredi, former National Chief, Assembly of First Nations, raised this issue in 1996 when arguing for assistance to improve economic conditions on Native reserves; "We were willing to share – but instead they took and took and took, and they took so much that we did not have enough resources left to meet our own basic needs.... Had the treaties been honoured, had our people been treated as partners, we would be able to provide for our own needs."[4]

Why the continuation of such a partnership in the history of relations has not figured prominently in the subsequent relations between Natives and non-Natives is unclear. The Indian Act, however, established the Bloods as wards of the Crown and thus ensured that economic ties would not be free and unencumbered.[5] In the words of one DIA official, the Indian's "position seems like that of a child for whom the state stands *in loco parentis*," a view held by the late Prime Minister Pierre Elliott Trudeau and reflected in the 1969 White Paper.[6] Making the Native population wards of the state brought the Canadian government responsibility to ensure that their basic needs were met and fundamental rights protected. Cultural isolation on reserves was an ideal, but economically separating Natives from the remainder of the community was neither practical nor possible. How else could the cash and goods promised in the treaty be redeemed or otherwise provided except through participation in the local economic infrastructure?[7]

When the Bloods selected their reserve and a sedentary existence, they were forced into the local market economy. They became participants in a macro-economic arrangement externally driven and over which they had, depending on the nature of the commercial activity, limited control. Initially, lacking the means to effectively sustain themselves, not unlike their non-Native neighbours, they played out their consumer role on the promise of tomorrow and a cycle of credit and debt. The next 'harvest' or 'sale' held the key to future prosperity and independence while today's needs required satisfaction. The Bloods' participation in the market place as consumers will therefore be discussed for the period from the 1880s to the 1930s. In the process, an analysis of business views of the importance of the Bloods as consumers will be given. The positions of the Indian agents and DIA, as intermediaries between the Bloods and local businesses, will also be revealed. The discussion will shed light on the varying economic fortunes of the Blood reserve and the region.

THE MERCHANT ENVIRONMENT

Entrepreneurs quickly followed 'official' Anglo-Canadian presence in southern Alberta. Merchants appeared in Fort Macleod and Cardston soon after the towns were established. Fort Macleod, for example, could boast twenty-six retail businesses by 1887.[8] Local merchants eventually faced competition from itinerant salesmen, who wandered at will and plied their wares, as well as catalogue shopping organized by the likes of T. Eaton Company.[9] The initial intent of businesses was to cater to the needs of the North West Mounted Police and settlers, but the value of the Bloods was soon appreciated. The trails, roads, and especially railroads tied the towns to the national economy and brought needed merchandise to the local area.[10] Travel for individuals was still sufficiently difficult, however, to force customers to patronize local businesses for many of their immediate needs. Those businesses that survived adapted their sales practices to suit local circumstances and served Native and non-Native customers alike. Such adaptation included enticing or welcoming customers with a combination of barter, money purchases, and credit all under one roof.[11] Henry Klassen points out that some of Alberta's general merchants had diverse interests extending much beyond the general retail trade and indeed might cater to a variety of commercial and financial services to ensure a steady and diversified clientele.[12]

Credit, to sustain market activity, is a commercial finance policy of long standing directed at Natives and as a ploy to encourage consumerism and enhance profits, especially in rural economies. Morantz, for example, views credit arrangements in the James Bay area of Quebec, in the 1600s, as a sensible business arrangement "given that the harvests of fur bearing animals, like those of agricultural crops, were subject to fluctuations beyond the control of the harvester."[13] Recognition of this fact caused the Hudson's Bay Company to extend credit to Natives, a practice, which Ray notes, was carried into the twentieth-century fur trade.[14] Clark has illustrated that in eighteenth- and nineteenth-century Massachusetts the economy was based on a complex combination of cash and credit where the motives and desires of both borrower and lender affected one another.[15] In southern Alberta during the first decade of the twentieth century, Voisey observes, the High River *Times* sold its newspapers on credit, recognizing local farmers' argument "that they only received income at highly irregular intervals." During the Great Depression of the 1930s, the paper resorted to barter, accepting wheat and other foodstuffs in payment for subscriptions.[16]

Into this mix of entrepreneurial adaptation was thrown DIA policy, which set the rules of Native engagement with capitalism. Accordingly, Natives could purchase locally, with the Indian agent's consent, goods that were 'needed' or which provided basic requirements of daily existence or for individual economic functions. A listing signed by Agent J.T. Faunt,

image not available

Figure 5.1.
"Trading Post, Stand Off, Alberta [ca. 1886]." Glenbow Archives, NA-2928-50. An early trading post at Stand Off on the Blood Reserve.

circa 1921, shows orders for hardware implements, blacksmith services, harness, lumber and building supplies, horses, and 'machinery.' More personal purchases were groceries, especially beef and flour, clothing, medical services, and undertaker services.[17] Such approved purchases became 'legitimate' debt for the Natives and 'legitimate' sales for the merchants, a significant distinction with regard to eventual collections on the debt.

Similarly, the sale of reserve produce by individual Bloods required, to be legal, the agent's consent through a 'permit.' In this case, however, enforcement likely proved difficult, as illustrated by the activities of Blood reserve resident Tom Three Persons, who surreptitiously engaged in disposing of grain, livestock, and meat.[18] The extent of these black market activities, however, is exceedingly difficult to gauge.

Inevitably, with common usage, credit transactions with the Bloods were constantly appraised. One resident of the Blood Reserve praised the fairness of Cardston business practices with the Bloods. He especially noted the one price policy for non-Native and Indian alike and the 10 per cent discount for cash purchases. As a result, the Bloods did much business there.[19] Cardston entrepreneur Charles Ora Card stressed his fairness with the Natives, treating them "with the same consideration as white people."[20]

By 1899 the variety and location of businesses the Bloods patronized suggests they were discriminating shoppers who purchased goods and services where they could get the best bargain. Agent Wilson's records of the Bloods' accounts for August show they were indebted to businesses in both Cardston and Fort Macleod. There was a decided preference in the number of transactions in favour of Fort Macleod, probably because at this time most Bloods occupied the reserve area closest to that community.[21]

In keeping with its policy of isolating the Natives from the negative consequences of direct association with Euro-Canadian society, especially while on shopping 'sprees,' the DIA granted the Hudson's Bay Company permission to establish trading facilities on selected reserves.[22] This move was eventually judged unsatisfactory as, in the Department's opinion, the Indians all too quickly parted with their money. Consequently the Department decided that where reserves were situated close to towns, such as the Bloods were with Macleod, Cardston, and Lethbridge, it was just as well to let them visit and trade in town or with the numerous independent traders near the reserve as necessary. The Bloods became such heavy purchasers that in 1897 the DIA briefly experimented with providing businesses intent on collecting Native debts access to the reserve at treaty payment time. This was conditional on the Indians not being unduly influenced or coerced by the merchants and provided DIA officials rendered the merchants no assistance.[23]

Some merchants took advantage of market conditions to inflate the price of goods sold to Native customers pleading the added risk of non-payment. In one instance, the agent, as a suitable response to any such unfairness, suggested purchasing at wholesale rates for cash.[24] Indeed, this approach to doing business may have been very much a universal practice in colonial-driven economies and Colin Bundy has noted similar merchant behaviour in South Africa. Bundy observed that; "The Native, particularly in the rural areas, has to pay more for the same article than would a European, while for the same class of goods of the same quality he would receive less than a European."[25] There were other ways to discriminate and favour non-Native customers. Elder Joe Crop Eared Wolf (born 1920) recalled: "Clothing like men's overalls were hard to buy. Storekeepers hid their supplies for their favourite customers who were often non-Natives. Some of our wives solved the problem by buying denim by the yard and sewing their husband's and children's pants."[26]

During the early years of western Canadian development, non-Natives too were subjected to this business tactic. Barry Broadfoot has noted that there was a difference in country stores between "the price marked ... and the price the customer had in her head, and the real price might be somewhere in between. That's called haggling. You'd haggle."[27]

The Department's view was that credit purchasing was not conducive to the development of wholesome attitudes among its Native wards, a view much in keeping with public perceptions at this time. The *Macleod Gazette*, for example, proposed that credit-based business, encouraged by merchants and offered to Indian and homesteader alike, was unacceptable. However, ending such a solidly entrenched practice, the paper admitted, was likely difficult if not impossible. Nevertheless, the *Gazette* proposed that credit be gradually limited until business on a cash basis only was established. The ending of credit, the paper speculated, would "solve the dead-beat problem," that is, the incurring of debt, and end an "evil" system. The origin of the *Gazette's* view of the evils of credit is unclear, but it may have been related to the collapse of the speculative land market in Manitoba and an estimated failure rate of 30 per cent among Canadian banks between 1880 and 1910.[28]

image not available

NEIGHBOURS AND NETWORKS

Figure 5.2.
"Blood People on the Street, Cardston, Alberta, [ca. 1917]." Glenbow Archives, NA-4611-37. The town of Cardston, sharing a border with the Blood Reserve, provided the Bloods with access to services provided in an urbanized environment.

To oppose credit purchases, however, was to deny the efficacy of the basic economic practice that sustained much of prairie development.[29] Harry Buckwold, the owner of a general store at Admiral, Saskatchewan, indicated that credit was important to all customers to carry them from one harvest or sale to the next. Patrons used this option to run up bills at several stores at once or to play one business against the other. In response, merchants kept and shared customer lists of amounts due and habits of payment and accepted payment in cash or goods.[30]

It is not surprising, then, that in 1907 Cardston's *Alberta Star* considered the credit system bad for both the merchant and the customer as administrative costs and risk necessitated an estimated 20 per cent price increase.[31] The *Star* reflected the local variation of a region-wide movement to eliminate the credit aspect of business operations. The May 24 edition of the *Star* listed eleven Cardston merchant houses wishing to reduce both costs and risks and declaring that as of June 1, goods would be sold on a "cash or produce" basis only. The promised benefit to the consumer was cheaper goods. Among the companies participating in the new policy were H.S. Allen and Co. Ltd., and the Cardston Implement Co. Ltd., both of which did business with the Blood reserve.[32] Interestingly, during this brief campaign, no criticism was directed specifically at Blood customers. Ultimately merchants facing competitive pressure could not resist the established practices and continued to advance credit to their patrons. Competition, therefore, made credit advances with the attendant default and capital flow restrictions an essential risk of doing business in local entrepreneurial environments.[33]

As national mail order houses made significant inroads into the prairie communities' purchasing habits, they caused a backlash by local interests. The southern Alberta press began to advocate, and practically demand, loyalty to home-grown businesses.[34] The merchant community faced the formidable challenge of curbing the demand for credit and at the same time enhancing shopper loyalty. True, mail order houses, such as Eaton's, did not extend credit, but the convenience they offered along with competitive pricing based on volume purchasing was attractive.[35] The presence of mail order businesses invited criticism from local boosters well into the decade of the 1920s. For example, in its effort to boost community enterprise, the *Cardston Globe* refused to sell advertising space to mail order houses that, in the paper's view, posed a significant threat to local enterprise. The *Globe* admonished businesses to effectively increase their commerce by resorting to the more competitive practices of discounting, smaller markup, and sale on a cash basis only. By eliminating the expense incurred from direct loss and the management of credit accounts, local merchants could, said the *Globe*, drive mail order houses out of business.[36]

Suspicion with regard to the efficacy of credit financing juxtaposed with the promotion of the more financially sound cash transactions surfaced from time to time. In response to the heavy financing of farm expansion, the *Cardston News*, February 3, 1927, carried the views of one critic who argued that "unrestricted credit," combined with a flawed banking system along with dependence on "next year's crop" were responsible for the current credit crisis. The writer pointed out that short-term personal credit had developed to assist businessmen for periods of thirty to ninety days. Such a system was obviously not suited to agriculture where the time needed to grow and market a crop took from six to ten months and depended on the vagaries of both weather and markets. Historian David Jones has also pointed out the inconsistency in the time element of a short-term loan of three to four months when farm operations take twice that long.[37] The inevitable consequence of rampant credit was the crisis of 1920–21, which left the farmer owing "land vendors, mortgage companies, banks, machine companies, stores, garages, arrear taxes, seed and feed distributing centres, neighbours, friends and enemies."[38] Little wonder the *Star* branded farmers as the most ungrateful beneficiaries of the credit system.[39] Voisey notes that the High River *Times* extended credit because "farmers insisted on it."[40]

Businesses, no doubt, accepted the wisdom of a credit-free economy. This, however, was a highly unlikely solution to both their cash-flow problems and credit risks and could prove eminently unprofitable in a local economy largely based on seasonal and sporadic employment. Credit was, therefore, available to the Bloods and to settler/farmers because the market value of their produce, be it goods or labour, was significant enough to invite such risks.

The initial view that local merchants held of Blood purchasing power is unclear. It is evident, however, that the Bloods so successfully promoted their limited means that businesses eagerly sought out Blood patronage when they had money and liberally extended credit when they did not. The annuities promised in treaty were very important in enabling the Bloods to provide themselves with daily necessities. Local merchants were certainly aware of the August 1881, annuity payments of some $26,000.00 received by 2,892 Bloods. By October, 3,640 of the tribe were reported settled on the reserve with the promise of more lucrative business to come.[41]

Statements of reserve expenditures for May 1885, show that $14,656.44 was spent for a variety of purposes such as stage fare, salary, wages, and travel allowance. By far the biggest cash outlay, $13,279.51, was to the I.G. Baker Company for beef, $8,639.95 of it spent on the Bloods. The expenditure for June approached $12,700.00 with the Bloods receiving the lion's share at $11,289.67. A.B. McCullough has estimated that the value of government beef purchases in the Treaty 7 area between 1886 and 1900 amounted to $2,097,793.50.[42] Similarly $6,933.65 had been spent on hardware for the reserve and most of this was likely purchased locally.[43] Clearly the spending of so much money raised the profile of the Bloods with the cash-hungry business community.

The Bloods were too significant an economic force to be ignored or alienated. Agent James Wilson noted that, after receipt of their treaty annuity in the fall of 1893, the Bloods went on their usual spending spree in Fort Macleod and Lethbridge.[44] In his report for March 1895, Wilson noted that their earnings for the previous nine months were $5,989.00, the largest to date.[45] Total earnings for 1896 saw yet another increase at $7,510.11.[46] Even at this early stage of reserve development, the Bloods were a growing economic force. Merchants, no doubt, wished to assure themselves a portion of the Bloods' annual treaty payments, individually earned incomes and government expenditures on their behalf.

The Blood Agency report for 1904 gives three major divisions of the Blood population of 1,202. There were twenty-five self-supporting men with seventy-five dependents for a total of 100, or slightly more than 8 per cent of the reserve population. Add to these the 166 men considered partially self-supporting, with their 362 dependents; then slightly under 44 per cent of the reserve had some or significant purchasing power. There were 574 persons classed as destitute or infirm, a significant group for which the DIA assumed responsibility. For the fiscal year ending June 30, 1904, the 'working' group earned $36,154.78 from wages, the sale of beef, hay and ponies, freighting coal and supplies, and coal mining and other occupations and income for the reserve was in excess of $40,000.00.[47] Moreover, at a time when the Department was cutting spending the business transactions of Bloods of independent means became even more important to local merchants.[48] The income reported above is, of course, 'official' or agent approved and monitored income only. This does not account for income earned by Natives through individual contract agreement and which was thus beyond the agent's purview. The money earned, from such sources as cutting hay, freighting coal, and working the Raymond sugar beet fields must be considered substantial.

Despite a decade of fluctuating economic growth on the prairies, the Bloods experienced substantially increased prosperity beginning in 1911. Total income for that year was $56,750.00 and by 1920 reached $254,332.00, over a four-fold increase.[49] A synopsis of the Department's 1913 report for the Blood reserve contained some revealing facts about Blood income and resources. The population was now 1,140, down sixty-two from the 1904 figure. Of this population fifty-one Bloods were grain growers and 305 were engaged in stock raising. Clearly the great majority of working males were officially ranchers or farmers and as such were likely absent from the reserve for brief occasions only. The reserve was 354,000 acres valued at $5,306,990.00. Total income was given at $61,600.00, an increase of approximately $20,000.00 over the 1904 figure. The total of real and personal property owned by the band was $5,674,000.00 or about $5,000.00 per capita.[50] According to Agent W.J. Dilworth, 124 of the Bloods had incurred an authorized debt of $9,053.60 as of December 1913 for a per capita debt of $73.00 for those listed or an average debt of $7.94 per person for the entire tribe.[51] It is little wonder that businesses failed to single out the Bloods as a problem when discussing their discontent with the credit system. The failure to point their fingers at the Bloods suggests that the delinquency rate on debt was not so great as to alienate the Bloods or the agency.

POLICY AND BUSINESS

Treaty 7 promised both sustenance and assistance that could only be provided through the non-Native market economy. With the need to replace the buffalo economy, the Bloods were driven to the business community as consumers in need of credit and were thus tied to mercantile interests through contracted debt. How familiar they were with the workings and trappings of a frontier capitalist economy is an important point as the Bloods had little trouble satisfying their basic needs. The result was that the Bloods, a people presumed to have so little in the way of personal wealth, were readily granted uninsured credit. The general acceptance of Native credit trade was, by 1891, so extensive, and so contrary to the government's ideal of a self-supporting Native population, that the DIA issued a circular "forbidding" orders on credit.[52]

The treaties had saddled the federal government with responsibility for the Indians' economic well-being. Initially this was largely done through the government acting as a welfare agency and doling out sufficient goods to meet their minimal needs. The government was aware, however, of the long-term costs of such maintenance. One of the principles of the management of Indian affairs in Canada was, therefore, to direct Indian development towards eventual economic independence or at least, as Beal argues, 'self support' sufficient to reduce government expenditures "to an absolute minimum."[53] The key was to teach Natives a healthy appreciation for the value of amassing wealth through individually owned property and forsaking their cultural commitment to community well-being. They had to be taught to live within their means today to achieve financial independence tomorrow. The DIA and Indian agents, therefore, initially went to great lengths to keep the Indians from buying on credit.

The Department's policy on credit purchasing was straightforward: to be legitimate, all Indian purchases had to be 'authorized' through the agency office. Once approved, the Native took the official permission to purchase specified goods directly to a merchant who was often predetermined by the agent. The cost for 'needed' purchases was subsequently collected from that person's individual earnings by the agent and forwarded to the merchant.[54] Since the agent managed Indian income earned on the reserve, the DIA's policies were thus fulfilled.

This system of controlling purchases, however, had limitations. Not all individual earnings resulted from reserve employment or sales, and the agent had little or no control over money earned off the reserve. The appropriateness of purchases was then left to individual discretion. With their own money, and not needing a 'guarantee' from the agent, the Natives could exercise more freedom of choice in their purchase of goods and services. For example, Natives visited pool halls when in towns such as Fort Macleod, Cardston, or Raymond.[55] The behaviour of Blood rancher Tom Three Persons is a good illustration of the limitations of the DIA to control individuals. He kept a personal bank account, sold goods and produce without permission, and spent his own money at his pleasure.[56] In the 1930s one agent complained that the Bloods spent money on cars that unfortunately required costly maintenance.[57] Such behaviour served to reinforce, among government officials, the belief that Natives were not yet ready for free choice and that without supervision would quickly spend themselves deeper into debt.[58]

Another significant limitation of the DIA policy was the independence of the merchant. They could voluntarily undermine the Department's goals by extending 'unauthorized' credit to Natives.[59] Defying the Department's wishes, however, was not without its attendant risks. In 1904, for example, Blood Indian Agent James Wilson advised one Magrath business that, instead of calling on him, it should look to the collection of its accounts when the Indians returned to work in that community the following year.[60] Thus this creditor was forced to carry the accounts on his books for a full year, risking the possibility that the individuals concerned were either deeper in debt, had not returned to work, or had died.

The collection of debt from Natives was likewise difficult in cases where the debtor was unwilling or unable to pay. The problem was rooted in the Indian Act, which established the wardship status of the Indians, and in the communal nature of their property holding. Land, their most valuable commodity, could be alienated or sold only in right of the Crown. It has been argued that this fact alone severely restricts the Indians' access to credit in the market place: "Because of the legal restrictions on the alienation of reserves, Indians are usually unable to obtain long-term or mortgage loans by pledging land or buildings."[61] Natives were also protected from liens and mortgages against their property, except by another Indian and only against taxable property.[62] It is unclear how well local entrepreneurs understood the legal position of the Natives when they so readily extended credit. The agent, however, was frequently asked to assist with debt collection or to render an account of delinquent creditors. Most merchants believed the DIA responsible for legitimate claims against Natives defaulting on accounts.

THE BUSINESS OF DEBT

It is clear that although incurring debt was against DIA policy, the Bloods did not meekly accept the intended restrictions. The Bloods were offered the convenience of credit by local merchants unwilling to lose this important source of revenue. Thus the agent reported in November 1904, that the Bloods owed $4,750.40 for materials purchased from thirteen dealers in Macleod, Cardston, and Lethbridge on orders issued under authority of the agency. The merchants in all three communities granted credit, Agent James Wilson said, with the knowledge that payment would occur when the agent could collect. To remove some of the uncertainty of repayment,

Wilson suggested that the debt be paid by "vouchers against the tribal fund."[63]

In a letter to H.S. Allen & Co., Cardston, Wilson clarified his position with regard to collection of funds due creditors, "I only undertake to pay you (and others) upon the Indians paying me – that is I simply act as your collecting agent using due diligence in effecting collection as quickly as the Indians earn or otherwise acquire money over which my official position gives me control."[64] The collection of debt from the Bloods, though based on the agent's good will, was hampered by the restrictions of his powers. Only if the debtor co-operated could moneys be collected with the agent's assistance. In one case in 1915 an attempt to collect on a debt was turned aside by Agent W.J. Dilworth. Because the account had not been officially authorized, Dilworth said, he could only "advise" the debtor to pay. Indeed Dilworth's advice to creditors in like circumstance was "that the Department will not recognize such orders and will not be responsible for their payment."[65]

Interestingly, an account submitted by Massey-Harris, September 1914, listed seventy-two different orders for a total of $3,022.12. The amount for individual accounts was $2,950.81 and for the Agency $71.31. Clearly individuals were transacting a preponderance of the business. Of these, thirteen had no order number, suggesting that they were unauthorized. Two were for the agency and eleven for individuals. Of the eleven listed to individual Bloods, only five were entered in Dilworth's register of debtors, again suggesting that the remaining were unauthorized accounts. With regard to these five, Massey-Harris's statements do not agree with Dilworth's, Dilworth showing more than the company billed in three cases. Though Dilworth's statement is not dated, differing dates in issue and the possibility that individuals had made payments to reduce their debts may account for this discrepancy. In the case of A.D. Cairncross [Company], Cardston, only two of the eight accounts submitted are entered in Dilworth's ledger, and in the case of George Tanner only one of the seventeen account purchases made from him are registered with Dilworth.[66]

Credit was essential for a Native or farmer/homesteader to establish operations and to continue them in the face of poor crops, poor prices, or both. Farm yields for southern Alberta, for example, plummeted from an average thirty-five bushels of wheat to the acre in 1915, to 10.7 in 1917, 4.9 in 1918, and 1.4 in 1919.[67] The Fort Macleod area had a lower average of thirty-one bushels to the acre in 1915, followed by twenty-four, thirteen, four, and nil, respectively. The 1920 and 1921 season showed only marginal recovery with four and two bushels of wheat to the acre. Although the total bushels marketed from Fort Macleod in 1918–19, some 707,000 bushels, was greater than that from some other regions, it was a substantial reduction from the amounts marketed in 1915–16, 1916–17, and 1917–18 at 4,244,000, 3,1197,000 and 2,318,000 bushels, respectively, and is a good indication of the generally declining fortunes of the area.[68] Beginning in 1918, however, wheat prices declined and never again reached the 1918 levels during the subsequent two decades. Prices collapsed to as low as thirty cents per bushel for 1931–32.[69]

Comments by Indian Commissioner W.M. Graham in 1927 suggest why, even in the most distressing circumstances, merchants were willing to advance credit to the Bloods. Graham noted "Considering that there are over 200 farmers on the Blood Reserve and the indebtedness to the merchants is only $5,000.00 from the two previous years, the amount, when divided amongst the many farmers, is very small." Graham believed that this was not even one-tenth of the total value of business done.[70]

It is difficult to gauge the accuracy of Graham's statement, but it was his opinion that the Agency was a responsible customer, more prompt in the repayment of credit than most. Graham believed that the merchants were well aware of the Department's methods of business and they willingly assumed the risks of the uncertainty of prompt repayment. His conclusion was that, generally speaking, the Cardston merchants "were highly pleased with the treatment that they had received."[71]

Despite Graham's disclaimers, however, merchants often held the local agent personally responsible for the difficulty experienced with both authorized and unauthorized debt collection. By 1915, for example, Agent W.J. Dilworth's popularity was at a low ebb in Fort Macleod with complaints made that he was directing the agency's business, and thereby the Bloods' patronage, to Cardston.[72] Similarly, in 1924, the Bloods accused Agent T.J. Faunt of directing reserve business to Cardston through his purchasing orders. The result, it was charged, was that the Bloods sometimes paid more for the same article purchased in Cardston than if obtained in Fort Macleod.[73]

Although Dilworth made reasonable efforts to retire agency-sanctioned debts, he was less helpful with unauthorized debts. He advised the Riverside Lumber Co., Cardston, that their unauthorized credit to Bloods had been advanced at their own risk, and he informed them that in one case the individual concerned had little property, though some income. The income, however, Dilworth said, was beyond his control.[74]

Granting the Bloods credit without proof of agency approval, however, appears to have been a common practice. Dilworth found himself mostly in agreement with M.A. Coombs, Cardston, regarding his statement of account showing twenty-six individual Blood accounts totalling $1,031.54, but he protested he had no record of accounts for three others and insisted that the accounts were not authorized through his office. Although he might wish to collect the debt, the varying fortunes of the individuals interfered with Dilworth's ability to do so. Peter Heavy Shield, for example, suffered from tuberculosis and could not work his farm. Joe Bullshields, though "a good boy and a good worker," had suffered a crop failure.[75]

Consequently, the demands made of Dilworth to facilitate the swift repayment of debts were futile, and he angrily vented his frustration to the Department. He stipulated that he had only one rule with regard to debt collection, "Collect every time an Indian owing has funds to his credit in this office and pay in the order of seniority."[76] Such a promise, however, did little to satisfy the merchants' need for repayment in order that they might keep their own creditors at bay.

BUSINESSES CRY FOUL

Though desiring both individual Blood and agency patronage, unpaid accounts were a matter of great distress for businesses. Merchants employed a variety of tactics to encourage the local agent or the DIA to assume responsibility for all unpaid Indian and agency credit. For example, the Western Lumber Company Ltd., Lethbridge, stipulated that business done with the Bloods had to be on the "ordinary terms of credit"; that is, paid in full within ninety days. Accounts in arrears were unacceptable and payment with interest was demanded.[77] J.M. Callie of the Pioneer Furniture Store, Fort Macleod, appealed directly to the DIA for redress. Callie's plea of pressing need for the funds prompted DIA Secretary McLean to urge Agent Faunt to get the funds and pay the bill if possible.[78]

Hard times, such as during the general crop failure of 1927, increased the merchants' debt load. Stress and anxiety led to increased though often unrewarded pleas to the Blood reserve and the DIA for a settlement of credit accounts. Cardston's Smith and Pitcher Limited's requested squaring of the reserves $14,000.00 account to allay pressure from its own creditors was met with a muted and unpromising response. The company was informed, "the account would be reduced as collections [from Indians] were made." For a larger company, perhaps, this assurance would have sufficed, or at least been tolerated, but in this case it spelled hardship and brought an appeal for redress directly to the Minister of the Interior:

> The above seems rather hard blow to us, as we have been forced to pay the Harvester Company every cent cash outlay, depending on the mentioned account being paid. This has been almost more than a small concern as we are to carry, because we presume you are aware of the fact, crops here were almost a failure, collections very poor, naturally the need of money for our present needs being necessary, we therefore appeal to you, is there anyway [*sic*] that this account can be realized? or arrangements be made with the bank giving collateral that we could use in order that we can carry on.[79]

As with all such submissions to the Minister, Scott was non-committal but required a full report from Agent Pugh on the likelihood of the debt being retired.[80]

For local businesses, getting 'their money' was something of a difficult proposition.[81] The solicitors for one company argued that the system of doing business with the Indians was restrictive, "the situation really is that the goods were furnished as much to the Department as to the Indian himself, the situation being that our clients were practically prohibited from dealing direct with the Indian." This was in essence a summation of the wardship legally conferred by the Indian Act. Some creditors, therefore, refused to see the position of the DIA as anything but the rightful debtor. The Department, however, accepted neither moral nor legal obligation.[82]

Such DIA reluctance led to attempts by some businesses to muddy distinctions between the Bloods and the DIA. Although the Massey-Harris Company had made credit sales to Blood individuals on the basis of crop returns, when subsequent harvests were insufficient to settle accounts, the company argued that its sales were to the DIA and not to individual Bloods. In the company's view, as the agent had the DIA's approval to make the purchases, the Department was therefore responsible for ensuring payment. The company suggested that it had given the DIA a bargain in quoting "a very special price," on the understanding that the Department would pay.[83] The Cardston Implement Co., with regard to its $6,000.00 of credit issued to the Bloods or the agency, denied any understanding that the repayment of debt was dependent on crop returns.[84] It is clear that even though merchants differed in their understanding or acceptance of the Department's responsibility for Native incurred debt, practically all of them tried for departmental guarantees.

R.N. Wilson of the Standoff Trading Co., Standoff, Alberta, however, best expressed the general view that business took in their dealings with the reserve. The account with his firm was for $792.38. As a former long-time agent of the Blood reserve, he knew the system and so directly wrote D.C. Scott and indicated that he did not wish to wait another year or two for payment. He pointed out the business pressure he was under, with wholesalers demanding monthly payment of their accounts. He clearly stated his understanding of doing business with the Bloods – that the government was responsible for the repayment of the debt. Debts that remained unpaid for years were, said Wilson, "a misfortune to the merchant and a disgrace to the Government of Canada." Getting at the crux of the matter, he pointed out to Scott, "You will readily perceive that if departmental assistance to Indians in seeding and harvesting their crops was considered necessary for the proper administration of the reserve, it was the business of the Department to finance it when the expected revenue failed or when it became other wise inconvenient to collect in due course." Scott, as always, was unmoved.[85]

Despite the Department's attitude, hesitations and views, and at a time when fundamental monetary policy questioned the extension of personal credit, the Bloods appeared to be incurring some of their heaviest debt. As farming income collapsed (Table 5.1), debt rose from $17,056.12 in 1926 to 36,173.22 in 1927 and $75,423.11 in 1928.[86] If business practices prevailing in other areas of the prairies are representative, Native and non-Native were treated very much alike. One dry land area farmer reported the ease with which creditors lent money during the good years and the subsequent ferocity with which they harassed farmers to pay up. This farmer admitted that the habit of "buying on time" spelled trouble for farmers.[87] Merchants and credit institutions, without distinction, harassed Indian and non-Indian alike to make good on their credit purchases. "In the long chain of creditors," writes David Jones, "local merchants were at the last link."[88] With bank liens against poor crops, there was often pitifully little left to be applied against the merchants' credit advances. Jones observes that in 1921: "Hotels were filled with collectors tracing across the countryside seeking to pry loose dollars from penniless farmers."[89] Because of the

Table 5.1. Blood income from the sale of wheat and oats for 1920–27.

YEAR	WHEAT/ BUSHELS	VALUE	OATS/ BUSHELS	VALUE	TOTAL VALUE
1920	32,598	65,196.00	16,260	6,504.00	71,700.00
1921	27,985	27,985.00	7,206	2,522.10	30,507.10
1922	60,537	54,483.30	12,899	4,514.65	58,997.95
1923	212,319	191,087.10	27,249	9,537.15	200,624.25
1924	197,642	187,859.90	29,598	8,879.40	196,739.30
1925	89,580	116,454.00	3,497	1,049.10	117,503.10
1926	120,825	97,000.00	5,191	1,557,30	98,557.30
1927	69,995	41,997.00	2,482	992.80	42,989.80
TOTAL					817,618.80

Figures taken from LAC, RG 10, vol. 7595, file 10103, pt. 5; M. Christianson to W.M. Graham, May 18, 1928.

Indian Act and their wardship status, this was, perhaps, a more difficult and less rewarding venture with regard to the Bloods.

Unlike the banks which were often 'visiting institutions,' merchants were more often members of the local community dealing with neighbours and friends who would be returning yet again to be provisioned against the next year's crop. Businesswoman Mrs. F.A. Moir, Milk River Alberta, wrote:

> As a business woman running the largest general store in this district and knowing how my customers were situated I simply held back this fall [1921] on collections, only to see the banker, lumberman or implement man grab it all by threatening suits or court action. There is no use my holding off only to let some other heartless creditor clean the debtor up.[90]

The tendency for local businesses to show mercy was somewhat curbed by their own operating constraints, which demanded that their own credit purchases from their suppliers be paid in thirty days while their "customers just paid when they could."[91]

Local businesses, however, generously extended credit to the Bloods despite the knowledge born of long experience that Department policy and the application of the Indian Act made such business transactions risky. It is an important consideration whether, in the long run, most of these accounts were paid, and so reduced the overall view of credit extension as more a short-term nuisance than a long-term risk. Perhaps businesses reduced their risk by employing the double pricing system, as discussed above. Since there were, by law, no liens against the Indians' property, all creditors were on a level playing field and each stood a chance to reap some benefit. Being the local supplier and having some knowledge about the ebb and flow of crops and currency, community businesses might possibly have had an edge. Regardless, many merchants probably looked upon the risks as the cost of doing business.

THE DEPARTMENT OF INDIAN AFFAIRS: EXPLANATION AND REACTION

Fortunately, because of the DIA preoccupation with debt and debt reduction, we can reconstruct the situation for the Bloods. Agent Faunt, in 1921, calculated Blood indebtedness at $4,590.18, down from approximately $37,000.00 five years earlier, certainly a notable achievement. Faunt's statement of debt listed twenty-nine businesses and the reasons for the debt but unfortunately not the location of the companies. Most were likely in Fort Macleod and Cardston, although some debt was with companies as far east as Winnipeg.[92] This was also 'guaranteed indebtedness,' that is, debt incurred through and with the approval of the agent's office since the objective of the DIA scrutiny was to prevent individuals assuming a debt load which, in the view of the DIA, they could not handle.

Subsequent attempts to raise the Bloods and the agency to debt-free status were frustrated in their entirety. The policy followed on the Blood reserve had been to issue purchasing orders and pay after harvesting. The DIA and the agent were banking on good harvests, as it were. Whether the incurred debt was as a consequence of unsound fiscal management or poor local purchasing policies is unclear, but of poor harvests there is little doubt. By the fall of 1926 the accumulated debt was so pressing that some creditors were not paid as the Bloods soon ran out of funds. Agent Pugh now asked the Department to pay about $5,000.00 in outstanding debt. With a seemingly minor financial crisis on its hands, the DIA cruelly instructed Pugh to curtail expenses by cutting the food bill from $3,500.00 to $2,500.00 monthly. The results were predictable, "the Indians became

image not available

Figure 5.3.
"John Pugh, Stand Off, Alberta [ca. 1930]." Glenbow Archives, PA-54-11. Indian Agent John Pugh managed Blood Reserve affairs during the difficult Great Depression years.

very ugly, and last week one Indian attempted to assault me, for which I laid a charge."[93] And matters were about to deteriorate quickly.

By 1927 with repeated crop failures and insufficient funds to meet their obligations, the 'guaranteed' debt accumulation was seriously in arrears for $21,017.00.[94] Predictably, merchants' collections from their Blood creditors now became practically impossible. The Bloods, like all of their neighbours in the vicinity, were also without a crop and Pugh was instructed to advise merchants that accounts could not be paid. Importantly, in a contradiction of the DIA's previously stated position, Pugh stated his belief that merchants operated under the assumption that in the event of crop failure the DIA would make good on Blood accounts.[95]

Faced with the reality of the Bloods' needs, available resources, the accumulated debt and the merchants expectations, the DIA now turned its attention to debt reduction, the ordering system, and the extent of the Department's responsibility in meeting credit-order-incurred debt. Secretary McLean feared that paying any such accounts would bring a flood of demands from creditors, an eventuality that was a concern given that neither departmental appropriation nor band funds were available to settle individual Blood accounts.[96] The alternatives were not to engage in the ordering system or to allow the Bloods or other Natives to incur debt.

It was Commissioner William Graham's opinion that the current debt crisis originated when credit borrowed against the 1925 crop was not repaid. Subsequently, the following year the Bloods were short of funds and had to be financed again, with the result that two years' operations had to be financed against the 1926 crop. Although the 1926 harvest looked promising, bad weather reduced the anticipated harvest from the 175,000 bushels expected to only 120,000 bushels. Much of this was graded as 'feed,' bringing only sixty-four cents a bushel for a net return of approximately $97,000.00. The bill for the threshing operations was estimated at $18,000.00 and, in Graham's words, "the Bloods had to have some money out of the proceeds of the crop to buy clothing for themselves and their families, as well as something to live on."[97] Consequently, little funds were left to finance the debt burden.

Although Graham believed that Natives could not responsibly handle their own financial affairs, he did recognize that farming Natives were no different than any farmers – both needed "a little financing" from both banks and merchants. Merchants in particular, Graham noted, wanted assurance of payment, which, in the name of the Department, he was willing to give. But perhaps to reduce his own culpability for the difficulty and tenuous position in which the Department now found itself mired, Graham also stated that merchants were well aware that orders were issued on the promise of crops. In an attempt at partial alleviation, Pugh was instructed to withhold funds from those Indians who could afford a contribution towards their debt.[98] Importantly, however, it was recognized that debt, even for Natives, was considered an essential part of surviving in prairie agriculture.[99]

The crop returns for 1927 were far worse than anticipated. Through a combination of frost, rain, and snow, an expected harvest worth an estimated $300,000.00 was reduced to $30,000.00.[100] Graham now found himself forced to resort to the same tactical retreat from responsibility for increased debt that he was quick to condemn in the agents. He held out the hope of a possible reduction of $15,000.00 in a $40,000.00 debt, "and the balance will possibly have to be carried by the merchants." The crop failure was so extreme that many Natives would have to be supported by the Department if severe hardship was to be avoided.[101] Yet Graham declared that, despite "crop failures or other contingent circumstances," the numbers of destitute should not increase "except by the addition of the aged and incapacitated." The DIA was well aware that some members of the reserve had fallen on hard times. The number of Bloods said to be destitute in 1928–29 was 110, down from the 250 reported for 1927–28. This was a substantial reduction and, given the economic decline, calls into question the criteria used to determine eligibility for relief and suggests that real hardship and destitution had increased.[102]

It is clear that it was not intended to now provision able-bodied Bloods without resources. To his credit, however, Pugh, felt that such an action was parsimoniousness taken to unacceptable levels. Economic opportunities were limited, and, unlike Graham, Pugh saw a connection between available work and the potential for individual destitution. With little alternative, however, he reluctantly responded that he would cut costs despite any hardship caused.[103]

Conceivably, Graham's narrow views were the result of his intimate knowledge of the financial circumstances of the Blood reserve and the appearance they should have been well off. According to Inspector of Reserves M. Christianson's calculations, the Bloods had realized from farming, stock-raising, and leasing more than a million dollars in the decade previous to 1928, certainly sufficient capital to now meet their immediate needs.[104] The reports of repeated crop failure on the reserve, however, make it clear that income was sporadic and not uniformly spread over the decade (Table 5.1). The danger was to see all the Bloods as beneficiaries of this apparent prosperity and to attribute a general well-being that was best credited to those individuals engaged in relatively prosperous farming and cattle-raising. Local merchants must have indeed been buoyed by the infusion of much of this money into the local economy encouraging the interdependence of debtor and creditor alike.

In January 1929, Pugh listed fifteen companies to which the Bloods owed a total of $19,676.19, the result of several years accumulation.[105] As in previous years, the 1928 crop was struck with frost, threshing costs were high, and, after twine, hail insurance, and repairs, insufficient funds remained to meet creditor demands and Blood needs. Pugh accepted responsibility for the apparent sorry state of the reserve's financial affairs, blaming his failure to terminate the "order on credit system." Commissioner Graham's solution was still to wait for "one good crop," an action that, he failed to see, was the original source of the accumulated indebtedness.[106]

The response to this crisis from local businesses was predictable, but their threats to cut credit to the reserve and dire warnings of their own imminent collapse or to appeal to higher authority left both Scott and Graham unmoved.[107] Scott eventually concluded that nothing could be done about these debts; they were an unfortunate, involuntary, but necessary circumstance. Credit, concluded Scott, was "one of the vices of our system."[108] Generally, however, accounts would have to await the realization of a bountiful harvest, as always, expected in the next fall.[109] In its expectation for credit financing for Indians, the DIA's attitude was no different than that of the farmer/settler. When it came time to pay the bills, the DIA, like the farmer/settler in 'next-year country,' looked to the elusive bumper crop.

DEPRESSION

By comparison with the two previous years, 1929 brought a bountiful harvest with 130,250 bushels of wheat average No. 2 grade. The sale of 110,000 bushels at an advance of eighty cents per bushel brought in $88,000.00. Approximately $42,200.00 of this amount was used to pay off old creditors. Fifteen thousand dollars were placed at the disposal of individuals for purchases such as wagons, furniture, or living expenses, and the balance of $20,000.00 was deposited in individual Blood bank accounts. The Bloods still owed some $11,533.84 on individual personal credit accounts. How much of this would ultimately be discharged was uncertain until the final payments from the sale of the grain. Even with further payments, Graham estimated that a debt of about $8,000.00 would remain on the books. Inspector Christianson, with a view to once and for all being rid of the debt, now advised that the merchants be paid in full out of collections for beef and seed grain. This would place the Bloods in debt to the Department rather than to the local merchants.[110]

Any possibility of such debt relief was subsequently dashed when the Bloods, like many others, were victimized by the fall in commodity prices during the Great Depression. The Bloods' tenuous position was further aggravated by the market speculations of Agent Pugh. Pugh believed he could get a better price for the Bloods' harvest and held the grain off the market as the price rose, eventually expecting to get $1.40 a bushel. When the markets subsequently collapsed and the grain was finally sold, the tribe received less than 77.5 cents per bushel or about $88,000.00. Pugh accepted responsibility for the disaster insofar as the decision not to sell had been his. But that was only the beginning. The onset of winter shut down ploughing and haying earlier than usual, even cutting short work in the sugar beet fields. This series of calamities severely limited the income of many Blood families and led to disillusionment on the part of reserve farmers and many quit. By 1932 acres under cultivation decreased by 50 per cent, while income from farming dropped from $100,000.00 in 1930 to $24,000.00 in 1932.[111] From a decade of prosperity for some and limited financial success for others, the reserve and surrounding communities had suddenly descended into economic chaos and depression.

In these circumstances, survival, not debt-restructuring, became the most urgent concern of the Blood reserve's residents. Yet the DIA's senior personnel remained singularly inflexible and insensitive to the Bloods' situation and refused to return to the order system as a means of temporarily alleviating the collective distress. Christianson still expected that future successive crops would square the Bloods' accounts. Unbelievably, given the circumstances, Graham wanted any moneys collected applied against accounts with creditors "and we would at least be square with the public at large." to which Scott gave approval.[112] This was a change but only in that some of the senior bureaucrats recognized Departmental responsibility for legitimately authorized Indian indebtedness.

However, the 1932 crop was so poor that only about $1,000.00 could be spared to pay on all debts. In 1933 the total indebtedness of the agency stood at approximately $10,000.00, excluding monies owed the DIA, an

Table 5.2. Blood Tribe Debt as of April 1934.

CLASS	DIA	OUTSIDE CREDITORS	BLOOD AGENCY	TOTAL
A – Deceased	3,079.92	512.00	826.21	4,418.13
B – Old/Destitute	15,442.96	2,742.39	3111.58	21,296.93
C – Able Bodied (F/C)	49,226.09	8,617.34	6,749.40	64,592.83
D – Able Bodied	20,758.77	5,852.52	5,602.13	32,213.42
TOTALS	**88,507.74**	**1,7724.25**	**1,6289.32**	**122,521.31**
% OF TOTAL	73.3	14.5	13.3	

LAC, RG 10, vol. 7899, file 40103-1, J.E. Pugh to Secretary, April 18, 1934, and attached details.

amount that Christianson felt would be very difficult to clear. Christianson believed that "The good farmers on the reserve have all paid their accounts in full." The deceased, farmers who had quit, or poor farmers owed the balance.[113]

The Bloods' debt, and agency debt incurred on their behalf, was a long-standing problem for merchants and concern for the Department and was without an apparent satisfactory solution. In 1934 Agent Pugh did a major inventory of the Blood accounts owing to the Department, agency, and to outside creditors. Pugh divided his study into four classes: Class A – Deceased Indians, Class B – Old and Destitute Indians, Class C – Able Bodied Indians Farming or Cattle Raising (F/C), Class D – Able Bodied Indians Not Farming or Cattle Raising (Table 5.2). According to his calculations, the Bloods were in debt to all creditors, including the Department, in April 1934, for a total of $122,521.31. He recommended that the balance owed by all classes to the Department be written off, plus what Class A and Class B owed to the agency, for a total write-off of $92,445.53 or 75.45 per cent of the total debt. He further recommended that what classes C and D owed the agency ($12,351.53) and what all classes owed outside creditors ($17,724.25) be collected. Pugh offered no suggestion about how to collect for Class A and from B for outside creditors.[114] Clearly, collecting debt from the deceased and the old and destitute presented a practically insoluble problem.

The $17,724.25 owed to outside creditors was 14.5 per cent of total debt. If Pugh's recommendation that the debt owed the Department and also what classes A and B owed the agency be forgiven, outside creditors, perhaps, stood a much better chance of having their debt repaid. In theory, this move would have placed less strain on the incomes of the individual indebted Bloods. Unfortunately, because of the Depression incomes were reduced as a result of both depressed prices and reduced harvests. Outside creditors now had to compete with the agency, which wanted to collect the portion of debt owed by Classes C and D. These creditors also stood to lose, or at least face great difficulty in collection, of the portion of the debt owed by Classes A and B, which amounted to $3,254.39 or 18.4 per cent of the total $17,724.25 debt owed.[115] (For a breakdown and summary of the debt by class/community see Tables 5.3 and 5.4.) Fortunately, the Department permitted Pugh to collect the debt owed the agency and use these funds to pay outside creditors.[116]

Pugh noted the unfairness of this approach, given that those owing the most, Classes A, B, and D (total of $9,106.91 or 51.4 per cent of the total of $17,724.25 owing Outside creditors), he would be able to collect the least from. He felt that the Class C would be more than compensated by being so penalized because they stood to gain the most if the debts owed to the Department were written off. Their saving would be $49,226.09 or 54.8 per cent of the total of $89,773.74). It is difficult to determine the fairness of this approach since how much each individual owed to the outside creditors or to the Department is unknown. Individuals with the least debt in both cases would not be receiving equitable savings from the cancellation of the debt to the Department and therefore would be subsidizing those more heavily in debt in both cases. To do what Pugh advocated meant that the agency was in fact foregoing collection of its debt, since the funds received were to be used to pay outside creditors, and therefore that portion of the debt was, in reality, also being cancelled.[117]

Table 5.3. Blood Tribe Debt on the Basis of Community Owed.

NO. OF COMPANIES OR INDIVIDUALS OWED	COMMUNITY	TOTAL	% OF TOTAL
14	Cardston	14,316.99	80.8
04	Macleod	458.85	2.6
04	Lethbridge	910.00	5.1
03	Calgary	1,012.33	5.7
01	Winnipeg	1,026.08	5.8
TOTAL		17,724.25	100.0

LAC, RG 10, vol. 7899, file 40103-1, J.E. Pugh to Secretary, April 18, 1934, and attached details.

Table 5.4. Summary of Blood Tribe Debt by Class.

YEAR	CLASS A	CLASS B	CLASS C	CLASS D	TOTAL
1922	232.65	22.00	1,056.17	1,032.48	2343.30
1923				370.00	370.00
1924	59.05	152.92		127.00	338.97
1925	648.46	2,915.18	6,677.46	4,800.01	15041.11
1926	782.23	3,115.34	8,455.15	6,584.23	18936.95
1927	847.99	3,204.67	6,548.44	5,631.36	16232.46
1928	820.30	2,816.46	7,369.79	3,888.27	14894.82
1929	295.00	2,138.74	5,435.39	2,252.30	10121.43
1930	569.63	3,971.47	17,104.61	3,628.17	25273.88
1931	76.24	798.65	2,828.81	741.21	4444.91
1932	57.60	1,121.40	4,909.81	1,393.13	7481.94
1933	28.98	1,022.62	4,160.26	1,765.08	6976.94
TOTALS	**4,418.13**	**21,279.45**	**64,545.89**	**32,213.24**	
*		21,296.43	64,592.83	32,213.42	

LAC, RG 10, vol. 7899, file 40103-1, J.E. Pugh to Secretary, April 18, 1934, and attached details.
* The official figures, which do no agree with my own calculations contained in the line above.

The winter of 1934–35 was a difficult one for the Bloods, with a chronic shortage of income only partly alleviated from the sale of horses. Sadly, the difficulty for some Bloods was compounded by their recent successes. Pugh went on to explain that some of those individuals currently experiencing difficulties were good workers with good incomes who had built up estates now requiring maintenance. Some of the Bloods did have personal means, and Pugh reported that, for the period of December 31, 1934, to December 31, 1935, the Bloods had transacted some $5,177.01 worth of private business, mostly for groceries and car repairs, through the agency.[118]

With frugality and caution watchwords for the Bloods, despite a poor harvest in 1936 the amount owing to the agency and outside creditors did not increase.[119] Pugh was encouraged in his tight-fisted approach because of the experience of the past decades and the Department's monitoring the Bloods' fiscal affairs. The Bloods, however, insisted on exercising any financial independence possible and for the period of January 1 to December 31, 1936, transacted $6,708.55 of private business. In 1936, 179 Bloods had active accounts and enjoyed a per capita income of $104.00, while the per capita income for the tribe was $15.00.[120]

After several years of disaster, the projected 1937 crop held the promise of a general recovery for the reserve and its environs with the *Cardston News* predicting more than $18 million in earnings for Cardston and its local commercial hinterland. Local merchants were challenged to turn their energies towards thwarting the attempts of Lethbridge and other areas to siphon off a share of this anticipated bounty. The paper speculated: "Unless Cardston merchants become active in the realization that this year presents an opportunity unparalleled for many years past much of this cash trade will glide over the graveled roads to distant points."[121] Coming at the end of several years of economic depression and bad crops, it is understandable that the *News* was reticent to have any portion of this projected local bonanza absorbed by Cardston's competitors.

The Bloods, like those around them, were reaping a share of the improving economy. Individually financed business transactions amounted to $24,978.43 for the period January 1 to December 31, 1937, of which local businesses undoubtedly reaped the largest portion.[122] Overall indebtedness for the period 1934 to 1942 experienced only minor fluctuations and the amount officially owing to outside creditors was reduced from just under one thousand dollars to just under one hundred dollars of total debt (Table 5.5.). It is not clear whether the Bloods were spending and financing less or whether there was simply less being done officially through the agency office. The Bloods' position was likely improved, however, by the more than $80,000.00 of debt forgiven by the DIA.[123]

image not available

Figure 5.4.
"Dwelling of Heavy Head, Blood, 1925." Glenbow Archives, NA-2908-11. An indication, perhaps, of success in acquiring property.

image not available

Table 5.5. Blood Tribe Debt, 1934–42.

YEAR	COLLECTABLE INDEBTEDNESS	COLLECTIONS ON DEBT	INCURRED DEBT	CURRENT DEBT	OWING OUTSIDE CREDITORS
1934	14,538.59	–	–	–	–
1935	14,538.59	960.64	671.85	14,249.80	989.79
1936	14,249.80	–	426.48	14,676.28	989.79
1937	14,676.28	1,325.20	1,056.18	14,407.26	989.79
1938	14,407.26	2,088.52	999.36	13,235.34	097.00
1939	13,235.34	–	–	13,187.59	097.00
1940	13,187.59	–	1,685.84	14,873.43	097.00
1941	14,873.43	–	–	14,873.43	097.00
1942	14,873.43	–	–	14,873.43	097.00

LAC, RG 10, vol. 7899, file 40103-1. Table compiled from statement of J.E. Pugh.

Individual fortunes seem to have improved late in the Depression and spending for those who could afford it was significant. In 1938 the Bloods spent $37,392.48 from individual accounts with the two largest expenditures being groceries at $10,882.57 and car repairs, etc., at $5,303.61.[124] Expenditure for 1939 was down at $33,312.45 but still significant. Again groceries, car repairs, gas, and oil accounted for most of this expenditure at $15,571.21 and $6,411.98, respectively.[125] The total sum spent did not dip below $31,000 during the following few years. There was, however, very little change in the amount of debt incurred or retired during eight years of records between 1934 and 1942 (Table 5.5.).

CONCLUSION

Though stated DIA policy on permitting Natives to purchase on credit and incur debt was clear, its application of that policy was less so. A number of factors intervened to cause variations in policy implementation. The feelings of the agent and DIA field personnel, political exigencies and the view from Ottawa, the personal wealth of the individual concerned, the amount of money on hand, economic circumstances in general, and the perception of urgency all played a part in decision making regarding debt-policy implementation. The fact that the Department was very restrictive in both releasing funds and in sanctioning purchases, for example, encouraged the Bloods to incur unauthorized debt. The one immutable fact is the general acceptance that the Bloods needed financing in order to make their reserve activities economically viable, especially with regard to farming.

From the beginning, the Bloods were planned into the economic strategies of the merchant community. Their patronage was both encouraged and appreciated. Attempts by the Department to limit or curtail this form of economic integration with the non-Native community had only limited success. Had the Bloods been simply a debtor society, their commercial involvement with local businesses might have been more easily and formally regulated – the DIA purchasing on their behalf and for their needs as it saw fit. Because the Bloods displayed both personal initiative and some commercial independence, however, they were in a position to maximize their efforts to use credit, a benefit that, like many of their neighbours, they insisted on having.

The difficulties that attended all settlers' attempts to succeed in 'next-year country' also attended the Bloods. Success could not be attained independent of national economic structures, such as banking institutions, or patterns of commercial exchange, such as credit. Depression-induced crop failures and environmental upheaval in the southern Alberta region and on the Blood reserve made the DIA realize that Natives were very much in the same position as others. The Bloods' attachment to their reserve could not mitigate this fact and in all likelihood compounded it. The boundaries of the reserve and departmental policy and supervision were no antidote to the changing economic fortunes of the region or the nation, or to the Bloods' own efforts. The result was that eventually Department bureaucrats at Ottawa came to the same realization as Blood reserve agents – policies had to bend with circumstances if the Bloods were not to be totally reduced to a commercially impotent and beggar society. The Bloods could neither be driven nor restrained without reference to the extended environmental and commercial community in which they lived.

Clearly the Bloods' personal spending habits, and Indian Affairs expenditures on their behalf, resulted in a significant cash transfer to merchants in Cardston, Fort Macleod, and the small businesses situated close to the reserve. In December 1928, the *Cardston News* recognized the special commercial relationship that existed between the Blood reserve and Cardston. The paper opined: "The Indian is a prospective citizen of no mean importance."[126] In March 1929, the *News* elaborated on this commercial bond, describing business relations with the Bloods as

... most cordial. It is true that the system sometimes causes annoyance to those who must give credit but generally speaking, the Indians' business is fully as well paid and as properly conducted as that of any similar group or community of white men. In fact some of our own business methods might well be remodeled to measure up to the standards of business ethics set by many of our Indian friends.[127]

This was the paper's perception, but it contained, no doubt, a least a kernel of truth to permit such a favourable comparison.

As the Depression ended, increased spending by the Bloods, as a whole, likely ended most of the complaints about the non-payment of debts by individual Bloods. The Bloods were but one portion of the consuming public, of necessity tolerated and, as any other group seasonally harassed or wooed by business as alternating economic fortunes dictated.

Local businesses eagerly sought both Department-sponsored and individually arranged expenditures, even though collecting on credit so freely extended often proved exceedingly frustrating, sometimes even impossible. Undoubtedly, the impact on some commercial establishments was considerable, but for most the benefits outweighed the risk. This was especially true where establishments were not totally dependent on the local area for their sales. Though, like others, individually the Bloods' fortunes varied, collectively they represented a financial opportunity too great to ignore.

6: Conclusion: Change Over Time

This study is a survey of one small area of southern Alberta containing an immigrant population encountering a host Native culture. It highlights inherent dangers in assumptions of Native isolation and exclusion from market processes. The intent was to ascertain how both Natives and newcomers fit together at the economically significant points of encounter, land and products from the land, labour and monetary exchange. This southern Alberta location fits historian W.L. Morton's definition of a 'site,' that is, an area having both significance of geographic position and economic function. Though the significance of a 'site' "varies with the nature of the environment and the state of technology," the region has been deemed more or less significant over time by its various inhabitants and for a variety of reasons.[1] Canada, driven by a dream of continental expansion, regarded the region and the surrounding expanse of prairie and parkland as necessary for its geographic and imperial ambitions. Settlers regarded the area as a homeland to sustain anticipated prosperity. The Bloods clearly indicated the significance of this region to themselves when they selected their reserve.

The significance of this site was rarely, if ever, questioned by the nation that viewed the West as a fount of wealth, a hinterland appendage to be exploited.[2] Those settlers who lived there came to question its suitability for their purposes only after the heady visions of progress and prosperity had been tempered by the bitter experience of failure. This in turn brought about a reassessment of the viability of this 'next-year country' to sustain their dreams. However, the fluctuating fortunes and altering circumstances threatening survival gave added critical significance to the area of the Blood reserve and its possessors. It seemed to be endowed with rescue potential, offering the possibility of the neighbouring individuals and communities to repair the frustrated hopes shattered by nature and the limitations imposed by the 160-acre homestead.[3] These hopes, however, were at times contingent on the Bloods being conscripted into a co-operative and reciprocal partnership with their neighbours.

The dynamic at work in this area both encapsulated the hopes and reflected the policies of Canada's expanding national influence: Fort Macleod founded by the NWMP represented the extension of authority, Lethbridge the grasp of expanded eastern enterprise, and communities such as Cardston and Raymond the reality of transplanted society and economy, the tramp of 'civilization' across the frontier.[4] The formation of the Blood reserve, and Native reserves in general, illustrated for the newcomers the dispossession of the Natives and foreshadowed their imminent assimilation or even extinction. Irene Spry, however, argued that, after the influx of immigrants into the Red River area, Natives collaborated with the new economy and gained an appreciation for "a cash calculation of well-being."[5] Similarly, in southern Alberta, the new economy created demands for land, materials, money and labour, all of which the Bloods possessed in varying degrees at various times. Thus the fortunes and history of the Natives and the Whites were of necessity intertwined. The needs of both the Bloods and their neighbours, though seen by some as competitive, rationally encouraged co-operation and integration of the 'white' neighbourhood with the reserve.

During the period of this study, the Bloods experienced continual change and adaptation as they had for millennia. The influx of non-Natives into the Bloods' Plains homeland occasioned reappraisal and realignment of commercial and cultural relationships. During this period, Euro-American presence overwhelmed Native populations just as their capitalist economies overwhelmed precapitalist Native behaviours. Crisis, however, was mitigated by the Bloods' adaptive capacity. Skills, ingenuity, and physical prowess were summoned to successfully meet various emergent circumstances. The Bloods looked to inclusion in commodity markets and embraced competition rather than resist it. The changed economic circumstances became their own version of an exterior imposed regimen. The Bloods were able to function this way because they saw adaptation and reciprocity as natural economic and cultural processes. The reserve land base with its cultural uniformity sustained their integrity and their limited self-determination.

Rolf Knight argues that the limited economic return from agriculture on the prairies stimulated an outward and diversified approach to earning income.[6] The Bloods took a much more diversified approach to work and income than is often credited. For example, as early as 1896, the DIA recognized that the area in which the Bloods resided was not particularly suited to crop agriculture and as a result the Department encouraged them to take up mixed farming or stock-raising.[7] Within two years, the Bloods had added freighting to their economic activities.[8] By 1903 the agent downplayed the significance of farming, noting that cattle, hay, and freighting, both for "the reserve and the neighbouring ranchers," returned more revenue.[9]

By 1904 the Bloods had diversified once again and added labour in the Raymond sugar beet fields to their income-earning opportunities. Crop agriculture may have been, as Hana Samek argues, unsuccessful, but its modest nature initially should not be construed to represent overall Blood economic achievement.[10] Even officially measured economic returns from these activities may not indicate the true measure of successful Blood economic endeavours as they responded to off-reserve demand for their labour and resources.

It may be more revealing, therefore, to compare the Bloods, not with prairie farmers who pursued cereal grain monoculture, but rather with Whites who practised subsistence farming and were required to follow a variety of seasonal occupations and with other Native groups such as the Cree. This included working for others and temporarily migrating, for some permanently, to other areas in order to eke out an existence. Thus a variety of occupations were followed in the completion of a work year. Geographer Larry McCann has pointed to the need for such an adaptive strategy among Atlantic Canadians responding to the failure of industrialism to bring full and permanent employment.[11] This chasing of a variety of occupations has similarly been noted by Beal for the Cree of Saskatchewan.[12]

Although the Canadian government recognized Aboriginal right or title to the lands they occupied, others did not.[13] Expansion to the westward, for the man on the street or behind the plough, simply meant the acquisition of free and available land. This view was totally at odds with Native perceptions that they owned the land and continued to have unimpeded rights confirmed by treaty. Once established, however, ranchers and settlers alike accepted reserves as inviolable Indian lands only as long as their borders could not be breached or the non-Native community did not need them. Efforts to breach Blood resilience specifically and Native resilience generally were supported by government policy. The attitudes and actions of both settlers and government placed intense pressure on the Indians to alienate large segments of their reserves in the interests of the incoming settler population.[14] The Bloods, however, stubbornly and generally successfully resisted such persuasion and pressure.

The influx of settlers after the turn of the century and the enthusiasm of town booster ideology resulted in a more integrated region. Towns vied for supremacy in the surrounding hinterland and insisted that communication and commerce required efficient transportation routes. The pressure on the Bloods to open their reserve's borders to provide access was strong and persistent. Cardston insistently regarded the reserve roadways as thoroughfares to more effectively extend its reach and became a troublesome neighbour to the Bloods. When in 1899, for example, the DIA granted a road allowance through the Blood Reserve from Cardston to the St. Mary River, Agent James Wilson wanted to close the old road allowance that he felt was now redundant. Wilson was perturbed to learn, however, that the new one was simply to be an addition to the two already existing, and that the White settlers considered all three roadways necessary. Wilson rightly concluded that since the Bloods had no use for such a road, and since it interfered with the reserve boundary, it was obviously intended solely for the benefit of the citizens of Cardston.[15]

As towns and villages such as Hillspring, Glenwood, Mountain View, Magrath, and Raymond extended their reach towards both the east and the west, the reserve was absorbed into the local transportation system by travellers and entrepreneurs who sought the most efficient and shortest means of communication and movement. Thus the reserve was drawn into a burgeoning complex of social and economic networks. The Bloods, however, were aware of their needs and were determined to set their own agenda. In 1899 the Bloods fenced the road connecting Cardston and Mountain View where it crossed the reserve, much to the chagrin of local residents who complained that it inconvenienced the travelling public and hindered mail delivery. Despite the fact there was clear trespass on the reserve, the DIA recommended that the fence be removed to grant unimpeded movement across the reserve. However, the DIA determined that the Government of the Territories could not secure road access without the consent or surrender of the Bloods.[16]

The demands for roads across the reserve, and reserve surrender to facilitate their construction, continued through the 1920s. Added pressure was exerted on the Bloods in the 1920s and 1930s by the province of Alberta as it sought to update and better integrate its transportation systems to accommodate rural and urban growth.[17] Ultimately these roadways proved beneficial to the Bloods as people and commerce used the right of ways.

Any attempt to socially and economically isolate the Bloods was frustrated by the demands and needs of the non-Native community and the governments that worked on their behalf. As late as 1926 DIA secretary J.D. McLean, on the occasion of turning down the most recent request for yet another road right of way across the Blood reserve, reassured the Province of Alberta that "the Department is willing to expedite the development of the country by allowing roads to be established anywhere necessary"[18] but would not necessarily accede to every request.

The Bloods clearly did not remain economically or physically isolated, despite attitudes relegating Natives to a menial social position or the existence of their reserve as a social and political entity.[19] They were almost immediately drawn into the newly emerging complex of economic patterns established by the rancher, farmer, town, and village regimes. The needs of the new settlers, both real and imagined, readily opened doors to mutual co-operation and exchange with the Bloods. Economics proved more potent than social attitudes and prejudice and ultimately more of a unifying force than a divisive one.

Penrose believes that the loss of the buffalo left Plains Natives "with very few options" except farming and ranching. Surely this is overstated. The assumption that Natives "were duly confined to small reserves ... [and] out of the way" as an all-inclusive assertion simply cannot be sustained.[20] More than anything, perhaps, we have to rethink the effectiveness of confinement with regard to Natives and their reserves and challenge the tendency to regard confinement as approaching the absolute. It thus becomes easy to internalize an ideology of "out of *site*, out of mind" with regard to Natives, endowing the various reserves with absolute isolationist properties, however unreal. This has permitted non-Natives to imagine control of Natives' daily patterns and micro-management of the economic agenda.

It is inconceivable that the Blood population, with their more than 500 square miles of territory, and the variety of resources and people skills contained therein, would have had no self-directed impact on, or part to play in, a local or regional economy. It is inconceivable, as well, that local business enterprises and mercantile interests, in general, would not recognize the benefits to be gained from tapping the resources of this land base and its people and be, therefore, content to let the Bloods remain in passive isolation. Though reserves were planned as isolation units in which social engineering and economic reorientation could take place, Natives and Whites could not be kept apart except through a rigorous application of the regulations. To believe they could denies the Bloods' participation in the economic life of the region. The reality is, however, that the Bloods did have a significant impact.

The Bloods entered the late nineteenth and the early twentieth centuries having to deal with a much different incoming society. Unlike early explorers and fur traders, the primary desire of the new arrivals was to directly integrate the region into the national economy and exchange agricultural products for the manufactured goods of central Canada. They quickly found that the Bloods had much to offer in fulfilling their individual or collective dreams for prosperity. With their traditional buffalo economy made obsolete, the Bloods themselves needed goods that could make their existence more tolerable. Whites needed both Blood land and labour and the purchasing power the tribe, and Natives in general, represented; hence, it was impossible for the Bloods to remain detached from the economic forces at play around them. Acts of mutual exchange occurred, not through default, but were deliberately sought out and generally welcomed by all parties.

Both the Bloods and the non-Native community recognized the potential each held for the other. Non-Natives were aware of the benefits that Blood land promised and recognized that the Blood people could supply needed raw materials. For the ranching industry, the increase in the number of cattle and the subsequent reduced grazing capacity, limitations imposed by variations in weather and natural disasters, made the large area of the Blood reserve important to its well-being. In a calculated response, the Bloods systematically and strategically offered their land as a market commodity. When direct access to the Bloods' land and its resources was denied to non-Natives, the Bloods were contracted to supply their labour and the desired produce. By all indications, the Bloods were not loath to accept such arrangements if they believed they could derive financial benefit. The intensity with which the payment of land rents was fought, or avoided, sustains the argument that access to the Blood reserve was perceived by many Whites as a *necessary right* with which they were reluctant to part. The voluminous correspondence on this issue suggests this access was regarded as a genuine need.

Ranchers could co-exist with the reserve as a political entity so long as they were not deprived of access to grazing land. Farming, however, was more land-use intensive and individual. Land that was separate and legally inalienable was simply not available for sustained and planned farming. The Bloods dismissed demands to surrender land, and the more insistent the demands became the more the Bloods refused to accommodate the needs of the non-Native community, preferring instead to move to large-scale land rental.

Land, as a commodity, became the focus of development both for the Indians and the non-Native interests. Opinions differed between the Government, seeking to realize a specific policy aimed at answering the needs of an immigrant population, and the Bloods, hoping to realize benefits from their titled possession. And although historians have often judged Indian agents as mean-spirited and neglectful of Native interests, agents defended the rights of the Bloods both against the Department's intent and against rancher and farmer interlopers.

It is clear that the land base of the Blood reserve played an important part in the economic well-being of ranching and subsequently the mixed farming enterprises of the region. When the non-Native needs did not clash with the Bloods' own requirements, an accommodation, though sometimes strained, could usually be worked out. Problems arose when over-exploitation exhausted the land to the detriment of the Bloods, as happened during the drought of the 1930s. Difficulties also occurred when the government failed to recognize or adequately protect the Bloods from the impact of illegal land use and the abuse of lease privileges.

The Bloods, through their agents, pressed the Department to protect their reserve from illegal and unwarranted intrusion and exploitation. The main problem was that the DIA felt it knew best what the Bloods needed and acted accordingly. Thus the reserve's resources were sometimes alienated despite the protests of both the Indians and the local agent. Though this at times occasioned bitterness on the part of the Bloods, neither they nor their customers lost sight of the value of each to the other. Clearly, the Bloods' needs, reserve politics, various agents' ambitions, Department policy and natural conditions; all had a part to play in determining the disposal of reserve resources. Drought conditions during the 1930s, for example, eventually led to a decision to curb outsider access, although it was implemented only in part.

Not only did the Bloods integrate their land into the growing economic system of their area but they also sold their produce and labour. Thus for a short time the Bloods' coal and hay sales and their contract freighting displaced those who were less competitive or who lacked the Bloods' connections. Significantly, despite official policy directed at curbing the Native competition with Whites, the Blood agents were forceful and energetic in acquiring off-reserve employment for their charges, opportunities that the Bloods were quick to seize. This was not seriously challenged by the DIA.

Attempts by the public to restrict the Bloods' market access all failed and indeed by the 1920s the DIA had accepted the Bloods' right to inclusion, if only because it now supported the government's policy of fiscal restraint.

Blood labour in the Raymond sugar beet fields provides perhaps the best example of their participation in the local economy through the labour market. They were aggressively recruited for this work and were deemed essential by the growers to the functioning of the industry. Despite repeated attempts by the industry, no suitable alternative labour could initially be found to replace them. The beet industry eventually went into decline, and, while critics blamed an inadequate labour supply, it is clear that market forces independent of labour supply were important contributing factors to the failure. A more detailed examination of the sugar beet industry in southern Alberta for this early period is clearly indicated.

Blood income was also important to the local economy. Both the DIA and the Bloods themselves could only meet their immediate needs through commerce with off-reserve businesses. Whether or not Natives possessed personal wealth, they generated wealth by their needs. Most non-Native entrepreneurs held the mistaken idea that the government was a bottomless purse on which the Bloods had call. Thus merchants in both Cardston and Fort Macleod curried Indian favour – in fact competed for it despite the obvious risks. Problems with debt collection, however, never resulted in a long-term denial of credit to the Bloods, though the Department did attempt to enforce its own restrictions by making such collection difficult.

Clearly, DIA policy was not cohesively dispersed. Its local impact on the Bloods was determined in some measure by the character of various agents, the Blood chiefs, and the Bloods' collective will. These factors also determined relations with non-Native neighbours, both rural and urban. This study offers such insights into practical motivations that also drove Blood economic adaptive capacity and desires and which influenced their economic relationships. Concerted campaigns and efforts to force Blood compliance or induce them to co-operate had limited success at best as illustrated by Blood behaviour in the sugar beet fields or with regard to leasing their land. Similarly, exclusion tactics as with commodity sales ended in non-Natives' frustrations.

What was striking, however, was that the Bloods, even though they became a numerical minority and faced an increasingly complex and more competitive market situation, maintained considerable local economic influence. Anthropologist Esther Goldfrank, for example, reported an annual Blood income of $7,500 in 1895. And where Samek envisioned agricultural failure, Goldfrank saw *change*, the partial abandonment of crop agriculture in favour of cattle-raising and the development of the more lucrative contract haying, with the result that by 1906 the annual income was $40,000. By 1920 the income was $254,332, more than a six-fold increase, and, as significant, less than one half of this was realized from agricultural products, including hay.[21] The implications of this dramatic increase can better be appreciated when one considers that during this period the Blood population remained fairly constant, a population of 1,168 in 1906 and 1,158 in 1924.[22] True, the Bloods' income collapsed with the onset of the Depression, declining from $100,000 in 1930 to $24,000 in 1932.[23] This dramatic collapse, however, did not set the Bloods apart; they simply suffered, as did all their neighbours, the misery of general national economic depression.[24]

The Bloods participated in the tremendous economic growth experienced by Canada's agricultural sector during the 1920s, and it is in this decade that agricultural production became a critical factor in the Blood reserve economy. Between 1911 and 1920, the percentage of income attributable to farm products, including hay was 52.2 per cent, 39.2 per cent, 42.6 per cent, 43.3 per cent, or less than 50 per cent, except for the year of least income.[25] This evidence contradicts the commonly held belief that the Bloods had been so continually poverty-stricken that they did not even notice the collapse of regional and national economies in the Great Depression.[26] The decade of 1911 to 1920 had been one of increased economic diversification and increasing, if limited, prosperity. It was not until the decade of the 1920s that reserve farming finally accounted for more reserve income than other revenue sources. Prior to this, therefore, one must not give too much weight to crop agriculture, as its importance was discounted by agents and that of hay was stressed. By 1924, however, the total value of farm products including hay was $209,000 or 74.6 per cent of total income of $280,332.[27] Consequently, agriculture only became substantially significant after the period in which Samek determined Blackfoot reservation economies to have failed. By 1920, Samek says, the Bloods "were back on rations, with their economy having turned full circle back to the destitution of forty years earlier."[28] It is inconceivable that they failed to realize that their hundreds of thousands of dollars in income in the 1920s had shrunk to mere thousands in the early 1930s. It is more likely that the misery of the 1930s was many times compounded because of the relative prosperity of the previous decade, a problem common to the entire region.

There exists the view that both the Bloods and other Natives were inconsequential to and isolated from the economic and social processes unfolding around them. This is largely a result of viewing the history of relations from the standpoint of what was officially desired, demanded, or perceived as ideal by government, especially in creating a western economy based on farming, and not in viewing particular circumstance of specific locations. There is also a tendency to see Natives as exploited rather than as competitive or exploitative, a view that does not recognize the reality of economic and social relationships with neighbours. The Bloods' self-interested behaviour in the leasing of their land, the sale of their labour and produce, the way they spent their money, and incurred debt provides sufficient evidence. Their actions in the Raymond area beet fields are simply a further proof. The Blood reserve could not, no more than the surrounding countryside, exist in 'splendid isolation,' functioning independently of national, local, or and individual forces and drives. Both communities accommodated each other's needs, while operating within the framework of a regional and national economic system.

During the period of this study, the Bloods overcame the calamitous loss of the buffalo, took advantage of market forces, and largely avoided becoming totally marginalized. What emerges is a clear indication that the Bloods were more or less disadvantaged depending on the general economic circumstances to which both Natives and Whites were subjected. Some Bloods were likely more economically marginalized than some of their White neighbours, and less than others. Whites who were suffering financially could either leave or seek help from financial institutions and banks, options not open to the Bloods because of legal and cultural restrictions. The Bloods' land and patronage, however, often determined the well-being of the industries developing around them, and thus they became an essential, and not an irrelevant factor, in the local economy. As a consequence the Bloods could sometimes pick and choose the means with which to define or modify the associations, a situation wholly out of keeping with an insignificant status.

The Bloods experienced dramatic though by no means complete change in that not all traditional behaviours or mores were abandoned. Some, however, were adapted to accommodate the new circumstances and grasp the opportunities offered by the new economy. It was in the economic sphere that great change occurred, much of it self-directed, reflecting the Bloods comprehension of altered circumstance. In *Common and Contested Ground*, Theodore Binnema has illustrated the ebb and flow of the Plains buffalo culture in which the Bloods participated. Clearly it is incorrect to think that, because the buffalo existed in large numbers, Plains people were provided with a life of ease. The fur trade economy, just as the post-buffalo economy, required constant orientation and accommodation.[29] Hugh Dempsey, in his study *Firewater*, has convincingly illustrated that the last days of the buffalo economy were filled with turmoil and destruction.[30] Indeed, the extent of this destruction necessitated economic readjustment. Treaty 7, and subsequent efforts to participate in new economic opportunities, offers evidence that the Bloods were fully cognizant of the new reality into which they had been thrust.

Many of the changes that the Bloods experienced and directed were transparent, many less so, but in the main the traditional yearly round of activities was increasingly altered with the passage of time. An excellent illustration of change was that, for the Bloods as for other Plains Natives, the "shopping spree" replaced the buffalo hunt and the general store, not the buffalo, became the 'emporium' for the Bloods' needs. Beef replaced buffalo as the staple meat and the vegetable garden and grains supplemented what could be dug from nature's garden. Wooden cottages replaced teepees as the primary living space, and movement was along well-trodden trails and roads to towns rather than with the intent of wide-ranging wanderings. Ranching, lease contracts, contract labour, share-cropping, mining, haulage, and credit purchasing were either new methods of economic behaviour or more formal and sophisticated adaptations of fur trade and buffalo robe trade customs. These were not absolute one-on-one transfers but indicate that the life of the Bloods in the post-buffalo era was in some ways substantially different from previous experience.

Life changed for the Bloods in the post-buffalo era. However, as far as human potential was concerned, skill, energy, foresight, and planning to maximize benefits from economic activities were still needed and used. True, Whites largely drove the economy. The Bloods, however, successfully responded to resource depletion and a new economic and political order. Unlike the Dakota, whom Peter Elias concluded suffered from an imposed isolation and therefore exclusion from the surrounding labour market, the attempt to impose the same on the Bloods did not succeed.[31]

The mistake has been to assume that all Plains Natives experienced the same fate following the loss of the buffalo and to accept the conclusion that somehow today's stereotypes either reflect a historical reality in all cases or represent a continuity of experience through time. To do so is to assume that the Bloods were submissive in the face of government repression, failed to appreciate the value of the wealth they possessed in their land and labour, had no need for material possessions that could improve their standard of living, and deliberately chose to remain outside the market economy. It is also to conclude that non-Natives did not recognize any potential in their Blood neighbours or, if they did so, chose to ignore it in favour of some perceived *status quo*. Neither conclusion is sensible or true. Each society had materials and skills the other needed, so an accommodation had to be worked out for both to thrive or simply function at only a sustainable level in their common environments.

Through diverse economic, environmental, social, and cultural changes, the Blood reserve and its people remained a constant in the fluctuating fortunes of the area. The reserve was an oasis, promising some limited respite from the shrinking economies of scale for those Whites who could access its benefits. The promise of the reserve's potential forged an economic link between the Bloods and their neighbours.

This work has attempted to illustrate an Indian reserve and the surrounding non-Native community as in some ways integrated. However, the extent of economic integration was not overwhelming, nor was it consistent for all the factors during this time period. There was a period, for example, when there was no coal mine and when sugar beet labour was not required or not available. Though limited, the extent of integration has not previously been appreciated for its significance. The Bloods were important first to the ranching community and then to the farmers and the towns for the produce, services, and capital they provided. Much more detailed work will have to be done to determine the extent to which this was common to other reserves. This work on the Bloods, as well as that of Beal on the Saskatchewan Cree, however, certainly suggest that alternative interpretations must be contemplated and investigated. It should be noted, however, that the size and location of the Blood reserve makes it difficult to apply conclusions reached here to other Native groups and communities. But there is no reason to suppose that the Bloods were exceptional in responding to the challenges of the post-buffalo period.

The southern Alberta area went through periods of economic highs and lows much like the economy of the rest of the country. Those economic downturns caused by nature, the national and the world economy generally, affected the region as a whole; when the surrounding White population suffered so did the Bloods, and vice versa. As the initial settlement phase ended, the Bloods had cast their lot with their neighbours. In consequence, Whites, the DIA, and individual tribal members sometimes victimized the Bloods as a collective. But they did not respond as helpless victims. Instead, the Bloods enjoyed the benefits of economic co-operation and also suffered setbacks while making their contribution to the general well-being of the region.

Clearly the Bloods strategically adapted to the new post-buffalo reality and refused to be made 'strangers' in their own land.[32] It was but the recurrence of an old theme in their tradition of experience, and their former experience had been one of success. Native reserves had a more important part to play in the local or regional history than has previously been credited. In this case, the Bloods' importance to the ranching and farming community and to commerce in Cardston, Fort Macleod, and Raymond is clear.

Notes

CHAPTER 1

1   Helen Buckley, *From Wooden Ploughs to Welfare: Why Indian Policy Failed in the Prairie Provinces* (Montreal: McGill-Queen's University Press, 1992), 11–12. Buckley believes that the process of moving to reserves resulted in the Indians "taking up a new life, but never becoming part of the larger society or regaining their independence." Buckley, *From Wooden Ploughs*, 3. Cam Mackie states: "In a sense, economic development on Indian reserves both ended and began with the establishment of reserves.... Some attempts were made to establish an agricultural base, but for the most part, until the early 1960s, little of substance occurred that would lead to any form of economic self-sufficiency." Cam Mackie, "Some Reflections on Indian Economic Development," in *Arduous Journey: Canadian Indians and Decolonization*, ed. J. Rick Ponting (Toronto: McClelland & Stewart, 1986), 214. Likewise Menno Boldt, *Surviving as Indians: The Challenge of Self-Government* (Toronto: University of Toronto Press, 1993), 235; Heather Robertson, *Reservations Are for Indians* (Toronto: James Lewis & Samuel, 1970), 27.

2   Mackie, "Some Reflections on Indian Economic Development," 214. Likewise, Boldt, *Surviving as Indians*, 235.

3   Angus McLaren, *Our Own Master Race: Eugenics in Canada, 1885–1945* (Toronto: Oxford University Press, 1990), chap. 1; Richard Hofstadter, *Social Darwinism in American Thought* (Boston: Beacon Press, 1955), chaps. 8 & 9; Robert F. Berkhoffer,

The White Man's Indian: Images of the American Indian from Columbus to the Present (New York: Vintage Books, 1979), 55–61.

4   Duncan C. Scott, "The Aboriginal Races," *Annals of the American Academy of Political and Social Science* 107 (May 1923): 63–64.

5   The attempts to re-educate Natives in White-run schools are among the most painful remembered experiences of Indians. Linda Pelly-Landrie, "First Nations Cultures, Now and in the Future," in *Three Hundred Prairie Years: Henry Kelsey's 'Inland Country of Good Report'*, ed. Henry Epp (Regina: Canadian Plains Research Center, 1993), 178. On a negative view of the education system as it was and is for Indians, see Kateri Akiwenzie-Damm, "We Belong to this Land: A View of 'Cultural Difference'," *Journal of Canadian Studies* 31, no. 3 (Fall 1996): 24–25; Celia Haig-Brown, *Resistance and Renewal: Surviving the Indian Residential School* (Vancouver: Tillacum, 1989), 76–79. See also the reminiscence in Basil H. Johnston, *Indian School Days* (Toronto: Key Porter, 1988). For the efforts to stamp out plains Indian religious practices, see Katherine Pettipas, *Severing the Ties that Bind: Government Repression of Indigenous Religious Ceremonies on the Prairies* (Winnipeg: University of Manitoba Press, 1994); especially chaps. 4 and 5. Similarly, see Douglas Cole and Ira Chaikin, *An Iron Hand upon the People: The Law against the Potlatch on the Northwest Coast* (Vancouver: Douglas & McIntyre, 1990), chap. 6.

6   George Manuel and Michael Posluns, "The Fourth World in Canada," in *Two Nations,*

Many Cultures: Ethnic Groups in Canada, ed. Jean Leonard Elliot (Scarborough: Prentice-Hall Canada, 1983), 15.

7   Daniel Francis, *The Imaginary Indian: The Image of the Indian in Canadian Culture* (Vancouver: Arsenal Pulp Press, 1992), 53–57.

8   Toby Morantz, "Recent Literature on Native Peoples: A Measure of Canada's Values and Goals," *Acadiensis* 18 (1988): 237.

9   James W. St. G. Walker, "The Indian in Canadian Historical Writing," Canadian Historical Association, *Historical Papers* (Ottawa, 1971), 38–40; James W. St. G. Walker, "The Indian in Canadian Historical Writing, 1971–1981," in *As Long as the Sun Shines and Water Flows: A Reader in Canadian Native Studies*, ed. Ian A.L. Getty and Antoine S. Lussier (Vancouver: University of British Columbia Press, 1983), 348 ff.; Heidi Tiedemann, "The Representation of Native Culture from Duncan Campbell Scott to Margaret Laurence," Canadian Studies Program, University College, University of Toronto, *Occasional Paper Series* (vol. 3, no. 1), 1.

10 George F.G. Stanley, *The Birth of Western Canada: A History of the Riel Rebellions* (Toronto: University of Toronto Press, 1961), 196–97; 217.

11 Stanley, *Birth*, 219.

12 For an American example, see Alan Trachtenberg, *The Incorporation of America: Culture and Society in the Gilded Age* (New York: Hill and Wang, 1982), 32.

13 Hugh A. Dempsey: *Crowfoot: Chief of the Blackfeet* (Edmonton: Hurtig, 1972); *Red Crow: Warrior Chief* (Saskatoon: Western Producer Prairie Books, 1980); *Big Bear: The End of Freedom* (Vancouver: Douglas & McIntyre, 1984); *The Gentle Persuader: A Biography of James Gladstone, Indian Senator* (Saskatoon: Western Producer Prairie Books, 1986); *Tom Three Persons: Legend of an Indian Cowboy* (Saskatoon: Purich Publishing, 1997).

14 Buckley, *From Wooden Ploughs*, 7.

15 Hana Samek, *The Blackfoot Confederacy, 1880–1920: A Comparative Study of Canadian and U.S. Indian Policy* (Albuquerque: University of New Mexico Press, 1987), chap. 4, 56–57, 70–105, 178–83.

16 Donald G. Wetherell and Irene R.A. Kmet, *Town Life: Main Street and the Evolution of Small Town Alberta, 1880–1947* (Edmonton: University of Alberta Press, 1995); David Hamer, *New Towns in the New World: Images and Perceptions of the Nineteenth-Century Urban Frontier* (New York: Columbia University Press, 1990), 214–23.

17 Esther S. Goldfrank, *Changing Configurations in the Social Organization of a Blackfoot Tribe during the Reserve Period: The Bloods of Alberta, Canada* (Seattle: University of Washington Press, 1966), 24, 27.

18 Goldfrank, *Changing Configurations*, 33.

19 L.M. Hanks Jr. and J.R. Hanks, *Tribe under Trust: A Study of the Blackfoot Reserve in Alberta* (Toronto: University of Toronto Press, 1950), 29–30.

20 A good example has been the debate generated by an essay by historians Jeremy Adelman and Stephen Aron. Jeremy Adelman and Stephen Aron, "From Borderlands to Borders: Empires, Nation-States, and the Peoples in Between in North American History," *American Historical Review* 104, no. 3 (June 1999): <http://www.historycoooperative.org/jorunals/ahr/104.3/ah000814.html>. For responses, see John R. Wunder and Pekka Hamalainen, "Of Lethal Places and Lethal Essays," *American Historical Review* 104, no. 4 (October 1999): <http://www.historycooperative.org/journals/ahr/104.4/ah001229.html>; Evan Haefeli, "A Note on the Use of North American Borderland," *American Historical Review* 104, no. 4 (October 1999): <http://www.historycooperative.org/journals/ahr/104.4/ah001222.html>; Jeremy Adelman and Stephen Aron, "Of Lively Exchanges and Larger Perspectives", *American Historical Review* 104, no. 4 (October

1999):   <http://www.historycooperative.
org/journals/ahr/104.4/ah001235.html>.

21   Trachtenberg, *Incorporation of America*,
     17, 22–23; Patricia Nelson Limerick, *The
     Legacy of Conquest: The Unbroken Past of the
     American West* (New York: W.W. Norton,
     1987), 182.

22   Trachtenberg, *Incorporation of America*, 27.

23   Trachtenberg, *Incorporation of America*, 37.

24   Limerick, *The Legacy of Conquest*, 210.

25   Daniel H. Calhoun, "Strategy as Lived:
     Mixed Communities in the Age of New
     Nations," *American Indian Quarterly* 22,
     nos. 1 & 2 (Winter/Spring 1998): 183,
     188.

26   Arthur J. Ray, *Indians in the Fur Trade:
     Their Role as Hunters, Trappers and Middle-
     men in the Lands Southwest of Hudson Bay
     1660–1870* (Toronto: University of Toronto
     Press, 1974), 125.

27   Ray, *Indians in the Fur Trade*, 131.

28   Ray, *Indians in the Fur Trade*, 134; Paul C.
     Thistle, *Indian-European Trade Relations
     in the Lower Saskatchewan River Region to
     1840* (Winnipeg: University of Manitoba
     Press, 1986), 25–27; Arthur J. Ray and
     Donald Freeman, *'Give Us Good Measure':
     An Economic Analysis of Relations between
     the Indians and the Hudson's Bay Company
     before 1763* (Toronto: University of Toronto
     Press, 1978), 218–21.

29   Ray, *Indians in the Fur Trade*, 166.

30   Walter Hildebrandt and Brian Hubner,
     The Cypress Hills: The Land and Its People
     (Saskatoon: Purich Publishing, 1994), 34.

31   Walter Hildebrandt, *Views from Fort
     Battleford: Constructed Visions of an Anglo-
     Canadian West* (Regina: Canadian Plains
     Research Center, 1994), 60.

32   R. Douglas Francis, "In Search of a Prairie
     Myth: A Survey of the Intellectual and
     Cultural Historiography of Prairie Cana-
     da," *Journal of Canadian Studies* 24, no. 3
     (Fall 1989): 46–56.

33   There are detailed historical and literary
     discussions of positive and negative views

of Indians in relation to the West and to
Canada as a whole. On the Indian image
in early history of the West, see: R. Douglas Francis, *Images of the West: Changing
Perceptions of the Prairies, 1690–1960* (Saskatoon: Western Producer Prairie Books,
1989), 10, 39–40, 79; R. Douglas Francis,
"From Wasteland to Utopia: Changing
Images of the Canadian West in the Nineteenth Century," *Great Plains Quarterly* 7,
no. 3 (Summer 1987): 184–86. For general
literary discussion, see: Leslie Monkman,
*A Native Heritage: Images of the Indian in
English-Canadian Literature* (Toronto:
University of Toronto Press, 1981), chap. 4,
65–95; Terry Goldie, *Fear and Temptation:
The Image of the Indigene in Canadian, Australian, and New Zealand Literature* (Montreal: McGill-Queen's University Press,
1989), chaps. 5 & 8; Gaile McGregor,
*The Wacousta Syndrome: Explorations in
the Canadian Landscape* (Toronto: University of Toronto Press, 1985), 216–29.
On stereotyping in art, see Ronald Rees,
"Images of the Prairie: Landscape Painting
and Perception in the Western Interior of
Canada'," *Canadian Geographer* 10, no. 3
(1976): 261.

34   J.R. Miller, *Skyscrapers Hide the Heavens:
     A History of Indian–White Relations in
     Canada* (Toronto: University of Toronto
     Press, 1990), 221.

35   Steven High, "Native Wage Labour and
     Independent Production during the 'Era of
     Irrelevance'," *Labour/Le Travail* 37 (Spring
     1996): 243, 263–64.

36   Sarah Carter, *Lost Harvests: Prairie In-
     dian Reserve Farmers and Government
     Policy* (Montreal: McGill-Queen's Uni-
     versity Press, 1990); Peter Douglas Elias,
     *The Dakota of the Canadian Northwest: Les-
     sons for Survival* (Winnipeg: University of
     Manitoba Press, 1988).

37   Paul Voisey, *Vulcan: The Making of a Prairie
     Community* (Toronto: University of To-
     ronto Press, 1988), 7.

38   In a telling comment, Fred White,
     NWMP Comptroller, wrote "Townspeople

encourage the redman when he has money to spend, and it frequently happens that settlers are glad to have an Indian family or two camped near them so that they may get the benefits of their labour; and unfortunately, white men have on more than one occasion taken up the defense of the Indians and their legal right to be off their Reserves if they behave themselves." Library and Archives Canada (LAC), RG 18, vol. 218, file 469, Fred White to Mr. [James] Smart, August 30, 1901.

39 William G. Robbins, *Colony and Empire: The Capitalist Transformation of the American West* (Lawrence: University Press of Kansas, 1994), 11 & 19.

40 Richard White, as cited in Robbins, *Colony and Empire*, 49.

41 Carl Beal, "Money, Markets and Economic Development in Saskatchewan Reserve Communities, 1870–1930s" (PhD diss., University of Saskatchewan, 1994), 56.

42 Beal, "Money, Markets and Economic Development," 59–61.

43 Rolf Knight, *Indians at Work: An Informal History of Native Indian Labour in British Columbia 1858–1930* (Vancouver: New Star Books, 1978), 7, 15, 19–23.

44 Ron Laliberté, "The 'Grab A Hoe Indians': The Canadian State and the Procurement of Aboriginal Labour for the Southern Alberta Sugar Beet Industry," *Prairie Forum* 31, no. 2 (Fall 2006): 306–7.

45 Dianne Newell, *Tangled Webs of History: Indians and the Law in Canada's Pacific Coast Fisheries* (Toronto: University of Toronto Press, 1993), 75–87; Ron Bourgeault, "Aboriginal Labour in the North-West," *Prairie Forum* 31, no. 2 (Fall 2006): 293, 295–96.

46 Bourgeault, "Aboriginal Labour," 275–76; Laliberté, "The 'Grab A Hoe Indians,'" 307.

47 Bourgeault, "Aboriginal Labour," 293–95.

48 Bourgeault, "Aboriginal Labour," 276.

49 Laliberté, "The 'Grab A Hoe Indians'," 309.

50 Frank Tough, "Indian Economic Behaviour, Exchange and Profits in Northern Manitoba during the Decline of Monopoly, 1870–1930," *Journal of Historical Geography* 16, no. 4 (1990): 386, 391–92; Arthur J. Ray, *The Canadian Fur Trade in the Industrial Age* (Toronto: University of Toronto Press, 1990), 211 ff.

51 Gerhard J. Ens, "Metis Ethnicity, Personal Identity and the Development of Capitalism in the Western Interior," in *From Rupert's Land to Canada*, ed. Theodore Binnema, Gerhard Ens and R.C. Macleod (Edmonton: University of Alberta Press, 2001), 162.

52 Gerhard J. Ens, *Homeland to Hinterland: The Changing Worlds of the Red River Metis in the Nineteenth Century* (Toronto: University of Toronto Press, 1996), 5.

53 Gerald Friesen, *The Canadian Prairies: A History* (Toronto: University of Toronto Press, 1987), 4.

54 John Herd Thompson, *Forging the Prairie West* (Toronto: Oxford University Press, 1998), 69.

55 Robin Fisher, *Contact and Conflict: Indian-European Relations in British Columbia, 1774–1890* (Vancouver: University of British Columbia Press, 1980), xv.

56 Deborah Doxtator, "The Implications of Canadian Nationalism for Aboriginal Cultural Autonomy." Canadian Museum of Civilization, *Curatorship: Indigenous Perspectives in Post-Colonial Societies* (Mercury Series: Paper 8, 1996), 61.

57 Peter Carstens, *The Queen's People: A Study of Hegemony, Coercion, and Accommodation among the Okanagan of Canada* (Toronto: University of Toronto Press, 1991), 103.

58 Wetherell and Kmet, *Town Life*, xvii.

59 The Bloods claim a larger number of 3,542. *Lethbridge Herald*, March 26, 1994, A5. The government's figure is down from the 2,892 that were paid annuities in 1881. NAC, RG 10, vol. 1549, 4, Indian Agent to E. Dewdney, August 29, 1881.

60 The low is achieved by comparing the Bloods' 1924 population of 1,158 with the total of Cardston, Fort Macleod, and Raymond for the 1926 census. The Blood population for 1926 is not available.

61 Wetherell and Kmet, *Town Life*, 234.

62 Paul Voisey points out that in the decade between 1881 and 1891 population increase for all of the prairies was only 118,000 with the majority of this growth in southern Manitoba. Paul Voisey, "The Urbanization of the Canadian Prairies, 1871–1916," *Histoire Sociale–Social History* 8 (1975): 82.

63 Howard Palmer, *Patterns of Prejudice: A History of Nativism in Alberta* (Toronto: McClelland & Stewart, 1982), 6–7.

64 There are several sources that offer excellent overviews of the administrative setup and intent of Canadian Indian policy: John Leonard Taylor, "Canada's North-West Indian Policy in the 1870s: Traditional Premises and Necessary Innovations," in *Sweet Promises: A Reader on Indian-White Relations in Canada*, ed. J.R. Miller (Toronto: University of Toronto Press, 1991), 207–11; John L. Tobias, "Protection, Civilization, Assimilation: An Outline History of Canada's Indian Policy," *Western Canadian Journal of Anthropology* 6, no. 2 (1976): 13–30; Allan G. Harper, "Canada's Indian Administration: The 'Indian Act'," *America Indigena* 6, no. 4 (October 1946): 297–314; Douglas Leighton, "A Victorian Civil Servant at Work: Lawrence Vankoughnet and the Canadian Indian Department, 1874–1893," in *As Long as the Sun Shines and Water Flows: A Reader in Canadian Native Studies*, ed. Ian A.L. Getty and Antoine S. Lussier (Vancouver: University of British Columbia Press, 1983), 104–19; David J. Hall, "Clifford Sifton and Canadian Indian Administration 1896–1905," *Prairie Forum* 2, no. 2 (November 1977): 127–51; E. Brian Titley, *A Narrow Vision: Duncan Campbell Scott and the Administration of Indian Affairs in Canada* (Vancouver: University of British Columbia Press, 1986), chaps. 1 and 3.

65 Titley, *A Narrow Vision*, 13–14. The powers of the agents were debated in the House of Commons in 1905 and concerns were expressed about the possibility of agents being prejudiced against Whites in cases where they were involved with Indians. *House of Commons Debates*, vol. IV, May 25, 1905, 6545–6546.

66 Treaties and Historical Research Centre, *The Historical Development of the Indian Act* (Ottawa: Indian and Northern Affairs, 1978), 52 ff.

67 J. McKenna, "The Indian Laws of Canada," *Catholic World* 54 (October 1891): 66–67; Titley, *A Narrow Vision*, 12.

68 Tobias, "Protection, Civilization, Assimilation," 20.

69 Sarah Carter, "Controlling Indian Movement: The Pass System," *NeWest Review* (May 1985): 8–9. Also Sarah Carter, *Aboriginal Peoples and Colonizers of Western Canada to 1900* (Toronto: University of Toronto Press, 1999), 162–64; Carter, *Lost Harvests*, 149–58.

70 Treaty 7; A. Blair Stonechild, "The Indian View of the 1885 Uprising," in *1885 and After: Native Society in Transition*, ed. F. Laurie Barron and James B. Waldram (Saskatoon: Canadian Plains Research Center, 1986), 168.

71 Sidney L. Harring, *White Man's Law: Native People in Nineteenth-Century Canadian Jurisprudence* (Toronto: University of Toronto Press, 1998), 265–68.

72 J.R. Miller, "Owen Glendower, Hotspur, and Canadian Indian Policy," in *The First Ones: Readings in Indian/Native Studies*, ed. David R. Miller, Carl Beal, James Dempsey, and R. Wesley Heber (Piapot Reserve #75: Saskatchewan Indian Federated College Press, 1992), 253–54.

73 *Indian Act and Amendments*, 1868–1950, Ottawa: Treaties and Historical Research Centre, 1981, 49.

74 Treaty Seven Elders and Tribal Council, Walter Hildebrandt, Dorothy First Rider, and Sarah Carter, *The True Spirit and*

Original Intent of Treaty 7 (Montreal: Mc-Gill-Queen's University Press, 1996), 148.

75 *Indian Act and Amendments*, 33.

76 W. Keith Regular, "'Red Backs and White Burdens': A Study of White Attitudes towards Indians in Southern Alberta 1896–1911" (Master's thesis, University of Calgary, 1985), 86–88. See Dempsey, *Red Crow*, 208–10.

77 Dempsey, *Gentle Persuader*, 32–33.

78 LAC, RG 10, vol. 1560, 117, James Wilson to Amos Rae, April 28, 1894; 126–28, James Wilson to Indian Commissioner, May 7, 1894; 199–200, James Wilson to A. McNab, June 5, 1894.

79 John D. Higinbotham, *When the West Was Young* (Lethbridge: The Herald Printers, 1978), 188, 264–65. Also see, for example, LAC, RG 10, vol. 3577, file 421, L. Vankoughnet to E. Dewdney, June 14, 1883.

80 Voisey, *Vulcan*, 33 and 128.

81 R.C. Macleod, *The North-West Mounted Police and Law Enforcement 1873–1905* (Toronto: University of Toronto Press, 1976), 25; David H. Breen, *The Canadian Prairie West and the Ranching Frontier 1874–1924* (Toronto: University of Toronto Press, 1983), 15; John W. Bennett and Seena B. Kohl, *Settling the Canadian–American West, 1890–1915* (Lincoln: University of Nebraska Press, 1995), 13–14.

82 Paul F. Sharp, *Whoop-Up Country: The Canadian-American West, 1865–1885* (Norman: University of Oklahoma Press, 1973), 7–8.

83 Hamer, *New Towns in the New World*, 11–12. This seems to have been very much universal wherever Europeans and their descendants have encroached on territory occupied by Native people. See: Hamer, *New Towns in the New World*, 214–23; Robert G. Athearn, *Westward the Briton* (Lincoln: University of Nebraska Press, 1953), 126 ff.; Robert Hughes, *The Fatal Shore: The Epic of Australia's Founding* (New York: Alfred A. Knopf, 1987), 280–81.

84 Ronald Atkin, *Maintain the Right: The Early History of the North West Mounted Police, 1873–1900* (Toronto: Macmillan, 1973), 85.

85 Alison K. Brown; Laura Peers, *'Pictures Bring Us Messages'/ Sinaakssiiksi aohtsimaahpihkookiyaawa: Photographs and Histories from the Kainai Nation* (Toronto: University of Toronto Press, 2006), 220; Lynn Hickey, Richard L. Lightning, and Gordon Lee, "T.A.R.R. Interview with Elders Program," in *The Spirit of the Alberta Indian Treaties*, ed. Richard Price (Montreal: Institute for Research on Public Policy, n.d.), 134.

86 *Cardston Record*, August 6, 1898, 1.

87 *House of Commons Debates*, vol. 1, 1909, col. 1005. Lethbridge's population in 1901 was 2,072. Wetherell and Kmet, *Town Life*, 305.

88 Wetherell and Kmet, *Town Life*, 81–82.

89 L.A. Rosenvall, "The Transfer of Mormon Culture to Alberta," *American Review of Canadian Studies* 12 (1982): 142–43.

90 Town of Raymond, *Settlers, Sugar and Stampedes: Raymond Remembered* (Raymond: Town of Raymond, 1993), 4–37.

91 Brigham Y. Card, "The Canadian Mormon Settlements, 1886–1925: A North-American Perspective," *Canadian Ethnic Studies* 26, no. 1 (1994): 25.

92 Wetherell and Kmet, *Town Life*, 82.

93 Fisher, *Contact and Conflict*; Samek, *The Blackfoot Confederacy*; Robin J. Browlie, *A Fatherly Eye: Indian Agents, Government Power and Aboriginal Resistance in Ontario, 1918–1939* (Don Mills: Oxford University Press, 2003); Hugh Shewell, *'Enough to Keep Them Alive': Indian Welfare in Canada, 1873–1965* (Toronto: University of Toronto Press, 2004); Brown and Peers, *'Pictures Bring Us Messages'*.

94 Warren N. Elofson, *Cowboys, Gentlemen, and Cattle Thieves: Ranching on the Western Frontier* (Montreal: McGill-Queen's University Press, 2000); Warren N. Elofson, *Western Cattle Ranching in the Land*

and *Times of Charlie Russell* (Montreal: McGill-Queen's University Press, 2004); Simon M. Evans, *The Bar U and Canadian Ranching History* (Calgary: University of Calgary Press, 2004).

95 Betty Bastien, *Blackfoot Ways of Knowing: The Worldview of the Siksikaitsitapi* (Calgary: University of Calgary Press, 2004), 12–18.

96 Lea Zuyderhoudt, "Accounts of the Past as Part of the Present: The Value of Divergent Interpretations of Blackfoot History," in *The Challenges of Native American Studies: Essays in Celebration of the Twenty-Fifth American Indian Workshop*, ed. Barbara Saunders and Lea Zuyderhoudt (Leuven: Leuven University Press, 2004), 166.

97 Shepherd Krech III. *The Ecological Indian: Myth and History* (New York: W.W. Norton, 1999), 127–28.

98 Elizabeth Vibert, *Traders' Tales: Narratives of Cultural Encounters in the Columbia Plateau, 1807–1846* (Norman: University of Oklahoma Press, 1997), 212–14.

99 Ray, *Indians in the Fur Trade*, 55–60; Ray and Freeman, *'Give Us Good Measure,'* 45.

100 John S. Milloy, *The Plains Cree: Trade, Diplomacy and War, 1790 to 1870* (Winnipeg: University of Manitoba Press, 1988), 85–92

101 Olive Patricia Dickason, *Canada's First Nations: A History of Founding Peoples from Earliest Times* (Toronto: Oxford University Press, 1997), 166–67.

102 Bastien, *Blackfoot Ways of Knowing*, 16–17.

103 Margaret A. Kennedy, *The Whiskey Trade of the Northwestern Plains: A Multidisciplinary Study* (New York: Peter Land, 1997), 23; Norman C. Conrad, *Reading the Entrails: An Alberta Ecohistory* (Calgary: University of Calgary Press, 1999), 31–34.

104 John Foster, "The Metis and the end of the Plains Buffalo in Alberta," in *Buffalo*, ed. John Foster, Dick Harrison and I.S. MacLaren (Edmonton: University of Alberta Press, 1992), 73.

105 Kennedy, *The Whiskey Trade*, 31.

106 Kennedy, *The Whiskey Trade*, 95–96.

107 Dickason, *Canada's First Nations*, 171–73.

108 Dickason, *Canada's First Nations*, 174.

109 Jill St. Germain, *Indian Treaty-Making Policy in the United States and Canada 1867–1877* (Toronto: University of Toronto Press, 2001), 66.

110 Zuyderhoudt, "Accounts of the Past," 171.

111 R.C. Macleod and Heather Rollason, "'Restrain the Lawless Savages': Defendants in the Criminal Courts of the North West Territories, 1878–1885," *Journal of Historical Sociology* 10, no. 2 (June 1997): 159, 176.

112 George D. Spindler and Louise S. Spindler, "Identity, Militancy, and Cultural Congruence: The Menominee and Kainai," *Annals of the American Academy of Political and Social Science* 436 (March 1978): 79.

113 Brown and Peers, *'Pictures Bring Us Messages,'* 19.

114 Treaty 7 Elders and Tribal Council et al., *The True Spirit and Original Intent of Treaty 7*, 315–16.

115 Maureen K. Lux, *Medicine That Walks: Disease, Medicine, and Canadian Plains Native People, 1880–1940* (Toronto: University of Toronto Press, 2001), 10–12; Alex Johnson, *Plants and the Blackfoot* (Lethbridge: Lethbridge Historical Society, 1987), 25.

116 Theodore Binnema, *Common and Contested Ground: A Human and Environmental History of the Northwestern Plains* (Norman: University of Oklahoma Press, 2001), 41, 43.

117 John C. Ewers, *Plains Indian History and Culture: Essays on Continuity and Change* (Norman: University of Oklahoma Press, 1997), 40 & 167; Binnema, *Common and Contested Ground*, 56.

118 Zuyderhoudt, "Accounts of the Past," 167.

119 J. Powell, *A History of the Canadian Dollar*, Bank of Canada. Retrieved January 9, 2008, from <http://www.bankofcanada.ca/en/dollar_book/appendixa.pdf>.

120 Powell, *A History of the Canadian Dollar*.

121 M.C. Urquhart and K.A.H. Buckley, eds., *Historical Statistics of Canada* (Toronto: Macmillan Canada, 1965).

CHAPTER 2

1 For a detailed discussion of these developments, see A.A. den Otter, "Adapting the Environment: Ranching, Irrigation, and Dry Land Farming in Southern Alberta, 1880–1914," *Great Plains Quarterly* 6 (Summer 1986): 171–89.

2 For one aspect of this, see Lawrence B. Lee, "The Canadian-American Irrigation Frontier, 1884–1914," *Agricultural History* 40 (October 1966): 271–84.

3 Beal, "Money, Markets and Economic Development," 177. For a discussion of overall policy, see Titley, *A Narrow Vision*, 37–59.

4 The best discussion of this policy to date is Carter, *Lost Harvests*, especially chaps. 3, 5, and 6; Sarah Carter, "Two Acres and a Cow: Peasant Farming for the Indians of the North-west, 1889–1897," *Canadian Historical Review* 70, no. 1 (1989): 27–52. E. Brian Titley also discusses this policy. E. Brian Titley, "Hayter Reed and Indian Administration in the West," in *Swords and Ploughshares: War and Agriculture in Western Canada*, ed. R.C. Macleod (Edmonton: University of Alberta Press, 1993), 121–23.

5 Sheilagh S. Jameson, "The Ranching Industry of Western Canada: Its Initial Epoch, 1873–1910," *Prairie Forum* 11, no. 2 (Fall 1986): 233. On this theme, see also: Edward Brado, *Cattle Kingdom: Early Ranching in Alberta* (Vancouver: Douglas & McIntyre, 1984), 43, 171–75; Sharp, *Whoop-Up Country*, 242–43.

6 L.V. Kelly, *The Range Men: The Story of the Ranchers and Indians of Alberta* (Toronto: Coles, 1980), 60.

7 David H. Breen, "The Turner Thesis and the Canadian West: A Closer Look at the Ranching Frontier," in *Essays on Western History*, ed. Lewis H. Thomas (Edmonton:

University of Alberta Press, 1976), 149; Breen, *The Canadian Prairie West*, 85; John Jennings, "Policemen and Poachers: Indian Relations on the Ranching Frontier," in *Frontier Calgary: Town, City, and Region 1875–1914*, ed. A.W. Rasporich and Henry Klassen (Calgary: McClelland & Stewart West, 1975), 88–90; John Nelson Jennings, "The North West Mounted Police and Indian Policy, 1874–96" (PhD diss., University of Toronto, 1979), 196–201.

8 R.C. Macleod and Heather Rollason Driscoll, "Natives, Newspapers and Crime Rates in the North-West Territories, 1878–1885," in *From Rupert's Land to Canada*, ed. Theodore Binnema, Gerhard J. Ens, and R.C. Macleod (Edmonton: University of Alberta Press, 2001), 252, 259–64; Macleod and Rollason, "'Restrain the Lawless Savages'," 165–74.

9 Elofson, *Frontier Cattle Ranching*, 13–22, 38–39; Elofson, *Cowboys, Gentlemen and Cattle Thieves*, 76–78, 135–37; Evans, *The Bar U*, 88–89, 91–92.

10 Simon M. Evans, "The Passing of a Frontier: Ranching in the Canadian West, 1882–1912" (PhD diss., University of Calgary, 1976), 73–80.

11 The major lease holders for the prairies were given as: D. McEachran, 16,391 acres; Cochrane 73,000, 60,000, and 33,000; New Oxley Canada Ranch Co., 80,000, 62,934, 7,000, 100,000; Waldron Ranche Co. 100,000. *Macleod Gazette*, April 28, 1893.

12 Jameson, "The Ranching Industry of Western Canada," 234–35.

13 Breen, *Ranching Frontier*, 16–19. On the regulations, see Chester Martin, *"Dominion Lands" Policy* (Toronto: McClelland & Stewart, 1973), 179.

14 Breen, *Ranching Frontier*, 19–20. There is no clear delineation between 'large' and 'small' ranching. The above is taken from discussion in W.M. Elofson, "Not Just a Cowboy: The Practice of Ranching in Southern Alberta, 1881–1914," in *Canadian Papers in Rural History*, vol. 10, ed. Donald Akenson (Gananoque: Langdale

Press, 1996), 206–12; Philip S. Long, *The Great Canadian Range* (Calgary: Bonanza Books, 1970), 4. On the era of the big ranches dominated by the 'big four,' see Sheilagh S. Jameson, "The CPR and the Ranching Industry of the West," in *The CPR West: The Iron Road and the Making of a Nation*, ed. Hugh A. Dempsey (Vancouver: Douglas & McIntyre, 1984), 76–77.

15 Glenbow Archives (GA), file 2, Diary of W.F. Cochrane, Cochrane Ranch, entries for January 20, 22, and 23, 1885. Informal for the Cochrane Ranche as there is no indication of written agreement. The Bloods, however, likely considered the agreement legal and binding.

16 Simon M. Evans has expertly detailed these developments. Simon Evans, "Spatial Aspects of the Cattle Kingdom: The First Decade, 1882–1892," in *Frontier Calgary*, ed. A.W. Rasporich and Henry Klassen, 41–50. On American incursions, see: Simon M. Evans, "American Cattlemen on the Canadian Range, 1874–1914," *Prairie Forum* 4, no. 1 (Spring 1979): 123–26; Jameson, "The CPR and the Ranching Industry of the West," 77.

17 Evans, "Spatial Aspects of the Cattle Kingdom," 44–51; Simon M. Evans, *Prince Charming Goes West: The Story of the E.P. Ranch* (Calgary: University of Calgary Press, 1993), 41. Jameson says that government policy and encroachment from settlers were the main factors at work in killing off the Cochrane's major sheep ranching operations under the guise of the British American Ranche Company. Jameson, "The Ranching Industry of Western Canada," 232–33.

18 Sharp, *Whoop-Up Country*, 238; Jameson, "The CPR and the Ranching Industry of the West," 76; Sheilagh S. Jameson, "Era of the Big Ranches," in *The Best from Alberta History*, ed. Hugh A. Dempsey (Saskatoon: Western Producer Prairie Books, 1981), 56; Elofson, *Cowboys, Gentlemen and Cattle Thieves*, 9–10. American historian William T. Hagan has discovered that large and small cattle interests determined to

avail of the grazing resources the reserves offered similarly invaded some American Indian reservations. William T. Hagan, *United States–Comanche Relations: The Reservation Years* (Norman: University of Oklahoma Press, 1990), 150–53, 175–76, and 236–40.

19 Evans, *The Bar U*, 103–4; Elofson, *Frontier Cattle Ranching*, 163.

20 Simon M. Evans, "Grazing the Grasslands: Exploring Conflicts, Relationships and Futures," *Prairie Forum* 26, no. 1 (Spring 2001): 73–74.

21 GA, File 2, Cochrane Ranche Letterbook, W.F. Cochrane to J.M. Browning, February 15, 1885; Diary of W.F. Cochrane, Cochrane Ranch, entry for January 21, 25 and 27; Cochrane Ranch Letterbook, W.F. Cochrane to J.M. Browning, February 7, 1885.

22 LAC, RG 10, vol. 1557, 444–46, W. Pocklington to Indian Commissioner, February 18, 1890.

23 LAC, RG 10, vol. 1558, 406, W. Pocklington to Indian Commissioner, August 3, 1891; 643, Indian Agent to Manager, Cochrane Ranche Co., December 30, 1891.

24 LAC, RG 10, vol. 1558, 380, W. Pocklington to Maunsell Bros., July 23, 1891; 381, W. Pocklington to James McNab, July 23, 1891; 382–90, W. Pocklington to Browning Brothers, July 23, 1891; 449–51, W. Pocklington to Indian Commissioner, August 31, 1891.

25 Breen, *Ranching Frontier*, 20; Jameson, "The Ranching Industry of Western Canada," 234–35.

26 LAC, RG 10, vol. 1559, 498–99, James Wilson to Hayter Reed, October 2, 1893; 88–89, James Wilson to T. Curry, January 20, 1893.

27 LAC, RG 10, vol. 1559, 546–47, James Wilson to Indian Commissioner, November 13, 1893.

28 LAC, RG 10, vol. 3894, file 97,443, Hayter Reed to T. Mayne Dayly, January 6, 1893. MacInnes says that the Indians

killed cattle in protest because they strayed onto the reserves. I found no evidence that this was the case with the Bloods. C.M. MacInnes, *In the Shadow of the Rockies* (London: Rivingtons, 1930), 163. On trespass, see also: LAC, RG 10, vol. 1560, 502–3, James Wilson to Indian Commissioner, September 18, 1894; 549, James Wilson to Indian Commissioner, October 9, 1894; Vic Satzewich, "'Where's the Beef?': Cattle Killing, Rations Policy and First Nations 'Criminality' in Southern Alberta, 1892–1895," *Journal of Historical Sociology* 9, no. 2 (June 1996): 201–3.

29 Elofson, *Frontier Cattle Ranching*, 88.

30 *Macleod Gazette*, March 24, 1893; Macleod and Rollason, "'Restrain the Lawless Savages'," 10; F. Laurie Barron argues that the pass system had its origins in Hayter Reed's desire to curb the movements of the Natives. If so, he struck on a policy that many in the ranching community agreed with. F. Laurie Barron, "The Indian Pass System in the Canadian West, 1882–1935," *Prairie Forum* 13, no. 1 (Spring 1988): 27–29.

31 Esther S. Goldfrank, "Administrative Programs and Changes in Blood Society during the Reserve Period," *Applied Anthropology* 2 (Jan.–Mar. 1943): 19. See also Goldfrank, *Changing Configurations*, 22; Hugh A. Dempsey, *Red Crow: Warrior Chief* (Saskatoon: Western Producer Prairie Books, 1980), 201. The horse herds were substantial enough to lose 250 head in a winter storm in 1892. LAC, RG 10, vol. 1558, 863, A.G. Irvine to Superintendent General of Indian Affairs, July 29, 1892.

32 LAC, RG 10, vol. 1560, 620–23, James Wilson to Superintendent, N.W.M. Police, Macleod, November 24, 1894.

33 LAC, RG 10, vol. 1560, 948–54, James Wilson to Indian Commissioner, June 10, 1895.

34 Fraser Taylor, *Standing Alone: A Contemporary Blackfoot Indian* (Halfmoon Bay: Arbutus Bay Publications, 1989), 31.

35 LAC, RG 10, vol. 1560, 948–54, James Wilson to Indian Commissioner, June 10, 1895.

36 LAC, RG 10, vol. 1561, 395–97, James Wilson to The Indian Commissioner, Winnipeg, January 11, 1896; 395–97, James Wilson to The Indian Commissioner, Winnipeg, January 11, 1896.

37 LAC, RG 10, vol. 1561, 501–2, James Wilson to Mr. Pat Masson[?], March 2, 1896. See also RG 10, vol. 3894, file, 97,443, James Wilson to Indian Commissioner, January 11, 1896; RG 10, vol. 1561, 527–31, Conrad Brothers also expressed reluctance to pay rents. James Wilson to Indian Commissioner, March 10, 1896.

38 LAC, RG 10, vol. 1561, 527–31, James Wilson to Indian Commissioner, March 10, 1896; LAC, RG 10, vol. 1562, 316, James Wilson to Indian Commissioner, February 24, 1897. Wilson may have, in part, been responsible for this situation with the Mormons as a result of a non-verbal agreement reached with them in February of the previous year when, after a meeting with C.O. Card and a committee, he agreed to "be as lenient as his superiors would let him" and agreed to accept fifty cents per head per annum for grazing. D.G. Godfrey and Brigham Y. Card, eds., *The Diaries of Charles Ora Card: The Canadian Years 1886–1903* (Salt Lake City: University of Utah Press, 1993), 329; LAC, RG 10, vol. 1572, 480–81, James Wilson to Sterling Williams, April 27, 1897. C.O. Card wrote Wilson regarding the matter but the nature of the response is unknown. Godfrey and Card, *The Diaries of Charles Ora Card*, 405.

39 LAC, RG 10, vol. 1562, 387–89, James Wilson to Indian Commissioner, March 17, 1897. Wilson did not indicate how he planned to determine who could and could not afford to pay.

40 LAC, RG 10, vol. 1572, 480–81, James Wilson to Sterling Williams, April 27, 1897. C.O. Card wrote Wilson regarding the matter but the nature of the response is

unknown. Godfrey and Card, *The Diaries of Charles Ora Card*, 405.

41 LAC, RG 10, vol. 1562, 332–33, James Wilson to [?], Kipp, Alberta, March 2, 1897; 335 – 337, James Wilson to Mr. Smith, March 2, 1897; James Wilson to Mr. Whitney, March 2, 1897; 493, James Wilson to Indian Commissioner, April 30, 1897; 379, James Wilson to Indian Commissioner, March 15, 1897. See also vol. 1562, 482.

42 For particulars, see: LAC, RG 10, vol. 1563, 29, Indian Agent to H.R. Springett, May 12, 1897; 30, Indian Agent to Glengarry Ranche, May 12, 1897. See letters from agent to various companies in RG 10, vol. 1563, 31–34. The quality of the microfilm reproduction makes it difficult to read the names.

43 Kirk N. Lambrecht, *The Administration of Dominion Lands, 1870–1930* (Regina: Canadian Plains Research Center, 1991), 39; Jameson, "The Ranching Industry of Western Canada," 239.

44 LAC, RG 10, vol. 1563, 168, James Wilson to Deputy Superintendent General of Indian Affairs, July 19, 1897; 169, James Wilson to Indian Commissioner, July 19, 1897.

45 LAC, RG 10, vol. 1563, 210–13, James Wilson to Indian Commissioner, August 10, 1897. For a similar case, also see: 257–58, James Wilson to Secretary, DIA, September 4, 1897; vol. 1564, 187–88, James Wilson to Messers Maunsell and Browning, December 27, 1898. See also pp. 197–98, James Wilson to E.A. Maunsell, January 13, 1899. On the inability to collect dues, see 193, Statement of Account with Alex McNab; 343, James Wilson to C.O. Card, June 20, 1899.

46 LAC, RG 10, vol. 1563; 371–74, James Wilson to Secretary, DIA, October 26, 1897. See, for example, 408–10, James Wilson to R. Urch[?], November 10, 1897; James Wilson to Alexander McNabb, November 10, 1897; James Wilson to John [?], November 10, 1897.

47 David C. Jones, *Empire of Dust: Settling and Abandoning the Prairie Dry Belt* (Edmonton: University of Alberta Press, 1987), 11.

48 den Otter, "Adapting the Environment," 173; David H. Breen, "The Canadian Prairie West and the 'Harmonious' Settlement Interpretation," *Agricultural History*, 47 no. 1 (January 1973): 72.

49 Jameson, "The Ranching Industry of Western Canada," 239; Evans, "Spatial Aspects of the Cattle Kingdom," 52.

50 den Otter, "Adapting the Environment," 175, 178.

51 den Otter, "Adapting the Environment," 182.

52 Paul Voisey has detailed the misplaced faith in mixed farming as a panacea for sure success in all areas. Paul Voisey, "A Mix-Up Over Mixed Farming: The Curious History of the Agricultural Diversification Movement in a Single Crop Area of Southern Alberta," in *Building Beyond the Homestead: Rural History on the Prairies*, ed. David C. Jones and Ian MacPherson (Calgary: University of Calgary Press, 1985), 179–206.

53 The shifting demographics are nicely illustrated by D.N. Sprague, Barry Kaye, and D. Wayne Moodie, "Dispersal of the Manitoba Metis and the Northwest Rebellion, 1870–1885," in *Historical Atlas of Canada:* vol. 2, *The Land Transformed 1800–1891*, ed. R. Louis Gentilcore (Toronto: University of Toronto Press, 1993), Plate 35; William J. Carlyle, John C. Lehr, and G.E. Mills, "Peopling the Prairies," in *The Historical Atlas of Canada:* vol. 3, *Addressing the Twentieth Century 1891–1961*, ed. Donald Kerr and Deryck W. Holdsworth (Toronto: University of Toronto Press, 1990), Plate 17; Philip D. Keddie and Simon Evans, "Prairie Agriculture," in Kerr and Holdsworth, *Historical Atlas of Canada:* vol. 3, Plate 18.

54 Clifford Sifton, "The Needs of the Northwest," *Canadian Magazine* 20, no. 5 (March 1903): 426.

55 Clara Middleton remembers greeting trainloads of settlers at the station in Cross-field, Alberta. Clara and J.E. Middleton, *Green Fields Afar: Memories of Alberta Days* (Toronto: Ryerson Press, 1947), 59.

56 Carlyle et al., "Peopling the Prairies," Plate 17.

57 Annual Report for the Royal North West Mounted Police for 1904, CSP 28, No. 12, 1905, 49.

58 Theodore M. Knappen, "Winning the Canadian West," *Worlds Work* 10 (1905): 6598.

59 John Craig says that anxiety in the face of settlement led ranchers to purchase lands. John R. Craig, *Ranching with Lords and Commons* (New York: AMS Press, 1971), 236.

60 *Cardston Record*, August 13, 1898, 1.

61 Evans, "Grazing the Grasslands," 74.

62 LAC, RG 10, vol. 1564, 177–78, James Wilson to Walter Gleuse[?], December 20, 1898. For similar occurrences, see 149, James Wilson to Messers Brigham and Wellman, November 11, 1898, 179–80; James Wilson to Geo. Hauks, December 20, 1898.

63 On December 24, 1898, Wilson wrote to R. Fuller of Browning, Montana, about the possibility of Indian Department cattle or Blood Indian cattle that may have strayed across the border. In fairness, however, references of this kind were exceedingly rare in the DIA files. LAC, RG 10, vol. 1564, 98, James Wilson to R. Fuller, December 24, 1898, 184, James Wilson to Jack Miller, December 23, 1898.

64 That this was expected to be the case was recognized by the pre-emption clauses, though later rescinded, of the Dominion Lands Act. Lambrecht, *The Administration of Dominion Lands*, 22–27. Voisey, *Vulcan*, 128, 33–52. Lyle Dick also noted the trend towards enlargement in his study of the Abernethy District of Saskatchewan. Lyle Dick, "Factors Affecting Prairie Settlement: A Case Study of Abernethy,

Saskatchewan, in the 1880s," *Canadian Historical Association* (Historical Papers, 1985), 23–24.

65 R.W. Murchie, *Agricultural Progress on the Prairie Frontier* (Toronto: Macmillan Canada, 1936), 58. The Rev. Martin Holdom noted the settlement process and the edging out of ranchers in the area of Stettler, Alberta, in 1910. Paul Voisey, ed., *A Preacher's Frontier: The Castor, Alberta Letters of Rev. Martin W. Holdom, 1909–1912* (Calgary: Historical Society of Alberta, 1996), 55–56.

66 LAC, RG 10, vol. 3992, file 185,143, [Frank Oliver] to James Smart, June 3, 1899; J.D. McLean to James Wilson, June 7, 1899.

67 LAC, RG 10, vol. 3992, file 185,143, James Wilson to Secretary, Dept. of Indian Affairs, June 7, 1889; Memorandum signed by Law Clerk Reginald Rimmer, June 28, 1899.

68 Hugh A. Dempsey, "Story of the Blood Reserve," *The Pioneer West* 2 (1970): 5–6.

69 LAC, RG 10, vol. 1723, 364–65, James Wilson to James P. Low, April 10, 1900; 370–73, James Wilson to James P. Low, April 23, 1900; 371, James Wilson to James P. Low, April 23, 1900; RG 18, vol. 1546, file 76, D. Laird to Col. Herchmer, December 15, 1899.

70 LAC, RG 10, vol. 1535, 247. Unsigned and undated handwritten account, likely by James Wilson, of cattle on reserve.

71 LAC, RG 10, vol. 1721, 273, J. Wilson to Post Master, Spring Coulee, December 12, 1902; 275, J. Wilson to Post Master, Magrath, December 12, 1902; RG 10, vol. 1725, 8–9, James Wilson to Secretary, DIA, February 24, 1903; 30–33, James Wilson to Secretary, DIA, March 11, 1903. For more correspondence on these problems, see 387, James Wilson to Robert Patterson, February 28, 1903; 402, James Wilson to Alberta Ranch Co. Pincher Creek, March 12, 1903; RG 10, vol. 1721, 415–17, J. Wilson to H.S. Allen, March 21, 1903; 311, J. Wilson to [?], Cardston, January 19, 1903;

LAC, RG 10, vol. 1721, 350, J. Wilson to Al. Whitney, February 12, 1903; 11–14, Indian Agent to Messers Wallace and Co., April 8, 1902; Indian Agent to H. Williams, April 8, 1902; Indian Agent to W.B. Whitney, April 8, 1902; Indian Agent to R. Urch, April 8, 1902.

72　Dempsey counts 2,000 head of cattle by 1900. Dempsey, *Red Crow*, 201. Agent James Wilson reported that the Bloods had 3,000 horses in 1902. LAC, RG 10, vol. 1724, 497, James Wilson to Indian Commissioner, April 3, 1902. On theft, see RG 10, vol. 1725, 8–9, James Wilson to Secretary, DIA, February 24, 1903. On horses and cattle for this period, see Goldfrank, *Social Organization*, 23–25.

73　A.A. Lupton, "Cattle Ranching in Alberta 1874–1910: Its Evolution and Migration," *Alberta Geographer* 3 (1967): 57. It was the decade after 1896 that cattlemen faced the full effects of homesteads. Breen, *Ranching Frontier*, 101. Craig briefly mentions this contest for land. Craig, *Lords and Commons*, 236.

74　LAC, RG 10, vol. 1725, 30–33, James Wilson to Secretary, DIA, March 11, 1903.

75　LAC, RG 10, vol. 3571, file 130, pt. 19. See Memorandum of Agreement, dated May 16, 1903.

76　LAC, RG 10, vol. 1721, 680–82, James Wilson to Supt. Irwin, September 25, 1903.

77　Dempsey, *Gentle Persuader*, 26.

78　LAC, RG. 10, vol. 3571, file 130, pt. 19, J.G. Turriff to Clifford Sifton, November 19, 1903; J.A.J. McKenna to Clifford Sifton, January 5, 1904.

79　LAC, RG. 10, vol. 3571, file 130, pt. 19, J.D. McLean to J.A.J. McKenna, July 18, 1904; J.A.J. McKenna to Secretary, DIA, July 22, 1904; Frank Pedley to Assistant Indian Commissioner, July 27, 1904.

80　LAC, RG 10, vol. 1725, 99–104, James Wilson to Secretary, DIA, April 22, 1903; vol. 3571, file 130, pt. 19, J.A.J. McKenna to Secretary, DIA, September 7, 1904.

81　J.A.J. McKenna hinted that Chief Crop Eared Wolf was bribed to consent to the lease. LAC, RG. 10, vol. 3571, file 130, pt. 19, J.A.J. McKenna to Superintendent General, January 5, 1904. For machinations involved in granting the lease, see Dempsey, *Gentle Persuader*, 26; LAC, RG. 10, vol. 3571, file 130, pt. 19, R.N. Wilson to J.A.J. McKenna, March 25, 1904.

82　LAC, RG. 10, vol. 1722, 279–81, Indian Agent to Secretary, DIA, August 4, 1904. It appears that the reserve may have been overstocked. Taylor says that because of the large numbers "that almost the entire reserve was needed for pasture." Taylor, *Standing Alone*, 62.

83　LAC, RG 10, vol. 1725, 103, James Wilson to Secretary, DIA, April 22, 1903; 105, a listing of owners of cattle grazing on Blood Reserve 670, Indian Agent to Indian Commissioner, May 19, 1904.

84　Rancher E.F. Hagell makes several references to apparently intentional and illegal trespass of stock on the Blood reserve. E.F. Hagell, *When the Grass Was Free* (Toronto: Ryerson Press, 1954), 13–14, 64, 74–77. Even if we conclude that with the arrival of McEwan cattle other stock would have been removed from the reserve, the reserve would still be overgrazed if McEwan stocked the reserve to the lease limit of 7,000 and the Bloods still retained their complement of 6,000. The reserve would then be overstocked by 23 per cent.

85　*Rocky Mountain Echo*, August 29, 1905.

86　Lupton, *Cattle Ranching* 3 (1967): 57.

87　Elofson, "Not Just a Cowboy," 205–16. See especially his discussion in Elofson, *Cowboys, Gentlemen, and Cattle Thieves*, 134–49, and Elofson, *Frontier Cattle Ranching*, 158–74. As Paul Voisey has pointed out, although perhaps universally promoted, mixed farming was not universally adopted. Voisey, "A Mix-Up Over Mixed Farming," 179–80. See also Voisey, *Vulcan*, 77–81, 96–97.

88　*Rocky Mountain Echo*, May 1906.

89   Breen, *The Canadian Prairie West*, 145–48, 164; Elofson, *Cowboys Gentlemen and Cattle Thieves*, 84–91; Kelly, *The Range Men*, chap. 19.

90   *Rocky Mountain Echo*, May 1906.

91   Friesen, *The Canadian Prairies*, 328. Similar views were expressed by ranchers in the Palliser's Triangle. See Barry Potyondi, *In Palliser's Triangle: Living in the Grasslands 1850–1930* (Saskatoon: Purich Publishing, 1995), 102.

92   The Rev. Martin Holdom noted that in the area of Castor, Alberta, in 1910, the farmers were ruined by an early drought and in 1911 by early frost. The lesson to farmers, he said was clear; engage in mixed farming, grow an early variety of grain and do not borrow against the crop. Voisey, *A Preacher's Frontier*, 114–15; Max Foran, *Trails and Trials: Markets and Land Use in Alberta Beef Cattle Industry 1881–1948* (Calgary: University of Calgary Press, 2003), 9, 50–52.

93   *Macleod Spectator*, November 5, 1912, 3.

94   *Macleod Advertiser*, May 29, 1913, 1.

95   *Macleod Spectator*, June 4, 1912, 7.

96   *Cardston Globe*, May 8, 1914, 1.

97   See, for example, Long, *The Great Canadian Range*, 4. In 1902 the company ran 30,000 head of cattle and was considered a giant in the cattle industry. Ed Gould, *Ranching in Western Canada* (Saanichton, BC: Hancock House, 1978), 103–4; Dempsey, *Tom Three Persons*, 67.

98   *Macleod Advertiser*, June 6, 1912, 1. Success in alienating reserve land "would mean the breaking of the restrictive bond which has hampered the development of the district to the south and east for so long." May 29, 1913, 4.

99   *Macleod Advertiser*, June 6, 1912, 1. The *Cardston Globe* echoed these sentiments by reprinting the same article. The *Cardston Globe*, June 13, 1912, 1.

100 *Macleod Spectator*, June 4, 1912, 7. For more on this debate, see: *Macleod Spectator*, October 1, 1912, 6; October 8, 1912, 7; October 29, 1912, 4, 7; November 5, 1912, 3; December 31, 1912, 4; January 7, 1913, 4; January 14, 1913, 7; January 21, 1913, 1.

101 *Macleod Spectator*, November 19, 1912, 1. On this idea, see *Macleod Advertiser*, June 5, 1913, 7.

102 *Macleod Advertiser*, July 3, 1913, 7. See also the *Family Herald*, July 2, 1913.

103 *Macleod Advertiser*, July 3, 1913, 7. If this was the case by 1915 Roche had changed his mind and was more inclined to follow the wishes of the Bloods in this matter. *House of Commons Debates*, March 22, 1915, 1323–1324.

104 GA, Blood Indian Agency Correspondence (BIAC), file 62, Indian Agent to Secretary, DIA, June 13, 1913. The Cardston application was rejected in part because of the continued trespass and destruction of the reserve fence. LAC, RG 10, vol. 1547, 43, Indian Agent to the Secretary, DIA, July 10, 1913; BIAC, GA, file 62, Indian Agent to Secretary, DIA, June 25, 1913. The Bloods also blamed Cardston residents for the deaths of Single Rider and his wife, who died after drinking Florida Water purchased at Cardston, though no conviction was made. The agent reported that "the Indians imagine that … it is a job on the Mormons' part to poison them all off to get the Reserve." On trespass, see: GA, BIAC, file 62 Indian Agent to W. Caldwell, November 13, 1913; Indian Agent to W. Blackmore, November 13, 1913.

105 LAC, RG 10, vol. 1547, 43, Indian Agent to the Secretary, DIA, July 10, 1913. Emphasis added. There was some discussion on whether the rental should be $2.50 or $3.00 per head. GA, BIAC, file 62, Indian Agent to Secretary, DIA, June 13, 1913.

106 The *Globe* expressed the belief that big business interests, specifically meat packing plants in Winnipeg, were influencing Minister of the Interior, William J. Roche. See *Cardston Globe*, September 5, 1913, 1.

107 *Cardston Globe*, May 30, 1913, 1; *Macleod Advertiser*, June 19, 1913, 1.

108 *Cardston Globe*, July 25, 1913, 1.

109 *Macleod Spectator*, June 17, 1913, 1.

110 *Macleod Spectator*, September 9, 1913, 1.

111 *Macleod Advertiser*, October 24, 1912, 2. A summary of this idea, along with the implications for large-scale ranching, was given in the *Raymond Leader*, 1915; "The west has settled back on its haunches so to speak, and a wild, untamed, limitless area, with boundless prairie to run at will on, has become a home for a home-building people.... The homesteader and the settler, the men who dig post holes, string barbed wire and follow the plough are, of course, responsible for the change." *Raymond Leader*, March 26, 1915, 2.

112 *Raymond Leader*, September 12, 1913, 1. On how to distribute the land should the reserve be opened, see the *Raymond Leader*, July 4, 1913, 1.

113 *Cardston Globe*, June 30, 1914, 4. LAC, R.G. 10, vol. 4024, file 290, 240-2A; LAC, RG 10, vol. 1537, 105, Indian Agent to D.C. Scott, January 25, 1918.

114 LAC, RG 10, vol. 1547, 238, Indian Agent to Assistant Deputy and Sec'y, DIA, December 2, 1914; Provincial Archives of Alberta (PAA), Accession No. 70.414/81, W.J. Dilworth to Provincial Live Stock Commissioner, December 29, 1913.

115 *Macleod Spectator*, March 19, 1914, 1; May 28, 1914, 1.

116 *Cardston Globe*, May 18, 1916, 1.

117 *Cardston Globe*, January 17, 1918, 5.

118 LAC, RG 10, vol. 1537, 105, Indian Agent to D.C. Scott, January 25, 1918. Dilworth estimated the reserve capacity at 20,000 head. The criteria he used to arrive at this estimation are unknown.

119 There were occasions when offenders were ordered to remove their animals. Some contractors abusing their rights, such as E.H. Maunsell, were ordered to remove their stock. See, for example, GA, Cross Family Papers (CFP), file 893, [?] to A.E. Cross, May 8, 1919; LAC, RG 10, vol. 1546, 48, Indian Agent to O.J. Stoddard, February 26, 1919.

120 *Cardston Globe*, August 21, 1920, 4.

121 A hair brand singes the outer hairs for temporary identification of stock. When the hair grows back the brand is gone. It was generally used on cattle drives when owners wanted to temporarily identify animals. This information was provided by Hank Pallister and passed along by Douglas E. Cass, Senior Archivist, Glenbow.

122 GA, Western Stock Grazing Association Papers, 1896–1972, file 48.

123 *Macleod Times*, April 20, 1922, 3. The roundup of strays continued on practically a yearly basis. See: *Macleod Times*, July 13, 1922, 7; June 28, 1923, 1; July 21, 1927, 3; June 14, 1928, 1; *Cardston News*, June 14, 1928, 6. The July roundup for 1927 netted approximately 580 animals. *Cardston News*, July 14, 1927, 2 & 7. For 1929, see the *Cardston News*, June 27, 1929, 2; July 4, 1929, 5.

124 GA, CFP, file 952, Report to R.H. Campbell, Director of Forestry, Department of the Interior, October 24, 1922; CFP, file 895, has substantial correspondence on the shortage of feed for cattle during this period.

125 GA, CFP, file 952, Report to R.H. Campbell, Director of Forestry, Department of the Interior, October 24, 1922. Breen attributes other factors such as depressed prices and market access. Breen, *Ranching Frontier*, 215 ff. Evans, *The Bar U*, 145, 198, 302.

126 LAC, RG 10, vol. 1546, 273, Indian Agent to Duncan C. Scott, July 3, 1922. Dempsey recounts an incident between James Gladstone and the cattle of Knight and Watson. Dempsey, *Gentle Persuader*, 66.

127 GA, BIAC, file 131, W.M. Graham to J.T. Faunt, April 20, 1923; W.M. Graham to J.T. Faunt, May 2, 1923.

128 John Leonard Taylor, *Canadian Indian Policy during the Inter-War Years, 1918–1939*

(Ottawa: Indian Affairs and Northern Development, 1984), 15–19.

129 Dempsey, *Gentle Persuader*, 51–52.

130 *Macleod Times*, March 8, 1923, 3. The *Times* saw a glimmer of hope in a federal government decision to "grant grazing leases of vacant Dominion lands unfit for agricultural purposes in Manitoba, Saskatchewan and Alberta, and which are encumbered by seed grain and relief indebtedness." *Macleod Times*, March 22, 1923, 1. Indian farmer James Gladstone quit his efforts in 1923 when for three years running cattle from nearby ranches invaded his fields and ruined his crops. Dempsey, *Gentle Persuader*, 67. On the competition for limited space, see David C. Jones, *"We'll all be buried down here": The Prairie Dryland Disaster, 1917–1926* (Calgary: Historical Society of Alberta, 1986), 13–15, 90.

131 Titley, *A Narrow Vision*: 40–41; E. Brian Titley, "William Morris Graham: Indian Agent Extraordinaire," *Prairie Forum* 8, no. 1 (1983): 30.

132 Taylor, *Canadian Indian Policy*, 16–19.

133 Bruce Dawson, "'Better Than a Few Squirrels': The Greater Production Campaign on the First Nations Reserves of the Canadian Prairies" in *Plain Speaking: Essays on Aboriginal Peoples and the Prairies*, ed. Patrick C. Douaud and Bruce W. Dawson (Regina: Canadian Plains Research Center, 2002), 14, 19; R.N. Wilson, *Our Betrayed Wards: A Story of 'Chicanery, Infidelity and the Prostitution of Trust'* (Ottawa, 1921), 7, 9.

134 Dawson, "'Better Than a Few Squirrels'," 16.

135 Taylor, *Standing Alone*, 33; Statements in RG 10, vol. 4069, file 427,063; A.D. Fisher, "Introducing "our Betrayed Wards," by R.N. Wilson, *Western Canadian Journal of Anthropology* (January 1974): 28.

136 Taylor, *Canadian Indian Policy*, 21.

137 Jones, *Empire of Dust*, 107–8.

138 Treaty Seven Elders and Tribal Council et al., *The True Spirit and Original Intent of Treaty 7*, 321–22.

139 Titley, *A Narrow Vision*, 41–41; Wilson, *Our Betrayed Wards* (Ottawa, 1921), 10–16.

140 Dempsey, *Gentle Persuader*, 53 and 56; Samek, *The Blackfoot Confederacy*, 85.

141 Taylor, *Canadian Indian Policy*, 22; Dawson, "'Better Than a Few Squirrels'," 18–19.

142 Taylor, *Canadian Indian Policy*, 25.

143 Deputy Superintendent to Wm. Graham, February 22, 1922, RG 10, vol. 4069, file 427,063.

144 Dawson, "'Better Than a Few Squirrels'," 18.

145 To my knowledge there are no records or minutes of this convention extant. *Lethbridge Herald*, November 13, 14, 15, 1924 in LAC, RG 10, vol. 4093, file 600,107; Mike Mountain Horse to J.T. Faunt, November 22, 1924; *Calgary Herald*, November 14, 1924, in LAC, RG 10, vol. 4093, file 600,107; Yale Belanger, "'An all round Indian affair': The Native Gatherings at Macleod, 1924 & 1925," *Alberta History* (06/22) 2005.

146 GA, George Gibson Coote Papers, 1907–1956 (GGCP), file 137, J.T. Faunt to Duncan C. Scott, May 31, 1923. McLean also had a lease on the Peigan Reserve and was said to be of the opinion that the Indians consent to a lease was not necessary. Coote charged that McLean got the Peigan lease for the "ridiculously low" price of six cents per acre for ten years, while at the same time some lease land brought thirty cents per acre. McLean politically well-connected was described by Coote as "a member of the late Stewart administration." GA, GGCP, file 137, G.G. Coote to the *[Lethbridge?] Herald*, n.d. (circa 1924); J.C. Caldwell to Deputy Superintendent General, DIA, April 17, 1924. See also: *Lethbridge Herald*, November 14, 1924; *Calgary Herald*, November 15, 1924, in LAC, RG 10, vol. 4093, file 600, 107.

147 LAC, RG 10, vol. 4093, file 600,107, A.F. Grady to C. Stewart, November 18, 1924; C. Stewart to A.G. Grady, November 24, 1924; Joseph Mountain Horse to Hon. W.L. Mackenzie King, February 7, 1925.

148 Dempsey, *Gentle Persuader*, 62 & 71.

149 Dempsey, *Gentle Persuader*, 62 & 71.

150 Gregory P. Marchildon, "Institutional Adaptation to Drought and the Special Areas of Alberta, 1909–1939," *Prairie Forum* 32, no. 2 (Fall 2007): 256.

151 Jones, *Empire of Dust*, 220.

152 M. Christianson to Secretary, DIA, May 29, 1933; Harold W. McGill, June, 1933; A.F. MacKenzie to M. Christianson, June 17, 1933. See itemized statement in LAC, RG 10, vol. 12648, file 103/32-1-2 (pt. 1) Arrears totalled $3,353.56. The total lease amount was for $4,973.28 so payments were 67 per cent in arrears. On the inherent confusion, see: M. Christianson to J.E. Pugh, February 28, 19[33]; J.E. Pugh to M. Christianson, March 4, 1933.

153 Max Foran, "The Impact of the Depression on Grazing Lease Policy in Alberta," in *Cowboys, Ranchers and the Cattle Business: Cross-Border Perspectives on Ranching History*, ed. Simon M. Evans, Sarah Carter, and Bill Yeo (Calgary: University of Calgary Press, 2000), 126–27, 130; Foran, *Trails and Trials*, 136–37.

154 LAC, RG 10, vol. 12648, file 103/32-1-2 (pt. 1), Harold W. McGill to J.E. Pugh, November 8, 1933.

155 LAC, RG 10, vol. 12648, file 103/32-1-2 (pt. 1), M. Christianson to Harold W. McGill, November 13, 1933; J.E. Pugh to M. Christianson, November 14, 1933. At this time there were twelve separate applications for grazing leases in the area.

156 LAC, RG 10, vol. 12648, file 103/32-1-2 (pt. 1), J.E. Pugh to M. Christianson, November 14, 1933.

157 LAC, RG 10, vol. 12648, file 103/32-1-2 (pt. 1), J.E. Pugh to M. Christianson, November 14, 1933; M. Christianson to J.E.

Pugh, November 16, 1933; J.E. Pugh to M. Christianson, November 14, 1933.

158 LAC, RG 10, vol. 12648, file 103/32-1-2 (pt. 1), M. Christianson to J.E. Pugh, November 16, 1933.

159 Perhaps the best illustration of this is the difficulty collecting lease rents. LAC, RG 10, vol. 12648, file 103/32-1-2 (pt. 1), J.E. Pugh to Secretary, DIA, October 24, 1933.

160 LAC, RG 10, vol. 1538, J.E. Pugh to W.T. McCaugherty, November 12, 1935. The matter was further complicated by the fact that some Bloods were pressing for 600 acres to be withdrawn from the lease, although they had not been living on the leased portion of the land when the lease had been granted. LAC, RG 10, vol. 1538, J.E. Pugh to Secretary, DIA, November 22, 1935; W.T. McCaugherty to J.E. Pugh, November 20, 1935.

161 LAC, RG 10, vol. 1538, J.E. Pugh to Secretary, DIA, January 13, 1936.

162 LAC, RG 10, vol. 1538, W.S. McCaugherty to J.E. Pugh, November 23, 1934.

163 LAC, RG 10, vol. 1538, J.E. Pugh to Secretary, DIA, January 13, 1936; A.F. Mackenzie to J.E. Pugh, January 23, 1936.

164 LAC, RG 10, vol. 12648, file 103/32-1-2 (pt. 1), J.E. Pugh to Secretary, DIA, January 13, 1936. The problems here, in part, stem from a lease transfer. This original lease had been with the now-defunct Cardston Grazing Co. and had stipulated that "The leasing of the above land will not interfere with the rights of the Indians at present residing within the limits of the proposed lease, nor will it interfere with the going to and from of the Indians of the reserve." For similar problems, see: J.E. Pugh to Secretary, DIA, June 24, 1937; J.E. Pugh to Messers. Smith & Kearl, July 14, 1937. See also: J.E. Pugh to Secretary DIA, May 16, 1938; J.E. Pugh to Secretary, DIA., July 14, 1937.

165 LAC, RG 10, vol. 12648, file 103/32-1-2 (pt. 1), M. Christianson to J.C. Caldwell, January 21, 1936.

166 A similar situation, also in 1935, occurred when the Town of Cardston raised objections to a portion of its desired lease being removed at the behest of Blood Indian Joe Devine who wished to live on the land. For details, see correspondence in LAC, RG 10, vol. 12649, file 103/32-1-2 (pt. 2). At least one scholar seems to suggest that the Bloods' behaviour with regard to lease land was suspect. Lawrence E. Kindt, "The Sheep Ranching Industry of Canada" (PhD diss., American University, 1939), 106. Indeed the agreement between the Bloods and the DIA stipulated that the lease agreements expire in 1934, but in 1935 they were still in effect. The extension was made necessary because of rent arrears in 1931 and that new contracts expired in 1937. Pugh observed that the latest contracts had to be reviewed by the Bloods in 1936 to allow for the mandatory one year notice to lessees before cancellation. LAC, RG 10, vol. 1538, J.E. Pugh to M. Christianson, December 16, 1935.

167 LAC, RG 10, vol. 1538, J.E. Pugh to Secretary, DIA, March 14, 1936; J.E. Pugh to M. Christianson, December 16, 1935.

168 LAC, RG 10, vol. 1538, J.E. Pugh to M. Christianson, December 16, 1935.

169 LAC, RG 10, vol. 1538, A.D. Wymbs to J.E. Pugh, January 20, 1936; J.E. Pugh to Secretary, DIA, April 27, 1936; A.F. MacKenzie to J.E. Pugh, April 28, 1936; A.F. MacKenzie to J.E. Pugh, May 27, 1936; H.W. McGill to Secretary-Treasurer, Town of Cardston, April 30, 1936.

170 LAC, RG 10, vol. 1538, Copy of vote; J.E. Pugh to Harold W. McGill, May 29, 1936. Pugh also noted that "the voters list carries 340 names, of these 322 were entitled to vote, 4 were incarcerated in jail, 14 were resident away from the reserve. A number of those who for sickness etc. were unable to attend sent in notes to express their vote, this was not allowed."

171 LAC, RG 10, vol. 12648, file 103/32-1-2 (pt. 1), J.E. Pugh to Harold W. McGill,

July 7, 1936; LAC, RG 10, vol. 1538, J.E. Pugh to Harold W. McGill, July 7, 1936.

172 LAC, RG 10, vol. 1538, J.E. Pugh to Secretary, DIA, September 18, 1936; J.E. Pugh to Representative of the Treasury, DIA, September 23, 1936. See also J.E. Pugh to Secretary, DIA, September 30, 1936.

173 LAC, RG 10, vol. 12648, file 103/32-1-2 (pt. 1), J.E. Pugh to H.W. McGill, August 3, 1936.

174 LAC, RG 10, vol. 1538, M. Christianson to J.E. Pugh, December 3, 1936.

175 LAC, RG 10, vol. 12648, file 103/32-1-2 (pt. 1), Billy Heavy Runner to Dr. McGill, September 21, 1936; J.E. Pugh to Secretary, DIA, October 15, 1936; J.E. Pugh to M. Christianson, November 18, 1936; L.E. Fairbairn to J.E. Pugh, November 30, 1936, RG 10, vol. 1538. In 1938 a request for a sheep lease was turned down on the basis of the poor condition of the grazing land and the constant "encroaching upon the Indians in one way or another." See N.E. Tanner to Agent Pugh, April 26, 1938; J.E. Pugh to N.E. Tanner, May 3, 1938; M. Christianson to Secretary, DIA, May 10, 1934.

176 LAC, RG 10, vol. 12648, file 103/32-1-2 (pt. 1), M. Christianson to General J.S. Stewart, August 23, 1935.

177 James H. Gray, *The Winter Years* (Toronto: Macmillan Canada, 1966), 109.

178 LAC, RG 10, vol. 12648, file 103/32-1-2 (pt. 1), J.E. Pugh to M. Christianson, December 16, 1935; J.C. Caldwell to M. Christianson, January 17, 1936.

179 LAC, RG 10, vol. 12648, file 103/32-1-2 (pt. 1), J.E. Pugh to M. Christianson, December 8, 1936.

180 See LAC, RG 10, vol. 12648, file 103/32-1-2 (pt. 1).

181 LAC, RG 10, vol. 12648, file 103/32-1-2 (pt. 1), C. Pant. Schmidt, December 17, 1937; C. Pant. Schmidt to John E. Pugh, December 17, 1937. For similar details and concerns, see LAC, RG 10, vol. 12648,

file 205/32-1, M. Christianson to C.P. Schmid:, November 26, 1937.

182 There was no correspondence in this file regarding leases for the year 1939.

183 LAC, RG 10, vol. 12648, file 103/32-1-2 (pt. 1), C. Pant. Schmidt to Secretary, D.I.A., March 25, 1941; Anthony Mc-Millan to C. Pant. Schmidt, September 24, 1942; C. Pant. Schmidt to J.E. Pugh, August 23, 1944; A. McMillan to Harold W. McGill, March 27, 1942; LAC, RG 10, vol. 12648, file 103/32-1-2 (pt. 1), J.E. Pugh to C. Pant Schmidt, February 8, 1940; LAC, RG 10, vol. 12648, file 103/32-1-2 (pt. 1), T.R.L. MacInnes, to C. Pant. Schmidt, February 20, 1940; LAC, RG 10, vol. 12648, file 103/32-1-2 (pt. 1), T.R.L. MacInnes to C. Pant. Schmidt, March 3, 1941.

184 LAC, RG 10, vol. 1535, 188-89, Petition for the keeping of Indian Horses on their own reserve, E. Hillzer, G. Pearson, E.J. Muldoon, Alf. H. Anderston, Geo. Anderton, John Smith, J.R. Allan, R.O. Sykes, John George Brown to Hon. Frank Oliver, n.d.

185 Harper, "Canada's Indian Administration," 307.

186 Beal, 'Money, Markets and Economic Develcpment," 57–58.

CHAPTER 3

1 Hildebrandt, *Views from Fort Battleford*, 49. Hildebrandt gave little attention to the Cree around Battleford.

2 Samek, *The Blackfoot Confederacy*, 70–86.

3 See, for example, Anthony G. Gulig, "Sizing Up the Catch: Native-Newcomer Resource Competition and the Early Years of Saskatchewan's Northern Commercial Fishery," *Saskatchewan History* (Fall 1995): 3–12. Complaints about Native competition in the marketplace led to the imposition of the permit system restrict-

ing off-reserve sales of Native produce. Carter, "Two Acres and a Cow," 36–37; Carter, *Lost Harvests*, 156–57; Samek, *The Blackfoot Confederacy*, 77; Fisher, *Contact and Conflict*, 109–11; Jane Gibson, "Native Responses to Bureaucratic Farm Management in Western Canadian Indian Reserves, 1880–1920," *Western Canadian Anthropologist* 7, nos. 1 & 2 (1990): 77.

4 John Lutz, "After the Fur Trade: The Aboriginal Labouring Class of British Columbia 1849–1890," *Journal of the Canadian Historical Association* (1992): 70; High, "Native Wage Labour and Independent Production during the 'Era of Irrelevance'," 243–44. The 'era of irrelevance' is the period from the end of the fur trade in the mid-nineteenth century to World War II. For a recent and detailed analysis of Native participation in local and extended economies, see Frank Tough, *'As Their Natural Resources Fail': Native Peoples and the Economic History of Northern Manitoba, 1870–1930* (Vancouver: UBC Press, 1996). See also Frank Tough, "Buying Out the Bay: Aboriginal Rights and the Economic Policies of the Department of Indian Affairs after 1870," in Miller et al., *The First Ones*, 405. Notable exceptions to the above are Stuart Jamieson, "Native Indians and the Trade Union Movement in British Columbia," *Human Organization* 20, no. 4 (Winter 1961–2): 219–25 and Rolf Knight, *Indians at Work: An Informal History of Native Indian Labour in British Columbia 1858–1930* (Vancouver: New Star Books, 1978). None of these studies emphasizes circumstances in southern Alberta.

5 Beal, "Money, Markets and Economic Development," 378.

6 Rob Innes, Breanda McDougall, and Frank Tough, "Band Economies 1897–1915," in *Atlas of Saskatchewan*, ed. Ka-iu Fung (Saskatoon: University of Saskatchewan, 1999), 59–60.

7 Beal, "Money, Markets and Economic Development," 70.

8   W.J.C. Cherwinski, "A Miniature Coxey's Army: The British Harvesters' Toronto-to-Ottawa Trek of 1924," *Labour/Le Travail* 32 (Fall 1993): 140–41; W.J.C. Cherwinski, "Wooden Horses and Rubber Cows: Training British Agricultural Labour for the Canadian Prairies, 1890–1930," Canadian Historical Association, *Historical Papers 1980*, 133. For particulars on the 1908 harvest season, see W.J.C. Cherwinski, "The Incredible Harvest Excursion of 1908," *Labour/Le Travailleur* 5 (Spring 1980): 57–80; Cecelia Danysk, *Hired Hands: Labour and the Development of Prairie Agriculture, 1880–1930* (Toronto: McClelland & Stewart, 1995), 24, 85; John Herd Thompson, "Bringing in the Sheaves: The Harvest Excursionists, 1890–1929," *Canadian Historical Review* 59, no. 4 (December 1978): 468; John Herd Thompson, *The Harvests of War: The Prairie West, 1914–1918* (Toronto: McClelland & Stewart, 1978), 62–63; R. Bruce Shepard, "The Mechanized Agricultural Frontier of the Canadian Plains," *Material History Bulletin* 7 (Spring 1979): 15.

9   Taylor, *Standing Alone*, 31–32. Commentary on Indian involvement in fairs and exhibitions tends to focus on social and cultural aspects of the events. Little information is contained in the public record of the financial or economic arrangements. On fairs and exhibitions, see Titley, *A Narrow Vision*, chap. 9; Keith Regular, "On Public Display," *Alberta History*, 34, no. 1 (Winter 1986): 1; Francis, *The Imaginary Indian*, 97–108; Donald G. Wetherell with Irene Kmet, *Useful Pleasures: The Shaping of Leisure in Alberta 1896–1945* (Regina: Canadian Plains Research Center, 1990), 328. Blood Indian Mike Mountain Horse, among others, did scout work for the Mounted Police. He also spent considerable time off the reserve living among White society. Mike Mountain Horse, *My People the Bloods* (Calgary: Glenbow-Alberta Institute, 1979), v–xi.

10   Taylor, *Standing Alone*, 31–32.

11   C.B. Beaty, "Geomorphology, Geology and Non-Agricultural Resources," in *Southern Alberta: A Regional Perspective*, ed. F. Jankunis (Lethbridge: University of Lethbridge, 1972), 18.

12   LAC, RG 10, vol. 7632, file 18103-1, James Wilson to Indian Commissioner, July 20, 1894, extract from copy of letter dated Blood Agency Macleod, December 6, 1895.

13   LAC, RG 10, vol. 7632, file 18103-1, A.E. Forget to Deputy of the Supt. Gen'l of Indian Affairs, June 21, 1890. For other commentary, see RG 10, vol. 1557, 575–76, W. Pocklington to Indian Commissioner, June 12, 1890. See letter dated June 30, 1890; A.E. Forget to Deputy of the Supt. Gen'l of Indian Affairs, January 21, 1892; RG 10, vol. 1557, 721–22, W. Pocklington to Indian Commissioner, August 30, 1890. See also 694–96, W. Pocklington to Indian Commissioner, August 12, 1890; RG 10, vol. 1558, 92–94, W. Pocklington to Indian Commissioner, December 1, 1890; Hugh A. Dempsey, *Red Crow: Warrior Chief* (Saskatoon: Western Producer Prairie Books, 1980), 198–99.

14   LAC, RG 10, vol. 1559, James Wilson to Indian Commissioner, August 22, 1893, 422–25.

15   LAC, RG 10, vol. 7632, file 18103-1, James Wilson to Indian Commissioner, December 24, 1896; Deputy Superintendent General to J.E. Pugh, December 18, 1933.

16   LAC, RG 10, vol. 7632, file 18103-1, news clipping, *Macleod Gazette*, February 16, 1894.

17   LAC, RG 10, vol. 1560, 321–25, James Wilson to Superintendent General of Indian Affairs, August 1, 1894.

18   Dempsey, *Red Crow*, 199. I have been unable to determine why the Galt Company would need to purchase this coal. The need to fill a small contract during a temporary coal shortage is, perhaps, an explanation.

19   LAC, RG 10, vol. 7632, file 18103-1, extract from copy of letter dated December

6, 1895, signed by Jas. Wilson. Because of the quality of the coal, eventually the Mounted Police refused to accept it for use at their posts. LAC, RG 10, vol. 7632, file 18103-1, A.E. Forget to Deputy of the Superintendent General of Indian Affairs, February, 17, 1896; James Wilson to Hayter Reed, September 17, 1896.

20   LAC, RG 10, vol. 7632, file 18103-1, R.N. Wilson to Secretary, DIA, June 30, 1909; John Harvie to Secretary, DIA, January 17, 1907; J.D. McLean to John Harvie, January 30, 1907; GA, BIAC, file 63, Indian Agent to A.G. McGuire, July 15, 1911; Agent to A.G. McGuire July 31, 1911.

21   GA, BIAC, file 63, A.G. McGuire[?] to William Hyde, July 27, 1911; *Lethbridge Herald*, June 15, 1911, 1.

22   *Raymond Leader*, January 23, 1913, 4.

23   LAC, RG 10, vol. 1547, 153–54, S. Swinford to Secretary, DIA, October 3, 1913.

24   David J. Bercuson, ed., *Alberta's Coal Industry 1919* (Calgary: Historical Society of Alberta, 1978), viii, x.

25   LAC, RG 10, vol. 7632, file 18103-1, Z.W. Jacobs to C.A. Magrath, January 3, 1918; C.W. Peterson to D.C. Scott, January 10, 1918; Duncan C. Scott to W.J. Dilworth, January 12, 1918; Deputy Superintendent General to W.J. Dilworth, January 21, 1918. Dilworth subsequently noted his belief that there was no coal shortage in the area.

26   Oliver was of the opinion that "educating these Indians to compete industrially with our own people" was a "very undesirable use of public money ...," *House of Commons Debates*, 1899, Cols. 5725–26, June 22, 1899; Hall, "Clifford Sifton and Canadian Indian Administration," 130.

27   LAC, RG 10, vol. 7632, file 18103-1, J.T. Faunt to Secretary, DIA, February 25, 1921. The coal was being sold at $8.50 per ton. Also see Duncan C. Scott to C.S. Finnie, March 14, 1921.

28   LAC, RG 10, vol. 7632, file 18103-1, M. Christianson to Doctor McGill, January 29, 1934.

29   LAC, RG 10, vol. 7632, file 18103-1, M. Christianson to Doctor McGill, January 29, 1934.

30   LAC, RG 10, vol. 7632, file 18103-1, Extract from a latter by J.E. Pugh, November 30, 1933; J.E. Pugh to H.W. McGill, December 22, 1933; F.W. Steel to H.W. McGill, January 12, 1934; H.W. McGill to The Superintendent General, January 16, 1934.

31   Barry Kaye, "'The Settlers' Grand Difficulty': Haying in the Economy of the Red River Settlement," *Prairie Forum* 9, no. 1 (Spring 1984): 7.

32   Tony Ward, "Farming Technology and Crop Area on Early Prairie Farms," *Prairie Forum* 20, no. 1 (Spring 1995): 25. With grain, for example, fifteen or twenty men were needed for a harvesting crew. Ernest B. Ingles, "The Custom Threshermen in Western Canada 1890–1925," in Jones and MacPherson, *Building beyond the Homestead*, 138–40.

33   LAC, RG 10, vol. 1557, 631–33, W. Pocklington to Indian Commissioner, July 10, 1890.

34   LAC, RG 10, vol. 1557, 723–25, J. Wilson, farmer, to W. Pocklington, August 27, 1890. On hay shortages, see also 680–82, W. Pocklington to Indian Commissioner, July 31, 1890.

35   LAC, RG 10, vol. 1557, 730–33, W. Pocklington to Indian Commissioner, September 4, 1890.

36   LAC, RG 10, vol. 1558, 370–71, W. Pocklington to Superintendent General of Indian Affairs, July 22, 1891; 405, W. Pocklington to Indian Commissioner, August 3, 1891.

37   LAC, RG 10, vol. 1558, 370–71, 405–6, W. Pocklington to Indian Commissioner, August 3, 1891; 449–51, W. Pocklington to Indian Commissioner, August 31, 1891; 650, S. Swinford to Indian Commissioner,

December 29, 1891; 370–71, 842, S. Swinford to Inspector Begin, July 20, 1892.

38 LAC, RG 10, vol. 1559, 373, James Wilson to R. Burton Deane, July 13, 1893; 387–88, James Wilson to S.B. Steele, July 25, 1893; 390, James Wilson to S.B. Steele, July 27, 1893. See 394, James Wilson to S.B. Steele, August 2, 1893.

39 LAC, RG 10, vol. 1559, 400, James Wilson to Indian Commissioner, August 3, 1893; 407, James Wilson to A.R. Springett, August 18, 1893.

40 LAC, RG 10, vol. 1559, 495–97, James Wilson to [Indian Commissioner], October 2, 1893.

41 LAC, RG 10, vol. 1564, 437, James Wilson to Commanding Officer, NWMP, Lethbridge, September 21, 1899.

42 On October 18, 1899, Wilson billed W.S. Anderton of Macleod for $250.96 for hay delivered. It is unclear whether or not this hay originated with the reserve or was just freighted under contract from some other source. LAC, RG 10, vol. 1564, 470, James Wilson to W.S. Anderton, October 18, 1899. See also pp. 471 and 473.

43 LAC, RG 10, vol. 1564, 336, James Wilson to R. Burton Deane, June 12, 1899; 347, James Wilson to Superintendent Commanding, NWMP, Macleod, June 27, 1899; 474, James Wilson to R. Burton Deane, October 25, 1899. See also *Annual Report of the Department of Indian Affairs*, CSP No. 27, 1900, 138.

44 *Lethbridge News*, March 7, 1901, 7; *Annual Report of the Department of Indian Affairs*, CSP, No. 27, 1902, 128. See also LAC, RG 18, vol. 218, file 469, H.S. Casey to Officer Commanding 'K' Division, N.W.M.P., August 8, 1901; Joseph Howe to Commissioner, N.W.M.P., August 30, 1901.

45 *Annual Report of the Royal North West Mounted Police*, CSP, 28, No. 11, 1904, 73; *Annual Report of the Department of Indian Affairs*, CSP, No. 27, 1904, 141 and *Annual Report of the Department of Indian Affairs*, CSP, No. 27, 1902, 128.

46 *Macleod Gazette*, February 27, 1906, 2.

47 *Annual Report of the Department of Indian Affairs*, CSP, No. 27, 1914, 70.

48 The previous year total contracts called for only 170 tons and haying was not completed until October 1, 1913. LAC, RG 10, vol. 1547, 222, Unsigned letter, August 22, 1914.

49 *Annual Report of the Department of Indian Affairs*, CSP, No. 27, 1915, 77.

50 LAC, RG 10, vol. 7595, file 10103, pt. 2; Contract between RNWM Police, Macleod and W.J. Dilworth, Blood Reserve, August 21, 1914.

51 There is no indication why, in this instance, the Bloods could not furnish the contract. LAC, RG 10, vol. 7595, file 10103, pt. 2, Laurence Fortescue to Duncan C. Scott, May 12, 1915; J.D. McLean to Laurence Fortescue, May 15, 1915; GA, BIAC, file 36, Indian Agent to Messers. Gordon Ironsides and Fares, August 24, 1915.

52 See GA, BIAC, file 36, Indian Agent to Messers. Gordon Ironsides and Fares, August 24, 1915.

53 Valerie K. Jobson, "The Blackfoot Farming Experiment 1880–1945," (Master's thesis, University of Calgary, 1990), 104.

54 *Sikotan* Flora Zaharia and *Makai'sto* Leo Fox, *Kitomahkitapiiminnooniksi: Stories from Our Elders*, vol. 3 (Edmonton: Kainai Board of Education, 1995), 77; *Sikotan* Flora Zaharia and *Makai'sto* Leo Fox, *Kitomahkitapiiminnooniksi: Stories from Our Elders*, vol. 1 (Edmonton: Kainai Board of Education, 1995), 53, 76.

55 See list in LAC, RG 10, vol. 7632, file 18103-1.

56 LAC, RG 10, vol. 1559, 372, James Wilson to Hayter Reed, July 13, 1893.

57 LAC, RG 10, vol. 1559, 535–37, James Wilson to Indian Commissioner, November 3, 1893.

58 LAC, RG 10, vol. 1563, 625–26, James Wilson to Secretary, DIA, February 11, 1898; RG 10, vol. 1562, 175–76, James Wilson to Indian Commissioner, December 31,

1896; 617–19, James Wilson to Commissioner, February 10, 1898.

59 LAC, RG 10, vol. 1562, 258, James Wilson to Indian Commissioner, January 27, 1897. See also statements of payment on pp. 256–57. Goldfrank, *Changing Configurations*, 21.

60 LAC, RG 10, vol. 7632, file 18103-1, James Wilson to Secretary, DIA, January 12, 1899. With regard to the delivery of coal to the police, see also: James Wilson to secretary, DIA, February 15, 1898; Fred White to J.D. McLean, April 15, 1898; Fred White to J.D. McLean, April 28, 1898; Fred White to J.D. McLean, May 13, 1898; James Wilson to Secretary, DIA, June 1, 1898.

61 LAC, RG 10, vol. 1564, 79, James Wilson to Ross Cuthbert, September 19, 1898; 430, James Wilson to R. Burton Deane, September 12, 1899; 457, James Wilson to R. Burton Deane, October 6, 1899.

62 *Lethbridge News*, March 7, 1901, 7.

63 *Lethbridge News*, March 7, 1901, 7.

64 *Annual Report of the Department of Indian Affairs*, CSP, No. 14, 1899, 133.

65 *Annual Report for the Department of Indian Affairs*, CSP, No. 27, 1915, 70; No. 27, 1917, 73–74.

66 Dempsey, *Gentle Persuader*, 85.

67 See Blair Stonechild and Bill Waiser, *Loyal till Death: Indians and the North-West Rebellion* (Calgary: Fifth House Publishing, 1997), 216, 250–53.

68 Commentary on the efficacy of the pass and permit systems is mixed. For the Indian view of this system, see Treaty Seven Elders and Tribal Council et al., *The True Spirit and Original Intent of Treaty 7*, 136–37, 146–47, 150–51, 152, 155. For other commentary about its intent and scope, see: Miller, "Owen Glendower, Hotspur, and Canadian Indian Policy," 253–54; Barron, "The Indian Pass System in the Canadian West," 34–37, on permits, see pp. 38–39; Rebecca B. Bateman, "Talking with the Plow: Agricultural Policy and Indian Farming in the Canadian and U.S. Prairies," *Canadian Journal of Native Studies* 16, no. 2 (1996): 217, 220. On the Indians as peasant farmers, see: Carter, "Two Acres and a Cow," 27; Arthur J. Ray, *I Have Lived Here Since the World Began: An Illustrated History of Canada's Native People* (Toronto: Lester Publishing, 1996), 256.

69 Ward, "Farming Technology," 25. Shepard says that the awareness of mechanization was such that "The early development of the Canadian Plains ... could be called a mechanized agricultural frontier." R. Bruce Shepard, "Tractors and Combines in the Second Stage of Agricultural Mechanization on the Canadian Plains," *Prairie Forum* 11, no. 2 (Fall 1986): 254. Machinery came increasingly into use with the advancing settlement of the West. Ingles, "The Custom Threshermen in Western Canada," 136–37.

70 Carter, "Two Acres and a Cow," 1.

71 LAC, RG 10, vol. 1558, 208, W. Pocklington to Indian Commissioner, March 18, 1891.

72 Shepard, "The Mechanized Agricultural Frontier," 2–3.

73 It is not immediately clear why the method of letting contracts was changed. It could have been in response to public pressures or may simply have been a part of efficiency measures. LAC, RG 10, vol. 1557, 635, W. Pocklington to Inspector Steele, July 14, 1890.

74 LAC, RG 10, vol. 1560, 243, James Wilson to S.B. Steele, June 29, 1894.

75 LAC, RG 10, vol. 1560, 244–45, James Wilson to Indian Commissioner, June 29, 1894; 313, James Wilson to S.B. Steele.

76 LAC, RG 10, vol. 1560, 416–17, James Wilson to Superintendent in command, Macleod, August 31, 1894; 316, James Wilson to W. Stafford, July 30, 1894; 317, James Wilson to Manager, Galt Mines, July 30, 1894.

77 LAC, RG 10, vol. 1564, 446, James Wilson to W.D. Barclay, September 5, 1894.

78 LAC, RG 10, vol. 1564, 691, James Wilson to Indian Commissioner, January 4, 1895. Wilson did not explain the difficult circumstances, but it may have been due to the ample supply of coal in the region. See A.A. den Otter, *Civilizing the West: The Galts and the Development of Western Canada* (Edmonton: University of Alberta Press, 1982), 320.

79 LAC, RG 10, vol. 1561, 187–89, James Wilson to Indian Commissioner, October 7, 1895.

80 LAC, RG 10, vol. 7632, file 18103-1, Hayter Reed to Indian Agent Wilson, August 29, 1896.

81 LAC, RG 10, vol. 7632, file 18103-1, Hayter Reed to Indian Agent Wilson, September 15, 1896; Dean Freeman to Deputy Supt. Genl. Indians Affairs, September 5, 1896; James Wilson to Hayter Reed, September 8, 1896.

82 LAC, RG 10, vol. 7632, file 18103-1, James Wilson to Hayter Reed, September 17, 1896; A.E. Forget to Deputy of the Superintendent General of Indian Affairs, February, 17, 1896.

83 LAC, RG 10, vol. 7632, file 18103-1, Extract from Agents Wilson's October Report, November 24, 1896.

84 On the pass system, see: Titley, "Hayter Reed and Indian Administration in the West,", 117–18; Barron, "The Indian Pass System in the Canadian West," 27–30; John Jennings, "The North West Mounted Police and Indian Policy after the 1885 Rebellion," in *1885 and After: Native Society in Transition*, ed. F. Laurie Barron and James B. Waldram (Regina: Canadian Plains Research Center, 1986), 228–30; Pettipas, *Severing the Ties that Bind*, 111–12. On permits, see: Barron, "The Indian Pass System in the Canadian West," 39; Carter, *Lost Harvests*, 156–58; Elias, *The Dakota of the Canadian Northwest*, 88–89, 94.

85 Pettipas, *Severing the Ties that Bind*, 111–12; Miller, *Skyscrapers Hide the Heavens*, 258–60.

86 LAC, RG 10, vol. 1561, 93–94, James Wilson to Indian Commissioner, August 14, 1895.

87 LAC, RG 10, vol. 1561, 93–94, James Wilson to Indian Commissioner, August 14, 1895.

88 *Macleod Gazette*, July 26, 1895. For complaints against Indian competition, see: Carter, "Two Acres and a Cow," 36; Carter, *Lost Harvests*, 184–90; Anthony G. Gulig, "Sizing up the Catch", 6–7.

89 *Macleod Gazette*, August 2, 1895.

90 *Annual Report of the Department of Indian Affairs*, CSP, 14, vol. XXXI, No. 11, 1897, 135.

91 *Annual Report of the Department of Indian Affairs*, CSP, 14, 1897, 155. The bulk of this hay was supplied to the Cochrane Ranche Company, North West Mounted Police, and for Agency needs. Interestingly, the agent noted that the 109 tons required for the agency farmers' horses and cattle, for the agency horses and cattle and for the hospital cows was hauled free of charge as it had been done in the two previous years. *Annual Report of the Department of Indian Affairs*, CSP, 14, 1897, 156. LAC, RG 10, vol. 1563, 875–76, James Wilson to Indian Commissioner, May 16, 1898. The hay brought ten to twelve dollars per ton. The amount sold was not given. The agent's report contained in the Sessional Papers states that 1139 tons was sold for approximately $5,695. At the minimum of ten dollars per ton, this should have netted $11,390. See *Annual Report of the Department of Indian Affairs*, CSP, No. 14, 1899, 133.

92 The license system was not in place to protect Whites but to enable the agent to properly protect the property and resources of the Indians. RG 10, vol. 1564, 39–40. James Wilson to Corporal in Charge Town Patrol, Lethbridge, July 23, 1898. Indians were not legally permitted to sell reserve resources without the permission of the agent. For a discussion

of the permit system, see Buckley, *From Wooden Ploughs to Welfare*, 53–54.

93   LAC, RG 10, vol. 1560, 244–45, James Wilson to Indian Commissioner, June 29, 1894; 313, James Wilson to S.B. Steele, July 28, 1894.

94   Bercuson, ed., *Alberta's Coal Industry 1919*, x.

95   LAC, RG 10, vol. 7632, file 18103-1, G. Finnie to D.C. Scott, February 13, 1921.

96   *Macleod Times*, July 21, 1920, 1. Amateur historian Bud Spencer also recalled this activity. Bud Spencer, *Go North, Young Man, Go North!: My Life's Story* (n.d.), 14.

97   Spencer, *Go North*, 14.

98   *Cardston News*, March 3, 1927, 1.

99   *Cardston News*, August 23, 1928, 1.

100   Dempsey, *Gentle Persuader*, 70–85.

CHAPTER 4

1   For discussion of the reserve economy, see Samek, *The Blackfoot Confederacy*, chap. 4. John Herd Thompson and Allen Seager briefly mention Indian involvement in the sugar beet industry. See John Herd Thompson and Allen Seager, "Workers, Growers and Monopolists: The 'Labour Problem' in the Alberta Beet Sugar Industry during the 1930s," in *The Depression in Canada: Responses to Economic Crisis*, ed. Michiel Horn (Toronto: Copp Clark Pitman, 1988), 32. Curiously, Ronald F. Laliberté states that from the beginning of the industry in the early 1900s "most of the hand labour" in the fields was done by immigrants from Europe, and this was the situation up until World War II, when that supply of labour was cut off. He does not recognize that the Bloods had any place in this industry. Ronald F. Laliberté, "The Canadian State and Native Migrant Labour in Southern Alberta's Sugar Beet Industry" (Master's thesis, University of Saskatchewan, 1994), 66.

2   Den Otter, *Civilizing the West*, 229–30; William G. Hartley, "Mormon Sugar in Alberta: E.P. Ellison and the Knight Sugar Factory, 1901–17," *Journal of Mormon History* 23 (Fall 1997): 7. See also Brado, *Cattle Kingdom*, 138. The plant itself was not of new manufacture but was a plant at Sunnyside, Washington, that was dismantled and moved to the Raymond site. See Fred G. Taylor, *A Saga of Sugar: Being a Story of the Romance and Development of Beet Sugar in the Rocky Mountain West* (Salt Lake City: Desert News Press, 1944), 175.

3   Hartley, "Mormon Sugar in Alberta," 7. The *Rustler* reported 52,000 acres. Raymond *Rustler*, May 31, 1911, 7.

4   On the growing importance of sugar in western society, see Ken Cruikshank, "Taking the Bitter with the Sweet: Sugar Refiners and the Canadian Regulatory State, 1904–20," *Canadian Historical Review* 74, no. 3 (September 1993): 369–71.

5   *Raymond Rustler*, May 31, 1911, 7.

6   *Alberta Star*, Cardston, April 2, 1909, 8.

7   C.A. Dawson, *Group Settlement: Ethnic Communities in Western Canada* (Toronto: Macmillan Canada, 1936), 233.

8   *Raymond Leader*, June 17 & 25, 1913.

9   *Raymond Leader*, January 23, 1914, 1.

10   *Raymond Leader*, July 31, 1913, 4.

11   *Raymond Leader*, October 17, 1913, 1.

12   *Raymond Leader*, December 18 & 24, 1914.

13   *Raymond Leader*, January 8, 1915, 1. See also *Raymond Leader*, December 24, 1914, 1.

14   On local developments immediately following this, see: *Raymond Leader*, January 15, 1915, 1; January 22, 1915, 4; February 26, 1915, 1; March 5, 1915, 4; March 12, 1915, 1; March 26, 1915, 1; *Cardston Globe*, January 7, 1915, 4; January 14, 1915, 1; March 11, 1915, 1; Leonard J. Arrington, *Beet Sugar in the West: A History of the Utah-Idaho Sugar Company, 1891–1966* (Seattle: University of Washington Press, 1966), 188.

15 *Annual Report of the Department of Indian Affairs*, CSP, vol. XXIX (No. 11, 1905), 203.

16 *Raymond Rustler*, May 31, 1911, 7.

17 LAC, RG 10, vol. 1535, document 214, H.S. Allen to Wilson, Nov. 28, 1902.

18 LAC, RG 10, vol. 1724, 947–48, James Wilson to E.P. Ellison, January 30, 1903.

19 LAC, RG 10, vol. 1721, 399, James Wilson to E.P. Ellison, March 10, 1903; 707, J. Wilson to Geo. Houks, October 22, 1903.

20 GA, BIAC, file 18, E.P Ellison to James Wilson, January 20, 1903; H.S. Allen to James Wilson, September 28, 1903.

21 LAC, RG 10, vol. 1535, 254, E.P. Ellison to J. Wilson, May 15, 1903.

22 LAC, RG 10, vol. 1725, 716, Indian Agent to Secretary, DIA, July 6, 1904.

23 D.J. Hall, *Clifford Sifton: The Young Napoleon, 1861–1900, vol. I* (Vancouver: University of British Columbia Press, 1981), 269–70; D.J. Hall, *Clifford Sifton: The Lonely Eminence 1901–1929*, vol. 2 (Vancouver: University of British Columbia Press, 1985), 43; Hall, "Clifford Sifton and Canadian Indian Administration," 128–29.

24 GA, BIAC, file 17, J.P. Jardine to R.N. Wilson March 19, 1904; Home-Seekers Association to R.N. Wilson, March 31, 1904.

25 LAC, RG 10, vol. 1147, 87, Frank Pedley to J.H. Gooderham, April 29, 1904; also GA, BIAC, file 17.

26 Hartley, "Mormon Sugar in Alberta," 16.

27 GA, BIAC, file 17, E.P. Ellison to John W. Jowett, May 12, 1905.

28 *Annual Report of the Department of Indian Affairs*, CSP, 27, No. 11, 1905, XXIX, 203. Dempsey says that the Bloods earned $2,182.25 for the 1905 season. Dempsey, *Gentle Persuader*, 26.

29 LAC, RG 10, vol. 1548, 561, Acting Indian Agent to Geo. Skelding, October 7, 1905; 580, Acting Agent to Peter McLaren, October 23, 1905; 595, Indian Agent to Peter McLaren, October 30, 1905.

30 *Calgary Herald*, January 6, 1906, 8; Thompson and Seager, "Workers, Growers and Monopolists," 32.

31 LAC, RG 10, vol. 1536, 105, E.P. Ellison to R.N. Wilson, August 5, 1906. The agent's report for the year ending March 31, 1907, gave a total income of $37,373.38 for the Bloods of which $9,000.00 was earned from work at the Raymond sugar beet fields. *Annual Report of the Department of Indian Affairs*, CSP, No. 27, 1907, 161.

32 LAC, RG 10, vol. 1539, 145, J.T. Smellie to R. Wilson, October 16, 1906. Emphasis added.

33 LAC, RG 10, vol. 1539, 146, E.P. Ellison to R. Wilson, October 24, 1906.

34 *Annual Report of the Department of Indian Affairs*, CSP, No. 27, 1908, 168.

35 T.J. O'Brien to James Wilson, March 8, 1906. These rates seem to be in keeping with rates charged in 1907, as indicated in a contract between Knight Sugar Company and Thos. Bennett. In fact, Prairie Chicken may have had a better deal considering that the contract with Bennett stipulated that he was to pay one dollar per acre rent and two dollars per acre ploughing. Bennett was to be paid $4.50 per ton for the beets but was to pay the company $2.35 per acre for the haulage of beets to the factory. GA, Knight Sugar Company Papers (KSCP), labour contract between Knight Sugar Company and Thos. Bennett, May 18, 1907. Also see Indian Agent to T.J. O'Brien, March 31, 1906.

36 GA, BIAC, file 21, T.J. O'Brien to R.N. Wilson, July 7, 1906.

37 Given the minimum estimated harvest above, Prairie Chicken stood to gross $400.00 on the sale of his beets for an initial outlay of $89.00.

38 *Annual Report of the North West Mounted Police*, CSP 28, XLII, 1907–8, 65, 82.

39 *Raymond Rustler*, May 31, 1911, 7; Arrington, *Beet Sugar in the West*, 23.

40 GA, BIAC, file 41, Ray Knight to W. Julius Hyde, September 22, 1911.

41 LAC, RG 10, vol. 1539, 273, J.W. Crane? to Mr. Hyde, October 19, 1911.

42 LAC, RG 10, vol. 1721, 685–86, J. Wilson to E. Ellison, October 2, 1903; 707, J. Wilson to Geo. Houks, October 22, 1903.

43 GA, BIAC, file 18, J.W. Woolf to James Wilson September 29, 1903. Likely Woolf's threat of foreign labour was a reference to Japanese labour from B.C.

44 Hartley, "Mormon Sugar in Alberta," 13.

45 GA, BIAC, file 17, E.P. Ellison to James Wilson, June 11, 1904; J.D. McLean to R.N. Wilson, June 29, 1904.

46 LAC, RG 10, vol., 1725, 716, Indian Agent to Secretary, DIA, July 6, 1904.

47 LAC, RG 10, vol., 1725, 717, Indian Agent to Secretary, DIA, July 6, 1904. To my knowledge nothing came of this idea.

48 GA, BIAC, file 17, E.P. Ellison to John W. Jowett, October 7, 1904.

49 GA, BIAC, file 16, Response to above letter dated Blood Agency December 5, 1906. Emphasis added.

50 H. Clare Pentland, *Labour and Capital in Canada: 1650–1860* (Toronto: James Lorimer, 1981), 188–89.

51 GA, BIAC, file 16, J.S. Smellie to R.N. Wilson, February 20, 1907; E.P. Ellison to R.N. Wilson February 25, 1907.

52 GA, BIAC, file 60, Indian Agent to J.O. Wilson, June 27, 1907.

53 LAC, RG 10, vol. 1539, 195, Indian Agent to Indian Commissioner, September 16, 1907.

54 Hartley, "Mormon Sugar in Alberta," 18.

55 GA, KSCP, Labour Contract between Knight Sugar Company and Thos. Bennett, May 18, 1907.

56 *Raymond Chronicle*, May 10, 1907, 1.

57 Jeremy Adelman, *Frontier Development: Land, Labour, and Capital on the Wheatlands of Argentina and Canada, 1890–1914* (Oxford: Clarendon Press, 1994), 165.

58 Thompson, "Bringing in the Sheaves," 468; W.J.C. Cherwinski, "A Miniature Coxey's Army," 140–41; Cherwinski, "Wooden Horses and Rubber Cows: Training British Agricultural Labour for the Canadian Prairies, 1890–1930," 133. For particulars on the 1908 harvest season, see: Cherwinski, "The Incredible Harvest Excursion of 1908," 57–80; Danysk, *Hired Hands*, 24, 85; Thompson, *The Harvests of War*, 62–63.

59 Adelman, *Frontier Development*, 165. E.P. Ellison also noted the preference of farmers for wheat and livestock over sugar beet during 1908. Hartley, "Mormon Sugar in Alberta," 19–20.

60 *Raymond Chronicle*, May 17, 1907, 1.

61 *Raymond Chronicle*, June 14, 1907, 1.

62 For their efforts in the 1907 season, they earned $9,000. Goldfrank, *Changing Configurations*, 24.

63 *Cardston Alberta Star*, April 18, 1908, 1.

64 *Cardston Alberta Star*, October 9, 1908, 5; Thompson and Seager, "Workers, Growers and Monopolists," 31.

65 Roger's Sugar Company Archives (RSCA), Vancouver, B.C., W.J. Hyde to Raymond Knight, October 12, 1911. I am indebted to Joanne Denton, Museum Co-Coordinator, Roger's Sugar Company Archives, for this and subsequent references from Roger's Sugar.

66 RSCA, W.J. Hyde to Raymond Knight, October 17, 1911; Knight Sugar Co. to W. Julius Hyde, October 26, 1911.

67 LAC, RG 10, vol. 1539, 307, J.W. Crane to Indian Officer, Blood Agency, January 13, 1912; 274, J.W. Crane to Mr. Hyde, October 19, 1911; RSCA, W.J. Hyde to Knight Sugar Co., October 23, 1911. Adelman notes that between 1907 and 1912 the cost of labour rose by nearly 60 per cent. It may have been in response to this that Crane was commenting on the farmers' ability to pay. Adelman, *Frontier Development*, 165.

68 *Raymond Leader*, October 27, 1911, 4.

69 RSCA, Knight Sugar Co. to W.J. Hyde, October 12, 1912.

70 RSCA, W.J. Hyde to The Knight Sugar Company, October 17, 1912.

71 Hartley, "Mormon Sugar in Alberta," 22.

72 GA, BIAC, file 96, Jas. E. Ellison to W. Julius Hyde, May 31, 1913; Indian Agent to J.E. Ellison, June 6, 1913.

73 RSCA, Knight Sugar Co. to W.J. Hyde, May 31, 1913.

74 *Cardston Globe*, April 26, 1917, 8.

75 Western Canada Irrigation Association, *Reports of the proceedings of the tenth annual convention held at Kamloops, B.C., July 25, 26 and 27, 1916*, Ottawa, Gov. Print Bureau, 1917, 141. In a neat twist on achieving 'market requirements' Arthur Dahl suggested the planting of fewer acres more intensely. The *Raymond Leader*, December 24, 1914, 1. The conference also promoted mixed farming. *The Kamloops Standard-Sentinel*, July 28, 1916.

76 Western Canada Irrigation Association, *Reports*, 144.

77 Western Canada Irrigation Association, *Reports*, 144–45. Emphasis added. Thompson and Seager also agree that the failure of the enterprise is attributable to the "'labour problem.'" Thompson and Seager, "Workers Growers and Monopolists," 31; Dawson, *Group Settlement*, 233–34.

78 *Raymond Leader*, October 14, 1916, 1. Emphasis added.

79 Stuart Marshall Jamieson, *Times of Trouble: Labour Unrest and Industrial Conflict in Canada, 1900–66* (Ottawa: Minister of Supply and Services, 1968), 148–50.

80 Dawson, *Group Settlement*, 233–34.

81 The above figures are given in the *Raymond Rustler* for the 1911 season. *Raymond Rustler*, May 31, 1911, 7.

82 *Raymond Leader*, December 24, 1914, 1.

83 L.A. Rosenvall, "The Transfer of Mormon Culture to Alberta," in *Essays on the Historical Geography of the Canadian West: Regional Perspectives on the Settlement Process*, ed. L.A. Rosenvall and S.M. Evans (Calgary: University of Calgary, 1987), 143.

84 Thompson and Seager, "Workers, Growers and Monopolists," 31. Paul Voisey has convincingly illustrated the misplaced faith in the profitability of mixed farming. Voisey, "A Mix-Up Over Mixed Farming,", 179–206; Voisey, *Vulcan*, 85–87, 90–92.

85 On the shortage of crop, see Dawson, *Group Settlement*, 233; Thompson and Seager, "Workers, Growers and Monopolists," 31. GA, KSCP, President to Board of Directors, March 31, 1908.

86 Jeremy Adelman has argued, "The shortage of labour was the overwhelming constraint on frontier development in Argentina and Canada. Workers had to come from outside the region of settlement." Adelman, *Frontier Development*, 184. On the "absorptive power of the land" with which employers had to compete, see Adelman, *Frontier Development*, 159–60.

87 Thompson and Seager, "Workers, Growers and Monopolists," 32–33.

88 GA, KSCP, Thos. H. Woolford to William Knight, October 18, 1905.

89 GA, KSCP, H.C. Andrews to Knight Sugar Co. Ltd., July 16, 1906; [Bedlington & Fisher] to Knight Sugar Company, July 17, 1906.

90 GA, KSCP, Knight Sugar Company Letterbook, April 2, 1906.

91 GA, KSCP, Knight Sugar Co. to Beet Growers of Magrath, October 10, 1907; GA, KSCP, Knight Sugar Co. Letterbook, Minutes of Directors Meeting, April 2, 1906, 37.

92 Cecilia Danysk, "'A Bachelor's Paradise': Homesteaders, Hired Hands, and the Construction of Masculinity, 1880–1930," in *Making Western Canada: Essays on European Colonization and Settlement*, ed. Catherine Cavanaugh and Jeremy Mouat (Toronto: Garamond Press, 1996), 177. See also the experience of a hired hand in Stettler, Alberta, in Voisey, *A Preacher's Frontier*, 52–53. Danysk, *Hired Hands*, 11.

93 Dawson, *Group Settlement*, 234; Arrington, *Beet Sugar*, 108; Laliberté, "The Canadian State," 39.

94 *Raymond Recorder*, September 7 & 25, 1925.

95 It is unclear whether or not the Bloods were considered part of this 'transient' labour. *Cardston News*, March 17, 1927, 1.

96 *UID News*, October 6, 20, 1927.

97 *UID News*, October 27, 1927, 1.

98 *Cardston News*, October 11, 1928, 1; *UID News*, October 11, 1928, 1.

99 *UID News*, November 8, 1928, 1.

100 Zaharia and Fox, *Stories from Our Elders*, vol. 1 (Edmonton: Kainai Board of Education, 1995), 112, 93, 102, 109. See also *Stories from Our Elders*, vol. 2, 47; vol. 3, 77.

101 Dempsey, *Tom Three Persons*, 106; Taylor, *Standing Alone*, 78–79, 84.

102 William M. Baker, William J. Lodge, and James D. Tagg, eds., *Weddings, Work and War. Lethbridge 1914–1945: A Scrapbook History* (Lethbridge: University of Lethbridge, 1994), 77, 107; Ron Laliberté and Vic Satzewich, "Native Migrant Labour in the Southern Alberta Sugar-beet Industry: Coercion and paternalism in the Recruitment of Labour," *Canadian Review of Sociology and Anthropology* 36, no. 1 (February 1999): 72–73; Laliberté, "The Canadian State," 67–68.

103 Laliberté and Satzewich, "Native Migrant Labour," 78–81.

104 Zaharia and Fox, *Stories from Our Elders*, vol. 2, 21.

105 Goldfrank, *Changing Configurations*, 35. Except to highlight disasters, Goldfrank does not discuss the economic activities of the Bloods in the twenties and thirties. See also Dempsey, *Gentle Persuader*, 54–57. Indian income was reduced by almost one half, from $2,388,485 to $1,269,510 between 1929 and 1933. Taylor, *Canadian Indian Policy*, 92.

CHAPTER 5

1 The latest presentation of this argument is Treaty 7 Elders and Tribal Council et al. *The True Spirit and Original Intent of Treaty 7*, 112–14, 127; Paul Williams, "The Act: Past, Present and Future," *Ontario Indian* 4, no. 4 (April 1981): 18. Dempsey, *Crowfoot*, 96, 106; Chief John Snow, *These Mountains Are Our Sacred Places* (Toronto: Samuel Stevens, 1977), 28–33; John Leonard Taylor, "Two Views on the Meaning of Treaties Six and Seven," in Price, *The Spirit of the Alberta Indian Treaties*, 43–45. Hickey et al., "T.A.R.R. Interview with Elders Program," 105–6, 132. Some scholars believe that the Natives were a sovereign people who have never been conquered. The treaties are, therefore, "'peace and friendship' treaties, which if anything reinforce the concept of the equal nationhood of First Nations." John Olthuis and Roger Townshend, "The Case for Native Sovereignty," in *Crosscurrents: Contemporary Political Issues*, ed. Mark Charlton and Paul Barker (Toronto: Nelson Canada, 1994), 65–66.

2 Sharon H. Venne, "Treaties Made in Good Faith," in *Natives and Settlers, Now and Then: Historical Issues and Current Perspectives on Treaties and Land Claims in Canada*, ed. Paul W. DePasquale (Edmonton: University of Alberta Press, 2007), 1–8.

3 Patricia Seed, "Three Treaty Nations Compared: Economic and Political Consequences for Indigenous Peoples in Canada, the United States, and New Zealand" in DePasquale, *Natives and Settlers, Now and Then*, 21–23.

4 *Western Native News*, September, 1996, vol. 9, no. 6, 2.

5 L.C. Green views the relationship between the Canadian government and Indians as one of trusteeship, Canada having the responsibility to act on behalf of its Natives who are subservient. L.C. Green "Trusteeship and Canada's Indians," *Dalhousie Law Journal* 3, no. 1 (May 1976): 104, 114–16. If the Indians are viewed as colonized a subservient economic relationship is

reinforced. is still the same. L.C. Green, "Legal Significance of Treaties affecting Canada's Indians," *Anglo-American Law Review* 1 (1972): 119.

6   McKenna, "The Indian Laws of Canada," 62; Green, *Dalhousie Law Journal*, 118; Harper, "Canada's Indian Administration," 298–99.

7   See the text of Treaty 7 in Alexander Morris, *The Treaties of Canada with the Indians of Manitoba and the North-West Territories* (Toronto: Coles, 1979), 368–75.

8   Wetherell and Kmet, *Town Life*, 115; Breen, *The Canadian Prairie West*, 15.

9   Thelma Dennis, "Eaton's Catalogue: Furnishings for Rural Alberta, 1886–1930," *Alberta History* (Spring 1989): 21; Wetherell and Kmet, *Town Life*, 126.

10   Wetherell and Kmet, *Town Life*, 80.

11   Annie L. Gaetz, *The Park Country: History of Red Deer (Alberta) and District* (Vancouver: Evergreen Press, 1948), 42. Similarly, see D.E. Macintyre, *Prairie Storekeeper* (Toronto: Peter Martin Associates, 1970), 39–42.

12   Henry C. Klassen, *A Business History of Alberta* (Calgary: University of Calgary Press, 1999), 48–49.

13   Toby Morantz, "'So Evil a Practice': A Look at the Debt System in the James Bay Fur Trade." In *Merchant Credit and Labour Strategies in Historical Perspective*, ed. Rosemary E. Ommer (Fredericton: Acadiensis Press, 1990), 204–5.

14   Ray and Freeman, *'Give Us Good Measure'*, 186–87; Arthur J. Ray, *The Canadian Fur Trade in the Industrial Age* (Toronto: University of Toronto Press, 1990), 105–6, 108–9.

15   Christopher Clark, *The Roots of Rural Capitalism: Western Massachusetts 1780–1860* (Ithaca, NY: Cornell University Press, 1990), 220–27.

16   Paul Voisey, *High River and the 'Times': An Alberta Community and Its Weekly Newspaper, 1905–1966* (Edmonton: University of Alberta Press, 2004), 62, 100.

17   See statement of Indian Indebtedness signed by J.T. Faunt, in LAC, RG 10, vol. 7881, file 35103.

18   Dempsey, *Tom Three Persons*, 97, 99.

19   *Cardston Record*, April 7, 1899, 1. The discount for cash purchasing was in effect a two-price policy to discourage credit purchases.

20   Godfrey and Card *The Diaries of Charles Ora Card*, 369.

21   LAC, RG 10, vol. 1564, 405, James Wilson to Messers. H.S. Allen Co., August 31, 1899; 406, James Wilson to Messers. Barker and Gardiner, August 31, 1899. See letters addressed to various businesses by Wilson, 404–30.

22   See, for example, letters granting permission for HBC to trade on reserves: LAC, RG 10, vol. 3582, file 1024, by L. Vankoughnet, January 16, 1891; L. Vankoughnet to Indian Commissioner, January 20, 1891; Letter signed by L. Vankoughnet, May 21, 1891. Also permission granted to George F. Tupper trade on Saddle Lake Reserve, No. 125 and Blue Quill's Reserve, No. 127, L. Vankoughnet, April 20, 1891.

23   LAC, RG 10, vol. 3582, file 1024, F.H.P. to Deputy Superintendent General of Indian Affairs, September 10, 1896. However, Indian Commissioner Hayter Reed disagreed with this new approach. He believed that prices were more open to influence by the Indians on the reserve than in the town or village store. LAC, RG 10, vol. 3582, file 1024, Hayter Reed to A.E. Forget, September 17, 1896. Desiring to restrict the Indians to the reserve as much as possible was in keeping with Reed's overall isolationist views. Barron, "The Indian Pass System in the Canadian West," 27–28. LAC, RG 10, vol. 3582, file 1024, James Wilson to Indian Commissioner, February 17, 1897. The documents do not reveal who these independent traders were. Though eventually reversed, the policy of permitting shopping off the reserve was kept for the Bloods. See: RG 10, vol. 3582, file 1024, A.E.F to The Deputy of the

Superintendent General of Indian Affairs, June 4, 1897; LAC, RG 10, vol. 3582, file 1024, Circular Letter signed J.D. McLean, April 7, 1897.

24 LAC, RG 10, vol. 1722, 227, Indian Agent to Secretary, Department of Indians Affairs, July 20, 1904. Hanks noted that the Blackfeet were subjected to this business policy in the 1940s and in fact could not get credit locally. Hanks and Hanks, *Tribe under Trust*, 83.

25 Colin Bundy, *The Rise and Fall of the South African Peasantry* (Berkeley: University of California Press, 1979), 129–30.

26 Zaharia and Fox, *Stories from Our Elders*, vol. 2, 49.

27 Barry Broadfoot, *The Pioneer Years 1895–1914* (Toronto: Doubleday Canada, 1976), 279.

28 *Macleod Gazette*, March 15, 1894; R. Craig McIvor, *Canadian Monetary Banking and Fiscal Development* (Toronto: Macmillan Canada, 1961), 76–77.

29 See, for example, T.D. Regehr, "Bankers and Farmers in Western Canada, 1900–1939," in *The Developing West*, ed. John E. Foster (Edmonton: University of Alberta Press, 1983), 306, 316; Jeremy Adelman, "Prairie Farm Debt and the Financial Crisis of 1914," *Canadian Historical Review* 71, no. 4 (December 1990): 494–95.

30 Heather Robertson, *Salt of the Earth: The Story of the Homesteaders in Western Canada* (Toronto: James Lorimer, 1974), 180.

31 *Cardston Alberta Star*, May 10, 1907, 9.

32 *Cardston Alberta Star*, May 24, 1907, 4. Selling for produce was akin to barter or 'trade.' There was, however, very little discussion of this aspect of doing business. If the diary of Wallace Weiss is any indication, this aspect of commercial exchange with one's neighbours is deserving of attention. Weiss lived south of Medicine Hat and his diary for January, February, and March 1937, shows he 'traded' with neighbours on twenty different occasions and made several other unsuccessful attempts.

Items traded included services, livestock, personal items such as rings and watches, and a radio. *Diary of Wallace Weiss*, January, February, March, 1937. Courtesy of Robert Weiss Family. Copy in possession of author.

33 Michael Bliss, *Northern Enterprise: Five Centuries of Canadian Business* (Toronto: McClelland & Stewart, 1987), 292. On Eaton's and its competitiveness, see Joy L. Santink, *Timothy Eaton and the Rise of His Department Store* (Toronto: University of Toronto Press, 1990), 155–58, 205, 251.

34 *Rocky Mountain Echo*, April 16, 1906; RG 10, vol. 4035, file 306,458; Voisey, *High River and the 'Times'*, 66–67.

35 Broadfoot, *Pioneer Years*, 287–82. See also 275–77.

36 The *Cardston Globe*, November 12, 1914, 1.

37 John S. Smith, "The Question of Credit," *Cardston News*, February 3, 1927, 7; Jones, *"We'll all be buried down here,"* lxi.

38 *Cardston News*, January 26, 1928, 1.

39 *Cardston Alberta Star*, May 10, 1907, 9.

40 Voisey, *High River and the 'Times'*, 62.

41 LAC, RG 10, vol. 1549, 4, Indian Agent to E. Dewdney, August 29, 1881; 16, N. Macleod, to [?], October 31, 1881.

42 LAC, RG 10, vol. 1552, 671 ff., Statement by W. Pocklington, June 6, 1885; 728 ff., Statement by W. Pocklington, July 14, 1885; A.B. McCullough, "Eastern Capital, Government Purchases and the Development of Canadian Ranching," *Prairie Forum* 22, no. 2 (Fall 1997): 230–33. See, for example, a statement of supplies issued in LAC, RG 10, vol. 1550, 836 ff.; RG 10, vol. 1551, 46–48, Indian Agent to Indian Commissioner, January 13, 1884; 172, Statement by C.E. Denny July 7, 1883.

43 LAC, RG 10, vol. 1553, 34, Statement by W. Pocklington for July, 1885; 324, Statements by W. Pocklington November, 1885; 491–92, W. Pocklington to E. Dewdney, February 9, 1886. See RG 10, vols. 1552, 1553, 1554, for further inventories of

purchases made on behalf of the Bloods. LAC, RG 10, vol. 1553, 35–44, Statements by W. Pocklington June 30, 1885.

44 LAC, RG 10, vol. 1560, 330, James Wilson to Superintendent General of Indian Affairs, August 1, 1894. Though the Department expressed a desire to end the credit system as early as 1904, it did not follow through with concerted action. See GA, BIAC, file 17, J.D. Mclean to R.N. Wilson, February 13, 1904.

45 LAC, RG 10, vol. 1560, 858, James Wilson to Indian Commissioner, April 4, 1895. A final tally for the income for 1895 could be $7,500. Fraser Taylor, *Standing Alone*, 31.

46 Goldfrank, *Changing Configurations*, 21.

47 LAC, RG 10, vol. 1722, 455, J.W. Jewett to Indian Commissioner, Winnipeg, October 13, 1904; LAC, RG 10, vol. 1548, 535, R.N. Wilson to Superintendent General of Indian Affairs, September 19, 1905; *Annual Report of the Department of Indian Affairs*, CSP 27, No. 11, 1905, vol. XXIX, 203.

48 LAC, RG 10, vol. 1548, 332, Indian Agent to Secretary, DIA, June 20, 1905.

49 Goldfrank, *Changing Configurations*, 32.

50 *Macleod Spectator*, December 18, 1913, 11.

51 See LAC, RG 10, vol. 7595, file 10103, pt. 2, Agent Dilworth's statement. We conclude that this was authorized debt as it was entered in the agent's accounts.

52 LAC, RG 10, vol. 1558, 592, W. Pocklington to deputy of the Superintendent of Indian Affairs, November 18, 1891. Agent J.A. Markle of the Manitoba Dakota was likewise opposed to credit as "detrimental" to the Indians interests. Elias, *The Dakota of the Canadian Northwest*, 89–90. An American historian referring to the commercial exchange between Indians and local merchants has noted: "Another group that stood to gain from the opening of reservation lands were merchants and others who did business with either Indians or whites near a reservation. Merchants with an established trade with Indians could expect increased sales after the opening of a reservation," to settlement. Leonard A. Carlson, *Indians, Bureaucrats, and Land: The Dawes Act and the Decline of Indian Farming* (Westport, CT: Greenwood Press, 1981), 38.

53 Beal, "Money, Markets and Economic Development," 177, 212.

54 LAC, RG 10, vol. 1722, 226–27, Indian Agent to Secretary, Department of Indians Affairs, July 20, 1904.

55 Wetherell and Kmet, *Useful Pleasures*, 359.

56 Dempsey, *Tom Three Persons*, 54, 72, 97, 99.

57 LAC, RG 10, vol. 7899, file 40103-1, Statement of J.E. Pugh.

58 See, for example, LAC, RG 10, vol. 1722, 226–27, Indian Agent to Secretary, Department of Indians Affairs, July 20, 1904.

59 Dempsey, *Tom Three Persons*, 54, 72, 97, 99.

60 LAC, RG 10, vol. 1722, 476, Indian Agent to R.W. Fletcher, November 29, 1904.

61 McKenna, *Catholic World*, 65. See also: Harper, "Canada's Indian Administration," 137; H.B. Hawthorn, C.S. Belshaw, and S.M. Jamieson, *The Indians of British Columbia: A Study of Contemporary Social Adjustment* (Berkeley: University of California Press, 1958), 189. See also Elias, *Dakota*, 120, 125.

62 Harper, "The Indian Act," 303.

63 LAC, RG 10, vol. 1722, 473, Indian Agent to Secretary, Department of Indian Affairs, November 29, 1904. Earlier in the year, Secretary J.D. McLean had written R.N. Wilson that the Department wished to abolish the order system of purchasing and encourage Indian purchasing on a cash basis only. GA, BIAC, file 17, J.D. McLean to R.N. Wilson, February 13, 1904.

64 LAC, RG 10, vol. 1723, 369, James Wilson to Messers. H.S. Allen & Co., April 9, 1900.

65 LAC, RG 10, vol. 7881, file 35103, W.J. Dilworth to Canadian Credit Men's Association, January 20, 1915; LAC, RG 10, vol. 7881, file 35103, W.J. Dilworth to Canadian Credit Men's Association, January 20, 1915. The Department concurred with Dilworth's decision. LAC, RG 10, vol. 7881, file 35103, J.D. McLean to Canadian Credit Men's Association, July 20, 1915; GA, BIAC, file 92, Indian Agent to Messers. Macleod and Gray, June 26, 1915; GA, BIAC, file 92, Indian Agent to Messers. Macleod and Gray, June 26, 1915.

66 GA, BIAC, file 96, Massey-Harris Statement in Blood Indian Agency Correspondence. See George Tanner Statement, October 28, 1914 Blood Indian Agency Correspondence, File [?], Glenbow Alberta Archives, M1788. The total for all of these was $887.75 or 29.37 per cent of total orders.

67 Jones, *"We'll all be buried down here,"* xxxvi.

68 Jones, *"We'll all be buried down here,"* 27 & 33.

69 Jones, *Empire of Dust*, 268–69.

70 LAC, RG 10, vol. 7881, file 35103, W.M. Graham to Secretary, DIA, June 28, 1927. We should not assume that only farmers were in debt.

71 LAC, RG 10, vol. 7881, file 35103, W.M. Graham to Secretary, DIA, June 28, 1927.

72 GA, BIAC, file 92, Indian Agent to Duncan C. Scott, August 14, 1915. *Macleod Spectator*, July 8, 1915, 2. Business in the previous year had been good. *Macleod Spectator*, November 12, 1914, 1. George Scott complained, through the local Conservative Association, that he did not get a fair share of Blood reserve patronage for his livery stable, a complaint rebutted by Dilworth. LAC, RG 10, vol. 1547, 248, W.S Gray to W.J. Dilworth, December 31, 1914; 255, Indian Agent to Sec'y, Conservative Executive, January 28, 1915. By 1916 the Bloods were again patronizing businesses in Macleod. *Macleod News*, December 7, 1916, 1.

73 LAC, RG 10, vol. 4035, file 306,458, J.A. Webbe to Officer Commanding, R.C. Mounted Police, Lethbridge, November 14, 1924.

74 GA, BIAC, file 92, Indian Agent to Assistant Deputy and Sec'y, DIA, September 2, 1915; Indian Agent to Riverside Lumber Co., September 4, 1915.

75 GA, BIAC, file 92, W.J. Dilworth to M.A. Coombs, September 17, 1915. One problem is that the amounts for unauthorized accounts are often not quoted, and so it is difficult to determine what percentage of the total business contracted was unauthorized and therefore, perhaps, not collectable.

76 GA, BIAC, file 92, Indian Agent to [DIA], May 20, 1915.

77 LAC, RG 10, vol. 4024, file 290,240-2A, Western Canada Lumber Co. Ltd. to Minister of the Interior, August 22, 1916. For other examples of late accounts, see: GA, BIAC, file 92, McLaren Lumber Co. to Indian Agent, November 24, 1915; W.H. Steed to W.J. Dilworth, December 15, 1915. The matter with the Western Canada Lumber Company was never satisfactorily resolved, and by 1917 the company was in receivership, the liquidator having no more success with Dilworth than did former management. LAC, RG 10, vol. 4024, file 290,240-2B, Western Canada Lumber Co. to Secretary, DIA, August 28, 1917.

78 LAC, RG 10, vol. 7881, file 35103, J.T. Faunt to Secretary, DIA, February 28, 1921; J.D. McLean to J.T. Faunt, February 22, 1921; J.M. Callie to Indian Department January 31, 1921; J.M. Callie to J.D. McLean, March 3, 1921; J.D. McLean to J.T. Faunt, March 9, 1921.

79 LAC, RG 10, vol. 7881, file 35103, W.E. Smith to Hon. Charles Stewart, December 23, 1927.

80 LAC, RG 10, vol. 7881, file 35103, Duncan C. Scott to J.E. Pugh, December 31, 1927.

81 See, for example, the correspondence regarding the Pioneer Lumber Company,

Lethbridge. LAC, RG 10, vol. 7881, file 35103, Pioneer Lumber Co. Ltd. to Secretary, DIA, October 7, 1930; Pioneer Lumber Co. Ltd. to Secretary, DIA, October 7, 1930. See bill in same file.

82   LAC, RG 10, vol. 7881, file 35103, Virtue, Paterson & Company to Superintendent, DIA, June 24, 1931. For other discussion on this disagreement, see: W.M. Graham to Secretary, DIA, August 31, 1931; A.F. MacKenzie to Virtue, Paterson & Beaumont, September 4, 1931; Virtue, Paterson & Company to Secretary, DIA, September 21, 1931; T.R.L. MacInnes to Virtue, Paterson and Company, September 28, 1931.

83   Based on these assumptions or understandings, the company now wanted payment of $2,931.82. LAC, RG 10, vol. 7881, file 35103, J.A. Rowat to Deputy Superintendent General, DIA, March 3, 1928. Scott's response was a perfunctory denial of responsibility. "These arrangements were," Scott wrote, "undoubtedly made with individual Indians, the payments to be made from crop returns. This, as you are no doubt aware, has been the usual practice." LAC, RG 10, vol. 7881, file 35103, Duncan C. Scott to J.A. Rowat, March 8, 1928.

84   LAC, RG 10, vol. 7881, file 35103, Cardston Implement Company to Honorable Charles Stewart, December 29, 1927. The Honourable Charles Stewart was asked to intervene in this matter. Charles Stewart to Cardston Implement Company, Ltd., January 27, 1928.

85   LAC, RG 10, vol. 7881, file 35103, R.N. Wilson to D.C. Scott, January 3, 1929; Duncan C. Scott to R.N. Wilson, January 16, 1929.

86   See Table 2 for the collapse of Blood farming income in 1927. GA, BIAC, Statement of Indebtedness As At Audit On Feb. 13, 1928, File 163.

87   Jones, *"We'll all be buried down here,"* lx, 39–41.

88   Jones, *Empire of Dust*, 155. Also see David C. Jones, "An Exceedingly Risky and Unremunerative Partnership: Farmers and

the Financial Interests Amid the Collapse of Southern Alberta," in Jones and MacPherson, *Building beyond the Homestead*, 210–11.

89   Jones, *"We'll all be buried down here,"* lx.

90   Jones, *"We'll all be buried down here,"* 55–56.

91   Barry Broadfoot, *Next-Year Country: Voices of Prairie People* (Toronto: McClelland & Stewart, 1988), 82.

92   LAC, RG 10, vol. 7881, file 35103, W.M. Graham to D.C. Scott, January 8, 1921; Statement of Indian indebtedness signed by Agent J.T. Faunt.

93   LAC, RG 10, vol. 7881, file 35103, J.E. Pugh to Secretary, DIA, June 7, 1927.

94   Pugh broke down the debt as follows; $6,000.00 due to the Cardston Implement Company, $3,200.00 due to Massey-Harris Company, $1,100.00 due the International Harvester Company. There was also a $2,000.00 twine debt and $1,400.00 for hail insurance. It was much the same situation for those companies who supplied the Indians with groceries; $2,700.00 due the Cardston Trading Company, $2,040.00 due Burt Brothers, $1,750.00 due E. McNeil and $827.00 due R.N. Wilson. LAC, RG 10, vol. 7881, file 35103, J.E. Pugh to Duncan C. Scott, January 6, 1928.

95   LAC, RG 10, vol. 7881, file 35103, J.E. Pugh to Duncan C. Scott, January 6, 1928.

96   LAC, RG 10, vol. 7881, file 35103, J.D. McLean to W.M. Graham, June 14, 1927.

97   LAC, RG 10, vol. 7881, file 35103, W.M. Graham to Secretary, DIA, June 28, 1927.

98   LAC, RG 10, vol. 7881, file 35103, W.M. Graham to Secretary, DIA, June 28, 1927; LAC, RG 10, vol. 7881, file 35103, W.M. Graham to Secretary, DIA, June 28, 1927.

99   On debt and prairie farmers, see: Voisey, *Vulcan*, 133–34; Jones, *Empire of Dust*, 169, 172–74; Adleman, "Prairie Farm Debt and the Financial Crisis of 1914," 493–502; Royden K. Loewen, *Family, Church, and Market: A Mennonite Community and the*

New Worlds, 1850–1930 (Urbana: University of Illinois Press, 1993), 206–7.

100 This figure does not entirely agree with the figure in Table 2.

101 LAC, RG 10, vol. 7881, file 35103, W.M. Graham to Secretary, DIA, December 13, 1927; W.M. Graham to Secretary, DIA, December 13, 1927; Report and Diary for month of November 1927, J.G. Pugh, December 2, 1927.

102 Provincial Archives of Alberta (PAA), Accession No. 70.189/SE., W.M. Graham to John E. Pugh, January 27, 1928.

103 PAA, Accession No. 70.189/SE., Indian Agent to W.M. Graham, January 30, 1928. The criteria for determining need were not consistent. Destitution was sometimes determined by the kind of assistance needed whether "tea, rice and soap," beef and flour, or clothing. For example, a list of "old destitute Indians" in need of underclothing for the winter of 1930 numbered 62 individuals. See also list dated Blood Agency, November 24, 1930.

104 Christianson gave the following: $907,618.80 from farming and stock-raising. Currently the grazing lease brought in $14,844.00 and a farming lease $5,780.00 for a total of $20,624.00, "which brings their total income derived from farming, stock-raising and leases to well over a million dollars." LAC, RG 10, vol. 7595, file 10103, pt. 5, M. Christianson to W.M. Graham, May 18, 1928.

105 LAC, RG 10, vol. 7881, file 35103. See list of firms carrying Indian indebtedness. Strangely the Marshall-Wells Hardware Co. was not listed among these. J.E. Pugh to Duncan C. Scott, January 26, 1929.

106 LAC, RG 10, vol. 7881, file 35103, J.E. Pugh to Duncan C. Scott, January 26, 1929; W.M. Graham to Duncan C. Scott, February 7, 1929.

107 LAC, RG 10, vol. 7881, file 35103, D.P. Sullivan to J.D. McLean, February 13, 1929; W.L. Smith to Duncan Scott, February 20, 1929. LAC, RG 10, vol. 7881, file 35103, D.C. Scott to J.E. Pugh, January 11, 1928. On the situation in the West at this time, see Jones *"We'll all be buried down here,"* 10–21; Jones, *Empire of Dust,* 151 ff.

108 LAC, RG 10, vol. 7881, file 35103, Memorandum, Duncan C. Scott to Mr. Pratt; May 23, 1929; Duncan C. Scott to W.L. Smith, February 26, 1929. Only in "a few cases of real hardship" to the government's friends might something be done. LAC, RG 10, vol. 7881, file 35103, Charles Stewart to W.A. Buchannan; June 21, 1929. Senator W.A. Buchannan of Lethbridge personally pleaded the case of the Cardston Implement Co. to the Hon. Charles Stewart. He said that the "MATTER IS A DISTURBING FACTOR AS OUR FRIENDS ARE AFFECTED." The account was subsequently paid. W.A. Buchanan to Chas. Stewart, June 17, 1929. Emphasis in original. Stewart reminded Buchanan that the accounts were owed by the Indians, not the Treasury. Duncan C. Scott to W.M. Graham, July 24, 1929. See also Duncan C. Scott to W.M. Graham, July 24, 1929.

109 LAC, RG 10, vol. 7881, file 35103, Duncan C. Scott to Marshall-Wells Company, Ltd., July 26, 1929.

110 LAC, RG 10, vol. 7881, file 35103, M. Christianson to W.M. Graham, November 30, 1929.

111 Goldfrank, "Administrative Programs and Changes," 21. Dempsey gives the income for 1929 as $97,000. Dempsey, *Gentle Persuader* 75–76.

112 LAC, RG 10, vol. 7881, file 35103, M. Christianson to W.M. Graham, November 30, 1929; W.M. Graham to Duncan C. Scott, December 4, 1929; M. Christianson to W.M. Graham, November 30, 1929. The DIA's Chief Accountant, F.M. Paget, pointed out that "collections made from Indians on account of Beef and Seed Grain, are due the Band's Interest Account, and not the Department." Though such payments "could be diverted towards paying off merchants [*sic*] indebtedness, and when

subsequently collected from the Indians would be credited to the Band's account as refunds due for seed and beef." Memorandum; F.M. Paget to Dr. Scott, December 18, 1929. Authorized debts to merchants were given preference over monies owed the Department and the band. LAC, RG 10, vol. 7881, file 35103, Duncan C. Scott to W.M. Graham, December 19, 1929.

113 LAC, RG 10, vol. 7881, file 35103, M. Christianson to Secretary, DIA, November 23, 1932; Memorandum for the Right Honourable The Prime Minister from Duncan C. Scott, October 19, 1931. Correspondence over this particular debt continued into 1933 with only $97.76 being paid on the account in a two year period. M. Christianson to Secretary, DIA, December 1, 1933. LAC, RG 10, vol. 7881, file 35103, M. Christianson to Secretary, DIA, December 1, 1933.

114 LAC, RG 10, vol. 7899, file 40103-1, J.E. Pugh to Secretary, April 18, 1934, and attached details.

115 Pugh judged most of the outside debt legitimate, with one qualification: the $7,798.14 owing the Cardston Implement Company. The debts owed to Massey-Harris Co., Smith & Pitcher, and the Cardston Trading Co., in particular, he said, were the result of "Orders issued to Indians *by Authority of the Department* and remained unpaid at the end of 1928, at which time this system was discarded and no orders issued after that year." LAC, RG 10, vol. 7899, file 40103-1, J.E. Pugh to Secretary, April 18, 1934. The Cardston Implement Co., the Bloods' largest creditor, was itself in debt and consigned its account of $7,798.14 with the Bloods to Marshall-Wells Co., Winnipeg. Marshall-Wells in turn was owed $1,026.08 by the agency. These two creditors alone accounted for $8,824.22 or 49.8 per cent of the total reported Blood outside debt. LAC, RG 10, vol. 7899, file 40103-1; see Cardston Implement Co. Ltd. and Marshall-Wells Ltd., Assignment of Blood Agency Account; Z.W. Jacobs, Barrister, and Solicitor, Cardston, Alberta.

116 LAC, RG 10, vol. 7899, file 40103-1, J.E. Pugh to Secretary, April 18, 1934, and attached details.

117 LAC, RG 10, vol. 7899, file 40103-1, J.E. Pugh to Secretary, April 18, 1934, and attached details.

118 LAC, RG 10, vol. 7899, file 40103-1, Report of J.E. Pugh, March 27, 1935. The two largest expenses of this sum were $862.88 for groceries and $341.91 for car repairs. Statement of J.E. Pugh.

119 LAC, RG 10, vol. 7899, file 40103-1, J.E. Pugh to L.W. McCutheson, December 11, 1936; N.C. Allen to J.E. Pugh, January 17, 1936. Another indication of difficult times is the reduced balance in the Blood Agency Bank Account, which "prior to 1929 this Trust Account would contain balances ranging from $20,000 to $70,000 for several months, generally from about September to January. It would rarely fall below $1,000 or $1,200." Since 1929, however, "owing to reduced prices for farm products and poor crop returns these monthly balances have dwindled, and during 1935 a further reduction has been caused by placing monies due the Receiver General in a separate Bank Account." As a consequence of the above conditions, the average monthly balance for the ten months of February to November, 1935, was $5,448.99 or approximately half of what it should have been. See RG 10, vol. 7899, file 40103-1, N.C. Allen to Dr. McGill, January 23, 1936.

120 LAC, RG 10, vol. 7899, file 40103-1, Statement of J.E. Pugh. The problem with these figures is that they do not show the business the Indians may have conducted through barter or through the expenditure of money in hand.

121 *Cardston News*, September 7, 1937, 1.

122 LAC, RG 10, vol. 7899, file 40103-1, Statements of J.E. Pugh and of Clerk Anthony McMillay.

123 Meanwhile, the uncollectible debt was put at $86,824.84 for 1934 and by 1942 still stood at $86,696.38. LAC, RG 10, vol.

7899, file 40103-1; see Statement of J.E. Pugh and Statement of Clerk Anthony McMillay.

124 LAC, RG 10, vol. 7899, file 40103-1, Statement of Clerk Anthony McMillay.

125 LAC, RG 10, vol. 7899, file 40103-1, Statements of Clerk Anthony McMillay and of J.E. Pugh.

126 *Cardston News*, December 27, 1928, 1.

127 *Cardston News*, March 21, 1929, 4.

CONCLUSION

1 W.L. Morton, "The Significance of Site in the Settlement of the American and Canadian Wests," in *Contexts of Canada's Past: Selected Essays of W.L. Morton*, ed. A.B. McKillop (Toronto: Macmillan Canada, 1980), 87.

2 For discussion of the West as national hinterland, see: J.M.S. Careless, *Frontier and Metropolis: Regions, Cities, and Identities in Canada before 1914* (Toronto: University of Toronto Press, 1989), 40 ff.; J.M.S. Careless, *Careless at Work: Selected Canadian Historical Studies* (Toronto: Dundurn Press, 1990), 120 ff.

3 Bennett and Kohl, *Settling the Canadian–American West*, 18.

4 For a complete discussion of this idea, see den Otter, *Civilizing the West*.

5 Irene M. Spry, "The Transition from a Nomadic to a Settled Economy in Western Canada. 1856–96," *Transactions of the Royal Society of Canada*, vol. 6, ser. 4 (June 1968): 190.

6 Rolf Knight, *Indians at Work: An Informal History of Native Indian Labour in British Columbia 1858–1930* (Vancouver: New Star Books, 1978), 169.

7 *Annual Report of the Department of Indian Affairs*, CSP 14, 1897, 155–56.

8 *Annual Report of the Department of Indian Affairs*, CSP 14, 1899, 133.

9 *Annual Report of the Department of Indian Affairs*, CSP 27, 1904, 141.

10 Samek, *The Blackfoot Confederacy*, 84–86.

11 Larry McCann, "The 1890s: Fragmentation and the New Social Order," in *The Atlantic Provinces in Confederation*, ed. E.R. Forbes and D.A. Muise (Toronto: University of Toronto Press, 1993), 122–23.

12 Beal, "Money, Markets and Economic Development," 355–56.

13 Christopher McKee, *Treaty Talks in British Columbia: Negotiating a Mutually Beneficial Future* (Vancouver: UBC Press, 1996), 5–10. Though recognized or acknowledged, the precise definition or character of Aboriginal title has eluded both politicians and jurors alike and in consequence is as much a problem today as it has been historically. Kent McNeil, "The Meaning of Aboriginal Title," in *Aboriginal and Treaty Rights in Canada: Essays on Law, Equality, and Respect for Difference*, ed. Michael Asch (Vancouver: UBC Press, 1997), 135–36, 141–52.

14 Friesen, *The Canadian Prairies*, 159–60.

15 LAC, RG 10, vol. 1564, 270–71, James Wilson to Deputy Minister of Public Works, April 10, 1899.

16 LAC, RG 10, vol. 1535, 11, Deputy Commissioner to Jas. Wilson, July 7, 1899; 39, J.D. McLean to Jas. Wilson, November 3, 1899.

17 See, in particular, correspondence in LAC, RG 10, vol. 7730, file 23103-1 and LAC, RG 10, vol. 7730, file 23103-1A.

18 LAC, RG 10, vol. 7730, file 23103-1A, J.D. McLean to Deputy Minister, Department of Public Works, Alberta, March 17, 1926.

19 For example, Sarah Carter, "Categories and Terrains of Exclusion: Constructing the 'Indian Woman' in the Early Settlement Era in Western Canada," *Great Plains Quarterly* 13 (Summer 1993): 147–48, 158.

20 J. Penrose, "When All the Cowboys Are Indians: The Nature of Race in All-Indian

Rodeo," *Annals of the Association of American Geographers* 93, no. 3 (2003): 691–92.

21 Goldfrank, "Administrative Programs and Changes," 19–20.

22 *Annual Report of the Department of Indian Affairs*, CSP, No. 27, 1907, 161; *Annual Report of the Department of Indian Affairs*, CSP, No. 14, 1925, 28. This population decline is most likely due to the influenza epidemic of 1919–20 and the probability that some Bloods were absent from the reserve doing work in the surrounding area. Dempsey, *Tom Three Persons*, 85.

23 Goldfrank, "Administrative Programs and Changes," 21.

24 The decade of 1911 to 1920 had been one of increased economic diversification and increasing, if limited, prosperity. Incomes for 1911, 1914, 1919, and 1920 were $56,750, $61,100, $233,746, and $254,332, respectively. Goldfrank, *Changing Configurations*, 32. It was not until the decade of the 1920s that reserve farming finally accounted for more reserve income than other revenue sources. Prior to this, therefore, one must not give too much weight to crop agriculture, as its importance was discounted by agents and that of hay was stressed. By 1921, however, the total value of farm products including hay was $80,000 or 60.2 per cent of total income of $132,989. *Annual Report of the Department of Indian Affairs*, CSP, No. 27, 1922, 58. In 1922 it was $50,000 or 41.8 per cent of $119,735; 1923, $108,300 or 61.5 per cent of total income of $176,070; and in 1924 it was $209,000 or 74.6 per cent of total income of $280,332. CSP No. 15, 1925, 78. The difficulty with the statistics is that the value of hay sales is generally included in agriculture returns and so it is not possible to determine its value relative to other agriculture income. For some years the Agents do give the value or the tonnage harvested.

25 *Annual Report of the Department of Indian Affairs*, CSP No. 27, 1922, 58.

26 See, for example, Taylor, *Standing Alone*, 35. Hugh A. Dempsey, "One Hundred Years of Treaty Seven," in *One Century Later: Western Canadian Reserve Indians since Treaty 7*, ed. Ian L. Getty and Donald Smith (Vancouver: University of British Columbia Press, 1978), 28.

27 *Annual Report of the Department of Indian Affairs*, CSP No. 15, 1925, 78.

28 Samek, *The Blackfoot Confederacy*, 85–86.

29 Binnema, *Common and Contested Ground*, 37–54.

30 Hugh A. Dempsey, *Firewater: The Impact of the Whisky Trade on the Blackfoot Nation* (Calgary: Fifth House Publishing, 2002). Especially see chap. 7.

31 Elias, *The Dakota of the Canadian Northwest*, 223.

32 Jennifer Reid, *Myth, Symbol, and Colonial Encounter: British and Mi'kmaq in Acadia, 1700–1867* (Ottawa: University of Ottawa Press, 1995), 110.

Select Bibliography

MANUSCRIPT SOURCES

Glenbow Archives, Calgary. Blood Indian Agency Correspondence

Glenbow. Cross Family Papers

Glenbow. Cochrane Ranche Letterbook

Glenbow. Diary of W.F. Cochrane, Cochrane Ranch

Glenbow. George Gibson Coote Papers, 1907–1956

Glenbow. Knight Sugar Company Papers

Glenbow. Western Stock Grazing Association Papers

Library and Archives Canada (LAC), Ottawa. RG 10 – Records of the Department of Indian Affairs, Black Series

LAC. RG 18 – Records of the North West Mounted Police

Provincial Archives of Alberta (PAA), Edmonton. Blood Indian Files

PAA. Legislative Assembly Records

Roger's Sugar Company Archives, Vancouver. Files relating to the Knight Sugar Company

Treaties and Historical Research Centre. *The Historical Development of the Indian Act.* Ottawa: Indian and Northern Affairs, 1978.

Treaties and Historical Research Centre, *Indian Act and Amendments, 1868–1950.* Ottawa: 1981.

OFFICIAL REPORTS

Canada. Parliament. House of Commons. *Debates: Official Report.*

Canada. Parliament. Sessional Papers. *Annual Reports of the Department of Indian Affairs.*

Canada. Parliament. Sessional Papers. *Annual Reports of the North West Mounted Police.*

Census of Prairie Provinces.

Dominion Bureau of Statistics. *Agriculture, Climate and Population of the Prairie Provinces of Canada.* Ottawa: F.A. Acland, 1931.

PRIVATE HOLDINGS

Wallace Weiss Diary. Courtesy of the Rob Weiss Family.

BOOKS, ARTICLES, AND PAMPHLETS

Adelman, Jeremy. *Frontier Development: Land, Labour, and Capital on the Wheatlands of Argentina and Canada, 1890–1914.* Oxford: Clarendon Press, 1994.

Adelman, Jeremy. "Prairie Farm Debt and the Financial Crisis of 1914." *Canadian Historical Review* 71, no. 4 (December 1990): 491–519.

Adelman, Jeremy, and Stephen Aron. "From Borderlands to Borders: Empires, Nation-States, and the Peoples in Between in North American History." *American Historical Review* 104, no. 3 (June 1999): 814–41.

Adelman, Jeremy, and Stephen Aron. "Of Lively Exchanges and Larger Perspectives." *American Historical Review* 104, no. 4 (October 1999): 1235–1239.

Akiwenzie-Damm, Kateri. "We Belong to This Land: A View of 'Cultural Difference.'" *Journal of Canadian Studies* 31, no. 3 (Fall 1996): 21–28.

Arrington, Leonard J. *Beet Sugar in the West: A History of the Utah-Idaho Sugar Company, 1891–1966.* Seattle: University of Washington Press, 1966.

Athearn, Robert G. *Westward the Briton.* Lincoln: University of Nebraska Press, 1953.

Atkin, Ronald. *Maintain the Right: The Early History of the North West Mounted Police, 1873–1900.* Toronto: Macmillan, 1973.

Baker, William M., William J. Lodge, and James D. Tagg, eds. *Weddings, Work and War. Lethbridge 1914–1945: A Scrapbook History.* Lethbridge: University of Lethbridge, 1994.

Barron, F. Laurie. "The Indian Pass System in the Canadian West, 1882–1935." *Prairie Forum* 13, no. 1 (Spring 1988): 25–42.

Bastien, Betty. *Blackfoot Ways of Knowing: The Worldview of the Siksikaitsitapi.* Calgary: University of Calgary Press, 2004.

Bateman, Rebecca B. "Talking With The Plow: Agricultural Policy and Indian Farming in the Canadian and U.S. Prairies." *Canadian Journal of Native Studies* 16, no. 2 (1996): 211–28.

Beal, Carl. "Money, Markets and Economic Development In Saskatchewan Reserve Communities, 1870- 1930s." PhD diss., University of Saskatchewan, 1994.

Beaty, C.B. "Geomorphology, Geology and Non-Agricultural Resources." In *Southern Alberta: A Regional Perspective*, edited by F. Jankunis, 11–19. Lethbridge: University of Lethbridge, 1972.

Belanger, Yale. "'An all round Indian affair': The Native Gatherings at Macleod, 1924 and 1925." *Alberta History* (June 2005): 13–24.

Bennett, John W., and Seena B. Kohl. *Settling the Canadian-American West, 1890–1915: Pioneer Adaptation and Community Building, An Anthropological History.* Lincoln: University of Nebraska Press, 1995.

Bercuson, David J., ed. *Alberta's Coal Industry 1919.* Calgary: Historical Society of Alberta, 1978.

Berkhoffer, Robert F. *The White Man's Indian: Images of the American Indian from Columbus to the Present.* New York: Vintage Books, 1979.

Binnema, Theodore. *Common and Contested Ground: A Human and Environmental History of the Northwestern Plains.* Norman: University of Oklahoma Press, 2001.

Bliss, Michael. *Northern Enterprise: Five Centuries of Canadian Business.* Toronto: McClelland & Stewart, 1987.

Boldt, Menno. *Surviving as Indians: The Challenge of Self-Government.* Toronto: University of Toronto Press, 1993.

Bourgeault, Ron. "Aboriginal Labour in the North-West." *Prairie Forum* 31, no. 2 (Fall 2006): 273–304.

Brado, Edward. *Cattle Kingdom: Early Ranching in Alberta.* Vancouver: Douglas & McIntyre, 1984.

Breen, David H. "The Canadian Prairie West and the 'Harmonious' Settlement Interpretation." *Agricultural History* 47, no. 1 (January 1973): 63–75.

Breen, David H. *The Canadian Prairie West and the Ranching Frontier, 1874–1924.* Toronto: University of Toronto Press, 1983.

Breen, David H. "The Turner Thesis and the Canadian West: A Closer Look at the Ranching Frontier." In *Essays on Western History,* edited by Lewis H. Thomas, 147–56. Edmonton: University of Alberta Press, 1976.

Broadfoot, Barry. *Next-Year Country: Voices of Prairie People.* Toronto: McClelland & Stewart, 1988.

Broadfoot, Barry. *The Pioneer Years 1895–1914.* Toronto: Doubleday Canada, 1976.

Browlie, Robin J. *A Fatherly Eye: Indian Agents, Government Power and Aboriginal Resistance in Ontario, 1918–1939.* Don Mills: Oxford University Press, 2003.

Brown, Alison K., and Laura Peers. *'Pictures Bring Us Messages/Sinaakssiiksi aohtsimaahpihkookiyaawa: Photographs and Histories from the Kainai Nation.* Toronto: University of Toronto Press, 2006.

Buckley, Helen. *From Wooden Ploughs to Welfare: Why Indian Policy Failed in the Prairie Provinces.* Montreal: McGill-Queen's University Press, 1992.

Bundy, Colin. *The Rise and Fall of the South African Peasantry.* Berkeley: University of California Press, 1979.

Calhoun, Daniel H. "Strategy As Lived: Mixed Communities in the Age of New Nations." *American Indian Quarterly* 22, nos. 1 & 2 (Winter/Spring 1998): 181–202.

Card, Brigham Y. "The Canadian Mormon Settlements, 1886–1925: A North-American Perspective." *Canadian Ethnic Studies* 26, no. 1 (1994): 19–39.

Careless, J.M.S. *Careless at Work: Selected Canadian Historical Studies*. Toronto: Dundurn Press, 1990.

Careless, J.M.S. *Frontier and Metropolis: Regions, Cities, and Identities in Canada before 1914*. Toronto: University of Toronto Press, 1989.

Carlson, Leonard A. *Indians, Bureaucrats, and Land: The Dawes Act and the Decline of Indian Farming*. Westport, CT: Greenwood Press, 1981.

Carstens, Peter. *The Queen's People: A Study of Hegemony, Coercion, and Accommodation among the Okanagan of Canada*. Toronto: University of Toronto Press, 1991.

Carter, Sarah. *Aboriginal Peoples and Colonizers of Western Canada to 1900*. Toronto: University of Toronto Press, 1999.

Carter, Sarah. "Categories And Terrains of Exclusion: Constructing the 'Indian Woman' in the Early Settlement Era in Western Canada." *Great Plains Quarterly* 13 (Summer 1993): 147–61.

Carter, Sarah. "Controlling Indian Movement: The Pass System." *NeWest Review* (May 1985): 8–9.

Carter, Sarah. *Lost Harvests: Prairie Indian Reserve Farmers and Government Policy*. Montreal: McGill-Queen's University Press, 1990.

Carter, Sarah. "Two Acres and a Cow: Peasant Farming for the Indians of the North-west, 1889–1897." *Canadian Historical Review* 70, no. 1 (March 1989): 27–52.

Cherwinski, W.J.C. "The Incredible Harvest Excursion of 1908." *Labour/Le Travailleur* 5 (Spring 1980): 57–80.

Cherwinski, W.J.C. "A Miniature Coxey's Army: The British Harvesters' Toronto-to-Ottawa Trek of 1924." *Labour/Le Travail* 32 (Fall 1993): 139–66.

Cherwinski, W.J.C. "Wooden Horses and Rubber Cows: Training British Agricultural Labour for the Canadian Prairies, 1890–1930." *Canadian Historical Association* (Historical Papers, 1980): 133–54.

Clark, Christopher. *The Roots of Rural Capitalism: Western Massachusetts 1780–1860*. Ithaca, NY: Cornell University Press, 1990.

Cole, D., and Ira Chaikin. *An Iron Hand upon the People: The Law against the Potlatch on the Northwest Coast*. Vancouver: Douglas & McIntyre, 1990.

Conrad, Norman C. *Reading the Entrails: An Alberta Ecohistory*. Calgary: University of Calgary Press, 1999.

Craig, John R. *Ranching with Lords and Commons*. New York: AMS Press, 1971.

Cruikshank, Ken. "Taking the Bitter with the Sweet: Sugar Refiners and the Canadian Regulatory State, 1904–20." *Canadian Historical Review* 74, no. 3 (September 1993): 367–94.

Danysk, Cecilia. "'A Bachelor's Paradise': Homesteaders, Hired Hands, and the Construction of Masculinity, 1880–1930." In *Making Western Canada: Essays on European Colonization and Settlement*, edited by Catherine Cavanaugh and Jeremy Mouat, 154–85. Toronto: Garamond Press, 1996.

Danysk, Cecilia. *Hired Hands: Labour and the Development of Prairie Agriculture, 1880–1930.* Toronto: McClelland & Stewart, 1995.

Dawson, Bruce. "'Better Than a Few Squirrels': The Greater Production Campaign on the First Nations Reserves of the Canadian Prairies." In *Plain Speaking: Essays on Aboriginal Peoples and the Prairies,* edited by Patrick C. Douaud and Bruce W. Dawson, 11–22. Regina: Canadian Plains Research Center, 2002.

Dawson, C.A. *Group Settlement: Ethnic Communities in Western Canada.* Toronto: Macmillan Canada, 1936.

Dempsey, Hugh A. *Big Bear: The End of Freedom.* Vancouver: Douglas & McIntyre, 1984.

Dempsey, Hugh A. *Crowfoot: Chief of the Blackfoot.* Edmonton: Hurtig, 1972.

Dempsey, Hugh A. *Firewater: The Impact of the Whisky Trade on the Blackfoot Nation.* Calgary: Fifth House Publishing, 2002.

Dempsey, Hugh A. *The Gentle Persuader: A Biography of James Gladstone, Indian Senator.* Saskatoon: Western Producer Prairie Books, 1986.

Dempsey, Hugh A. "One Hundred Years of Treaty Seven." In *One Century Later: Western Canadian Reserve Indians since Treaty 7,* edited by Ian L. Getty and Donald Smith, 20–30. Vancouver: University of British Columbia Press, 1978.

Dempsey, Hugh A. *Red Crow: Warrior Chief.* Saskatoon: Western Producer Prairie Books, 1980.

Dempsey, Hugh A. "Story of the Blood Reserve." *The Pioneer West* (No. 2): 1–6.

Dempsey, Hugh A. *Tom Three Persons: Legend of an Indian Cowboy.* Saskatoon: Purich Publishing, 1997.

den Otter, A.A. "Adapting The Environment: Ranching, Irrigation, and Dry Land Farming in Southern Alberta, 1880–1914." *Great Plains Quarterly* 6 (Summer 1986): 171–89.

den Otter, A.A. *Civilizing the West: The Galts and the Development of Western Canada.* Edmonton: University of Alberta Press, 1982.

Dennis, Thelma. "Eaton's Catalogue; Furnishings for Rural Alberta, 1886–1930." *Alberta History* 37, no. 2 (Spring 1989): 21–31.

Dick, Lyle. "Factors Affecting Prairie Settlement: A Case Study of Abernethy, Saskatchewan, in the 1880s." *Canadian Historical Association* (Historical Papers, 1985).

Dickason, Olive Praticia. *Canada's First Nations: A History of Founding Peoples from Earliest Times.* Toronto: Oxford University Press, 1997.

Doxtator, Deborah. "The Implications of Canadian Nationalism for Aboriginal Cultural Autonomy." In *Curatorship: Indigenous Perspectives in Post-Colonial Societies,* edited by E. Arinze and A. Cummins, 56–76. Hull: Canadian Museum of Civilization (Mercury Series: Paper 8, 1996).

Elias, Peter. *The Dakota of the Canadian Northwest: Lessons for Survival*. Winnipeg: University of Manitoba Press, 1988.

Ens, Gerhard J. *Homeland to Hinterland: The Changing Worlds of the Red River Metis in the Nineteenth Century*. Toronto: University of Toronto Press, 1996.

Ens, Gerhard J. "Metis Ethnicity, Personal Identity and the Development of Capitalism in the Western Interior." In *From Rupert's Land to Canada*, edited by Theodore Binnema, Gerhard Ens, and R.C. Macleod, 161–77. Edmonton: University of Alberta Press, 2001.

Elofson, Warren N. *Cowboys, Gentlemen and Cattle Thieves: Ranching on the Western Frontier*. Montreal: McGill-Queen's University Press, 2000.

Elofson, Warren N. *Frontier Cattle Ranching in the Land and Times of Charlie Russell*. Montreal: McGill-Queen's University Press, 2004.

Elofson, Warren N. "Not Just a Cowboy: the Practice of Ranching in Southern Alberta, 1881–1914." In *Canadian Papers In Rural History*, vol. 10, edited by Donald Akenson, 205–16. Gananoque: Langdale Press, 1996.

Evans, Simon M. "American Cattlemen on the Canadian Range, 1874–1914." *Prairie Forum* 4, no. 1 (Spring 1979): 121–35.

Evans, Simon M. *The Bar U and Canadian Ranching History*. Calgary: University of Calgary Press, 2004.

Evans, Simon M. "Grazing the Grasslands: Exploring Conflicts, Relationships and Futures." *Prairie Forum* 26, no. 1 (Spring 2001): 67–84.

Evans, Simon M. "The Passing of a Frontier: Ranching In the Canadian West, 1882–1912." PhD diss., University of Calgary, 1976.

Evans, Simon M. *Prince Charming Goes West: The Story of the E.P. Ranch*. Calgary: University of Calgary Press, 1993.

Evans, Simon M. "Spatial Aspects of the Cattle Kingdom: The First Decade, 1882–1892." In *Frontier Calgary: Town, City, and Region 1875–1914*, edited by A.W. Rasporich and Henry Klassen, 41–56. Calgary: McClelland & Stewart West, 1975.

Ewers, John C. *Plains Indian History and Culture: Essays on Continuity and Change*. Norman: University of Oklahoma Press, 1997.

Fisher, A.D. "Introducing 'Our Betrayed Wards,' By R.N. Wilson." *Western Canadian Journal of Anthropology* (January 1974): 21–59.

Fisher, Robin. *Contact And Conflict: Indian-European Relations in British Columbia, 1774–1890*. Vancouver: University of British Columbia Press, 1980.

Foran, Max. "The Impact of the Depression on Grazing Lease Policy in Alberta." In *Cowboys, Ranchers and the Cattle Business: Cross-Border Perspectives on Ranching History*, edited by Simon M. Evans, Sarah Carter, and Bill Yeo, 123–37. Calgary: University of Calgary Press, 2000.

Foran, Max. *Trails and Trials: Markets and Land Use in Alberta Beef Cattle Industry 1881–1948*. Calgary: University of Calgary Press, 2003.

Foster, John. "The Metis and the end of the Plains Buffalo in Alberta." In *Buffalo*, edited by John Foster, Dick Harrison, and I.S. MacLaren, 61–77. Edmonton: University of Alberta Press, 1992.

Francis, Daniel. *The Imaginary Indian: The Image of the Indian In Canadian Culture.* Vancouver: Arsenal Pulp Press, 1992.

Francis, R. Douglas. "In Search of a Prairie Myth: A Survey of the Intellectual and Cultural Historiography of Prairie Canada." *Journal of Canadian Studies* 24, no. 3 (Fall 1989): 44–69.

Francis, R. Douglas. *Images of the West: Changing Perceptions of the Prairies, 1690–1960.* Saskatoon: Western Producer Prairie Books, 1989.

Francis, R. Douglas. "From Wasteland To Utopia: Changing Images of the Canadian West in the Nineteenth Century." *Great Plains Quarterly* 7, no. 3 (Summer 1987): 178–94.

Friesen, Gerald. *The Prairies: A History.* Toronto: University of Toronto Press, 1987.

Fung, Ka-iu, ed. *Atlas of Saskatchewan.* Saskatoon: University of Saskatchewan, 1999.

Gaetz, Annie L. *The Park Country: History of Red Deer (Alberta) and District.* Vancouver: Evergreen Press, 1948.

Gentilcore, R. Louis, ed., *Historical Atlas of Canada: Vol. II, The Land Transformed 1800–1891.* Toronto: University of Toronto Press, 1993.

Germain, Jill St. *Indian Treaty-Making Policy in the United States and Canada 1867–1877.* Toronto: University of Toronto Press, 2001.

Gibson, Jane. "Native Responses to Bureaucratic Farm Management in Western Canadian Indian Reserves, 1880–1920." *Western Canadian Anthropologist* 7, nos. 1 & 2 (1990): 77–94.

Godfrey, D.G., and Brigham Y. Card, eds. *The Diaries of Charles Ora Card: The Canadian Years 1886–1903.* Salt Lake City: University of Utah Press, 1993.

Goldfrank, Esther S. "Administrative Programs and Changes in Blood Society During the Reserve Period." *Applied Anthropology* 2, no. 2 (Jan.–Mar. 1943):18–23.

Goldfrank, Esther S. *Changing Configurations in the Social Organization of a Blackfoot Tribe during the Reserve Period: The Blood of Alberta Canada.* Seattle: University of Washington Press, 1945.

Goldie, Terry. *Fear and Temptation: The Image of the Indigene in Canadian, Australian, and New Zealand Literature.* Montreal: McGill-Queen's University Press, 1989.

Gould, Ed. *Ranching in Western Canada.* Saanichton, BC: Hancock House, 1978.

Gray, James H. *The Winter Years.* Toronto: Macmillan Canada, 1966.

Green, L.C. "Legal Significance of Treaties affecting Canada's Indians." *Anglo-American Law Review* 1 (1972): 119–35.

Green, L.C. "Trusteeship and Canada's Indians." *Dalhousie Law Journal* 3, no. 1 (May 1976): 104–35.

Gulig, Anthony G. "Sizing up the Catch: Native-Newcomer Resource Competition and the Early Years of Saskatchewan's Northern Commercial Fishery." *Saskatchewan History* (Fall 1995): 3–12.

Haefeli, Evan. "A Note on the Use of North American Borderland." *American Historical Review* 104, no. 4 (October 1999): 1222, 1224.

Hagan, William T. *United States-Comanche Relations: The Reservation Years.* Norman: University of Oklahoma Press, 1990.

Hagell, E.F. *When the Grass Was Free.* Toronto: Ryerson Press, 1954.

Haig-Brown, Celia. *Resistance and Renewal: Surviving the Indian Residential School.* Vancouver: Tillacum, 1989.

Hall, David J. "Clifford Sifton and Canadian Indian Administration 1896–1905." *Prairie Forum* 2, no. 2 (November 1977): 127–51.

Hall, D.J. *Clifford Sifton:* vol. 1, *The Young Napoleon, 1861–1900.* Vancouver: University of British Columbia Press, 1981.

Hall, D.J. *Clifford Sifton:* vol. 2, *The Lonely Eminence 1901–1929.* Vancouver: University of British Columbia Press, 1985.

Hamer, David. *New Towns in the New World: Images and Perceptions of the Nineteenth-Century Urban Frontier.* New York: Columbia University Press, 1990.

Hanks, Lucien M. Jr., and Jane Richardson Hanks. *Tribe Under Trust: A Study of the Blackfoot Reserve of Alberta.* Toronto: University of Toronto Press, 1950.

Harper, Allan G. "Canada's Indian Administration: The 'Indian Act.'" *America Indigena* 6, no. 4 (October 1946): 297–314.

Harper, Allan G. "Canada's Indian Administration: The Treaty System." *America Indigena* 7, no. 2 (April 1947): 119–32.

Harring, Sidney L. *White Man's Law: Native People in Nineteenth-Century Canadian Jurisprudence.* Toronto: University of Toronto Press, 1998.

Hartley, William G. "Mormon Sugar in Alberta: E.P. Ellison and the Knight Sugar Factory, 1901–17." *Journal of Mormon History* 23 (Fall 1997): 1–29.

Hawthorn, H.B., C.S. Belshaw, and S.M. Jamieson. *The Indians of British Columbia: A Study of Contemporary Social Adjustment.* Berkeley: University of California Press, 1958.

High, Steven. "Native Wage Labour and Independent Production during the 'Era of Irrelevance.'" *Labour/Le Travail* 37 (Spring, 1996) 243–64.

Higinbotham, John D. *When the West Was Young: Historical Reminiscences of the Early Canadian West.* Lethbridge: The Herald Printers, 1978.

Hildebrandt, Walter. *Views from Fort Battleford: Constructed Visions of an Anglo-Canadian West.* Regina: Canadian Plains Research Center, 1994.

Hildebrandt, Walter, and Brian Hubner. *The Cypress Hills: The Land and Its People.* Saskatoon: Purich Publishing, 1994.

Hofstadter, Richard. *Social Darwinism in American Thought.* Boston: Beacon Press, 1955.

Hughes, Robert. *The Fatal Shore: The Epic of Australia's Founding*. New York: Alfred A. Knopf, 1987.

Ingles, Ernest B. "The Custom Threshermen In Western Canada 1890–1925." In *Building Beyond the Homestead: Rural History on the Prairies*, edited by David C. Jones and Ian MacPherson, 135–60. Calgary: University of Calgary Press, 1985.

Jameson, Sheilagh S. "The CPR and the Ranching Industry of the West." In *The CPR West: The Iron Road and the Making of a Nation*, edited by Hugh A. Dempsey, 71–86. Vancouver: Douglas & McIntyre, 1984.

Jameson, Sheilagh S. "Era of the Big Ranches." In *The Best from Alberta History*, edited by Hugh A. Dempsey, 53–64. Saskatoon: Western Producer Prairie Books, 1981.

Jameson, Sheilagh S. "The Ranching Industry of Western Canada: Its Initial Epoch, 1873–1910." *Prairie Forum* 11, no. 2 (Fall 1986): 229–42.

Jamieson, Stuart Marshall. "Native Indians and the Trade Union Movement in British Columbia." *Human Organization* 20, no. 4 (Winter 1961–2): 219–25.

Jamieson, Stuart. *Times of Trouble: Labour Unrest and Industrial Conflict in Canada, 1900–66*. Ottawa: Minister of Supply and Services, 1968.

Jennings, John Nelson. "The North West Mounted Police and Indian Policy, 1874–96." PhD diss., University of Toronto, 1979.

Jennings, John. "The North West Mounted Police and Indian Policy after the 1885 Rebellion." In *1885 and After: Native Society in Transition*, edited by F. Laurie Barron and James B. Waldram, 225–39. Regina: Canadian Plains Research Center, 1986.

Jennings, John. "Policemen And Poachers: Indian Relations on the Ranching Frontier." In *Frontier Calgary: Town, City, and Region 1875–1914*, edited by A.W. Rasporich and Henry Klassen, 87–99. Calgary: McClelland & Stewart West, 1975.

Jobson, Valerie K. "The Blackfoot Farming Experiment 1880–1945." Master's thesis, University of Calgary, 1990.

Johnson, Alex. *Plants and the Blackfoot*. Lethbridge: Lethbridge Historical Society, 1987.

Johnston, Basil H. *Indian School Days*. Toronto: Key Porter, 1988.

Jones, David C. *Empire of Dust: Settling and Abandoning the Prairie Dry Belt*. Edmonton: University of Alberta Press, 1987; reprinted by University of Calgary Press, 2002.

Jones, David C. "An Exceedingly Risky and Unremunerative Partnership: Farmers and the Financial Interests Amid the Collapse of Southern Alberta." In *Building Beyond the Homestead: Rural History on the Prairies*, edited by David C. Jones and Ian MacPherson, 207–27. Calgary: University of Calgary Press, 1985.

Jones, David C. *"We'll all be buried down here": The Prairie Dryland Disaster 1917–1926.* Calgary: Historical Society of Alberta, 1986.

Kaye, Barry. "'The Settlers' Grand Difficulty' Haying in the Economy of the Red River Settlement." *Prairie Forum* 9, no. 1 (Spring 1984): 1–11.

Kelly, L.V. *The Range Men: The Story of the Ranchers and Indians of Alberta.* Toronto: Coles, 1980.

Kennedy, Margaret A. *The Whiskey Trade of the Northwestern Plains: A Multidisciplinary Study.* New York: Peter Land, 1997.

Kerr, Donald, and Deryck W. Holdsworth, eds. *The Historical Atlas of Canada: Vol. III, Addressing the Twentieth Century 1891–1961.* Toronto: University of Toronto Press, 1990.

Kindt, Lawrence E. "The Sheep Ranching Industry of Canada." PhD diss., American University (Washington), 1939.

Knappen, Theodore M. "Winning the Canadian West." *Worlds Work* 10, 6595–6606.

Knight, Rolf. *Indians At Work: An Informal History of Native Indian Labour in British Columbia 1858–1930.* Vancouver: New Star Books, 1978.

Krech III, Shepherd. *The Ecological Indian: Myth and History.* New York: W.W. Norton, 1999.

Laliberte, Ronald F. "The Canadian State and Native Migrant Labour in Southern Alberta's Sugar Beet Industry." Master's thesis, University of Saskatchewan, 1994.

Laliberte, Ron. "The 'Grab a Hoe Indians': The Canadian State and the Procurement of Aboriginal Labour for the Southern Alberta Sugar Beet Industry." *Prairie Forum* 31, no. 2 (Fall 2006): 305–23.

Laliberte, Ron, and Vic Satzewich. "Native Migrant Labour in the Southern Alberta Sugar-beet Industry: Coercion and Paternalism in the Recruitment of Labour." *Canadian Review of Sociology and Anthropology* 36, no. 1 (February 1999): 65–85.

Lambrecht, Kirk N. *The Administration of Dominion Lands, 1870–1930.* Regina: Canadian Plains Research Center, 1991.

Lee, Lawrence B. "The Canadian-American Irrigation Frontier, 1884–1914." *Agricultural History* 40 (October 1966): 271–84.

Leighton, Douglas. "A Victorian Civil Servant at Work: Lawrence Vankoughnet and the Canadian Indian Department, 1874–1893." In *As Long as the Sun Shines and Water Flows: A Reader in Canadian Native Studies,* edited by Ian A.L. Getty and Antoine S. Lussier, 104–19. Vancouver: University of British Columbia Press, 1983.

Limerick, Patricia N. *The Legacy of Conquest: The Unbroken Past of the American West.* New York: W.W. Norton, 1987.

Loewen, Royden K. *Family, Church, and Market: A Mennonite Community in the Old and the New Worlds, 1850–1930.* Urbana: University of Illinois Press, 1993.

Long, Philip S. *The Great Canadian Range.* Calgary: Bonanza Books, 1970.

Lupton, A.A. "Cattle Ranching in Alberta 1874–1910: its evolution and migration." *Alberta Geographer* 3 (1967): 48–58.

Lutz, John. "After the fur trade: the aboriginal labouring class of British Columbia 1849–1890." *Journal of the Canadian Historical Association* 2 (1992): 69–93.

Lux, Maureen K. *Medicine that Walks: Disease, Medicine, and Canadian Plains Native People, 1880–1940.* Toronto: University of Toronto Press, 2001.

Mackie, Cam. "Some Reflections on Indian Economic Development." In *Arduous Journey: Canadian Indians and Decolonization*, edited by J. Rick Ponting, 211–27. Toronto: McClelland & Stewart, 1986.

Macintyre, D.E. *Prairie Storekeeper.* Toronto: Peter Martin Associates, 1970.

MacInnes, C.M. *In the Shadow of the Rockies.* London: Rivingtons, 1930.

Macleod, R.C. *The North-West Mounted Police and Law Enforcement 1873–1905.* Toronto: University of Toronto Press, 1976.

Macleod, R.C., and Heather Rollason. "'Restrain the Lawless Savages': Defendants in the Criminal Courts of the North West Territories, 1878–1885." *Journal of Historical Sociology* 10, no. 2 (June 1997):157–79.

Macleod, R.C., and Heather Rollason Driscoll. "Natives, Newspapers and Crime Rates in the North-West Terriotories, 1878–1885." In *From Rupert's Land to Canada*, edited by Theodore Binnema, Gerhard J. Ens, and R.C. Macleod, 249–69. Edmonton: University of Alberta Press, 2001.

Manuel, G., and Michael Posluns. "The Fourth World in Canada." In *Two Nations, Many Cultures: Ethnic Groups in Canada*, edited by Jean Leonard Elliot, 15–18. Scarborough: Prentice-Hall Canada, 1983.

Marchildon, Gregory P. "Instutional Adaptation to Drought and the Special Areas of Alberta, 1909–1939." *Prairie Forum* 32, no. 2 (Fall 2007): 251–71.

Martin, Chester. 'Dominion Lands' Policy. Toronto: McClelland and Stewart Ltd., 1973.

McCann, Larry. "The 1890s: Fragmentation and the New Social Order." In *The Atlantic Provinces in Confederation*, edited by E.R. Forbes, and D.A. Muise, 119–54. Toronto: University of Toronto Press, 1993.

McCullough, A.B. "Eastern Capital, Government Purchases and the Development of Canadian Ranching." *Prairie Forum* 22, no. 2 (Fall 1997): 213–36.

McGregor, Gaile. *The Wacousta Syndrome: Explorations in the Canadian Langscape.* Toronto: University of Toronto Press, 1985.

McIvor, R. *Canadian Monetary Banking and Fiscal Development.* Toronto: Macmillan Canada, 1961.

McKee, Christopher. *Treaty Talks in British Columbia: Negotiating a Mutually Beneficial Future.* Vancouver: UBC Press, 1996.

McKenna, J. "The Indian Laws of Canada." *Catholic World* 54 (October 1891): 62–68.

McLaren, Angus. *Our Own Master Race: Eugenics in Canada, 1885–1945*. Toronto: Oxford University Press, 1990.

McNeil, Kent. "The Meaning of Aboriginal Title." In *Aboriginal and Treaty Rights in Canada: Essays on Law, Equality, and Respect for Difference*, edited by Michael Asch, 135–54. Vancouver: UBC Press, 1997.

Middleton, Clara, and J.E. Middleton. *Green Fields Afar: Memories of Alberta Days*. Toronto: Ryerson Press, 1947.

Miller, J.R. "Owen Glendower, Hotspur, and Canadian Indian Policy." In *The First Ones: Readings in Indian/Native Studies*, edited by David R. Miller, Carl Beal, Jams Dempsey, and R. Wesley Heber, 252–65. Piapot Reserve #75: Saskatchewan Federated College, 1992.

Miller, J.R. *Skyscrapers Hide the Heavens: A History of Indian–White Relations in Canada*. Toronto: University of Toronto Press, 1990. Reprinted in 2000.

Milloy, John S. *The Plains Cree: Trade, Diplomacy and War, 1790 to 1870*. Winnipeg: University of Manitoba Press, 1988.

Monkman, Leslie. *A Native Heritage: Images of the Indian in English-Canadian Literature*. Toronto: University of Toronto Press, 1981.

Morantz, Toby. "Recent Literature on Native Peoples: A Measure of Canada's Values and Goals." *Acadiensis* 18 (1988): 237–57.

Morantz, Toby. "'So Evil a Practice': A Look at the Debt System in the James Bay Fur Trade." In *Merchant Credit and Labour Strategies in Historical Perspective*, edited by Rosemary E. Ommer, 203–22. Fredericton: Acadiensis Press, 1990.

Morris, Alexander. *The Treaties of Canada with the Indians of Manitoba and the North-West Territories*. Toronto: Coles, 1979.

Morton, W.L. "The Significance of Site in the Settlement of the American and Canadian Wests." In *Contexts of Canada's Past: Selected Essays of W.L. Morton*, edited by A.B. McKillop, 87–99. Toronto: Macmillan Canada, 1980.

Mountain Horse, Mike. *My People The Bloods*. Calgary: Glenbow-Alberta Institute, 1979.

Murchie, R.W. *Agricultural Progress on the Prairie Frontier: Volume V, Canadian Frontiers of Settlement*. Toronto: Macmillan Canada, 1936.

Newell, Dianne. *Tangled Webs of History: Indians and the Law in Canada's Pacific Coast Fisheries*. Toronto: University of Toronto Press, 1993.

Olthuis, John, and Roger Townshend. "The Case for Native Sovereignty." In *Crosscurrents: Contemporary Political Issues*, edited by Mark Charlton and Paul Barker, 5–8. Toronto: Nelson Canada, 1994.

Palmer, Howard. *Patterns of Prejudice: A History of Nativism in Alberta*. Toronto: McClelland & Stewart, 1982.

Pelly-Landrie, Linda. "First Nations Cultures, Now and In the Future," In *Three Hundred Prairie Years: Henry Kelsey's 'Inland Country of Good Report'*, edited by Henry Epp, 177–85. Regina: Canadian Plains Research Center, 1993.

Penrose, J. "When All the Cowboys Are Indians: The Nature of Race in All-Indian Rodeo." *Annals of the Association of American Geographers* 93, no. 3 (2003): 687–705.

Pentland, H. Clare. *Labour And Capital In Canada: 1650–1860.* Toronto: James Lorimer, 1981.

Pettipas, Katherine. *Severing the Ties that Bind: Government Repression of Indigenous Religious Ceremonies on the Prairies.* Winnipeg: University of Manitoba Press, 1994.

Potyondi, Barry. *In Palliser's Triangle: Living in the Grasslands 1850–1930.* Saskatoon: Purich Publishing, 1995.

Powell, J. *A History of the Canadian Dollar.* Ottawa: Bank of Canada, 2008.

Price, Richard., ed. *The Spirit of the Alberta Indian Treaties.* Montreal: Institute for Research on Public Policy, n.d.

Rasporich, A.W., and Henry Klassen, eds. *Frontier Calgary: Town, City, and Region 1875–1914.* Calgary: McClelland & Stewart West, 1975.

Ray, Arthur J. *The Canadian Fur Trade in the Industrial Age.* Toronto: University of Toronto Press, 1990.

Ray, Arthur J. *I Have Lived Here since the World Began: An Illustrated History of Canada's Native People.* Toronto: Lester Publishing, 1996.

Ray, Arthur J. *Indians In the Fur Trade: Their Role as Hunters, Trappers and Middlemen in the Lands Southwest of Hudson Bay 1660–1870.* Toronto: University of Toronto Press, 1974.

Ray, Arthur J., and Donald Freeman. *'Give Us Good Measure': An Economic Analysis of Relations Between the Indians and the Hudson's Bay Company Before 1763.* Toronto: University of Toronto Press, 1978.

Raymond, Town of. *Settlers, Sugar and Stampedes: Raymond Remembered.* Raymond: Town of Raymond, 1993.

Rees, Ronald. "Images of the Prairie: Landscape Painting and Perception in the Western Interior of Canada.'" *Canadian Geographer* 10, no. 3 (1976): 259–73.

Regehr, T.D. "Bankers and Farmers in Western Canada, 1900–1939." In *The Developing West*, edited by John E. Foster, 303–36. Edmonton: University of Alberta Press, 1983.

Regular, Keith. "On Public Display." *Alberta History* 34, no. 1 (Winter 1986): 1–10.

Regular, W. Keith. "'Red Backs and White Burdens': A Study of White Attitudes towards Indians In Southern Alberta 1896–1911." Master's thesis, University of Calgary, 1985.

Reid, Jennifer. *Myth, Symbol, and Colonial Encounter: British and Mi'kmaq in Acadia, 1700–1867.* Ottawa: University of Ottawa Press, 1995.

Robbins, William G. *Colony and Empire: The Capitalist Transformation of the American West.* Lawrence: University Press of Kansas, 1994.

Robertson, Heather. *Reservations are for Indians.* Toronto: James Lewis & Samuel, 1970.

Robertson, Heather. *Salt of the Earth: The Story of the Homesteaders in Western Canada.* Toronto: James Lorimer, 1974.

Rosenvall, L.A. "The Transfer of Mormon Culture to Alberta." *American Review of Canadian Studies* (1982): 122–44.

Rosenvall, L.A., and S.M. Evans, eds. *Essays on the Historical Geography of the Canadian West: Regional Perspectives on the Settlement Process.* Calgary: University of Calgary, 1987.

Samek, Hana. *The Blackfoot Confederacy 1880–1920: A Comparative Study of Canadian and U.S. Indian Policy.* Albuquerque: University of New Mexico Press, 1987.

Santink, Joy L. *Timothy Eaton and the Rise of His Department Store.* Toronto: University of Toronto Press, 1990.

Satzewich, Vic. "'Where's the Beef?': Cattle Killing, Rations Policy and First Nations 'Criminality' in Southern Alberta, 1892–1895." *Journal of Historical Sociology* 9, no. 2 (June 1996): 188–212.

Scott, Duncan C. "The Aboriginal Races." *Annals of the American Academy of Political and Social Science* 107 (May 1923): 63–66.

Seed, Patricia. "Three Treaty Nations Compared: Economic and Political Consequences for Indigenous Peoples in Canada, the United States, and New Zealand." In *Natives and Settlers, Now and Then: Historical Issues and Current Perspectives on Treaties and Land Claims in Canada*, edited by Paul W. DePasquale, 17–32. Edmonton: University of Alberta Press, 2007.

Sharp, Paul F. *Whoop-Up Country: The Canadian-American West, 1865–1885.* Norman: University of Oklahoma Press, 1973.

Shepard, R. Bruce. "The Mechanized Agricultural Frontier of the Canadian Plains." *Material History Bulletin* 7 (Spring 1979): 1–22.

Shepard, R. Bruce. "Tractors and Combines in the Second Stage of Agricultural Mechanization on the Canadian Plains." *Prairie Forum* 11, no. 2 (Fall 1986): 253–72.

Shewell, Hugh. *'Enough To Keep Them Alive': Indian Welfare in Canada, 1873–1965.* Toronto: University of Toronto Press, 2004.

Sifton, Clifford. "The Needs of the Northwest." *Canadian Magazine* 20, no. 5 (March 1903): 425–28.

Snow, Chief John. *These Mountains are our Sacred Places.* Toronto: Samuel Stevens, 1977.

Spencer, Bud. *Go North, Young Man, Go North!: My Life's Story.* n.p., n.d.

Spindler, George D., and Louise S. Spindler. "Identity, Militancy, and Cultural Congruence: The Menominee and Kainai." *Annals of the American Academy of Political and Social Science* 436 (March 1978): 73–85.

Spry, Irene M. "The Transition from a Nomadic to a Settled Economy in Western Canada, 1856–96." *Transactions of the Royal Society of Canada* 6, ser. 4 (June 1968): 187–201.

Stanley, George F.G. *The Birth of Western Canada: A History of the Riel Rebellions.* Toronto: University of Toronto Press, 1992.

Stonechild, A. Blair. "The Indian View of the 1885 Uprising." In *1885 and After: Native Society in Transition*, edited by F. Laurie Barron and James B. Waldram, 155–70. Regina: Canadian Plains Research Center, 1986.

Stonechild, Blair, and Bill Waiser. *Loyal till Death: Indians and the North-West Rebellion.* Calgary: Fifth House Publishing, 1997.

Taylor, Fraser. *Standing Alone: A Contemporary Blackfoot Indian.* Halfmoon Bay: Arbutus Bay Publications, 1989.

Taylor, Fred G. *A Saga of Sugar: Being a Story of the Romance and Development of Beet Sugar in the Rocky Mountain West.* Salt Lake City: Desert News Press, 1944.

Taylor, John Leonard. "Canada's North-West Indian Policy in the 1870s: Traditional Premises and Necessary Innovations." In *Sweet Promises: A Reader on Indian-White Relations in Canada*, edited by J.R. Miller, 207–11. Toronto: University of Toronto Press, 1991.

Taylor, John Leonard. *Canadian Indian Policy during the Inter-War Years, 1918–1939.* Ottawa: Indian Affairs and Northern Development, 1984.

Taylor, John Leonard. "Two Views on the Meaning of Treaties Six and Seven." In *The Spirit of the Alberta Indian Treaties*, edited by Richard Price, 3–7. Montreal: Institute for Research on Public Policy, n.d.

Thistle, Paul. C. *Indian-European Trade Relations in the Lower Saskatchewan River Region to 1840.* Winnipeg: University of Manitoba Press, 1986.

Thompson, John Herd. "Bringing in the Sheaves: The Harvest Excursionists, 1890–1929." *Canadian Historical Review* 59, no. 4 (December 1978): 467–89.

Thompson, John Herd. *Forging the Prairie West.* Toronto: Oxford University Press, 1998.

Thompson, John Herd. *The Harvests of War: The Prairie West, 1914–1918.* Toronto: McClelland & Stewart, 1978.

Thompson, John Herd, and Allen Seager. "Workers, Growers and Monopolists: the 'Labour Problem' in the Alberta Beet Sugar Industry During the 1930s." In *The Depression in Canada: Responses to Economic Crisis*, edited by Michiel Horn, 30–50. Toronto: Copp Clark Pitman, 1988.

Tiedemann, Heidi. "The Representation of Native Culture from Duncan Campbell Scott to Margaret Laurence." Canadian Studies Program, University College, University of Toronto, *Occasional Paper Series* 3, no. 1 (1993): 1–14.

Titley, E. Brian. "Hayter Reed and Indian Administration in the West." In *Swords and Ploughshares: War And Agriculture In Western Canada*, edited by R.C. Macleod, 109–47. Edmonton: University of Alberta Press, 1993.

Titley, E. Brian. *A Narrow Vision: Duncan Campbell Scott and the Administration of Indian Affairs in Canada*. Vancouver: University of British Columbia Press, 1986.

Titley, E. Brian. "William Morris Graham: Indian Agent Extraordinaire." *Prairie Forum* 8, no. 1 (1983): 25–41.

Tobias, John L. "Protection, Civilization, Assimilation: An Outline History of Canada's Indian Policy." *Western Canadian Journal of Anthropology* 6, no. 2 (1976): 13–30.

Tough, Frank. *'As Their Natural Resources Fail': Native Peoples and the Economic History of Northern Manitoba, 1870–1930*. Vancouver: UBC Press, 1996.

Tough, Frank. "Buying Out The Bay: Aboriginal Rights and the Economic Policies of the Department of Indian Affairs after 1870." In *The First Ones: Readings in Indian/Native Studies*, edited by David R. Miller, Carl Beal, James Dempsey, and R. Wesley Heber, 398–408. Piapot Reserve #75: Saskatchewan Indian Federated College Press, 1992.

Tough, Frank. "Indian economic behaviour, exchange and profits in northern Manitoba during the decline of monopoly, 1870–1930." *Journal of Historical Geography* 16, no. 4 (1990): 385–401.

Trachtenberg, Alan. *The Incorporation of America: Culture and Society in the Gilded Age*. New York: Hill and Wang, 1982.

Treaty Seven Elders and Tribal Council, Walter Hildebrandt, Dorothy First Rider, and Sarah Carter. *The True Spirit and Original Intent of Treaty 7*. Montreal: McGill-Queen's University Press, 1996.

Urquhart, M.C., and K.A.H. Buckley, eds., *Historical Statistics of Canada*. Toronto: Macmillan Canada, 1965.

Venne, Sharon H. "Treaties Made in Good Faith." In *Natives and Settlers, Now and Then: Historical Issues and Current Perspectives on Treaties and Land Claims in Canada*, edited by Paul W. DePasquale, 1–16. Edmonton: University of Alberta Press, 2007.

Vibert, Elizabeth. *Traders' Tales: Narratives of Cultural Encounters in the Columbia Plateau, 1807–1846*. Norman: University of Oklahoma Press, 1997.

Voisey, Paul. *High River and the 'Times': An Alberta Community and Its Weekly Newspaper, 1905–1966*. Edmonton: University of Alberta Press, 2004.

Voisey, Paul. "A Mix-Up Over Mixed Farming: The Curious History of the Agricultural Diversification Movement in a Single Crop Area of Southern Alberta." In *Building Beyond the Homestead: Rural History on the Prairies*, edited by David C. Jones and Ian MacPherson, 179–205. Calgary: University of Calgary Press, 1985.

Voisey, Paul. "The Urbanization of the Canadian Prairies, 1871–1916." *Histoire Sociale–Social History* 8 (1975): 77–101.

Voisey, Paul. *Vulcan: The Making of a Prairie Community*. Toronto: University of Toronto Press, 1988.

Voisey, Paul, ed. *A Preacher's Frontier: The Castor, Alberta Letters of Rev. Martin W. Holdom, 1909–1912*. Calgary: Historical Society of Alberta, 1996.

Walker, James W. St. G. "The Indian in Canadian Historical Writing." *Canadian Historical Association, Historical Papers* (1971): 21–51.

Walker, James W. St. G. "The Indian in Canadian Historical Writing, 1971–1981." In *As Long as the Sun Shines and Water Flows: A Reader in Canadian Native Studies*, edited by Ian A.L. Getty and Antoine S. Lussier, 340–57. Vancouver: University of British Columbia Press, 1983.

Ward, Tony. "Farming Technology and Crop Area on Early Prairie Farms." *Prairie Forum* 20, no. 1 (Spring 1995): 19–36.

Western Canada Irrigation Association. *Reports of the proceedings of the tenth annual convention held at Kamloops, B.C., July 25, 26 and 27, 1916*. Ottawa: Government Printing Bureau, 1917.

Wetherell, Donald G., and Irene R.A. Kmet. *Town Life: Main Street and the Evolution of Small Town Alberta, 1880–1947*. Edmonton: University of Alberta Press, 1995.

Wetherell, Donald G., with Irene Kmet. *Useful Pleasures: The Shaping of Leisure in Alberta 1896–1945*. Regina: Canadian Plains Research Center, 1990.

Williams, Paul. "The Act: Past, Present and Future." *Ontario Indian* 4, no. 4 (April 1981): 12–18.

Wilson, R.N. *Our Betrayed Wards: A Story of Chicanery, Infidelity and the Prostitution of Trust*. Ottawa, 1921.

Wunder John R., and Pekka Hamalainen. "Of Lethal Places and Lethal Essays." *American Historical Review* 104, no. 4 (October 1999).

Zaharia, *Sikotan* Flora, and *Makai'sto* Leo Fox. *Kitomahkitapiiminnooniksi: Stories from Our Elders*, vols. 1–3. Edmonton: Kainai Board of Education, 1995.

Zuyderhoudt, Lea. "Accounts of the Past as Part of the Present: The Value of Divergent Interpretations of Blackfoot History." In *The Challenges of Native American Studies: Essays in Celebration of the Twenty-Fifth American Indian Workshop*, edited by Barbara Saunders and Lea Zuyderhoudt, 161–83. Leuven: Leuven University Press, 2004.

NEWSPAPERS

Calgary Herald
Cardston Alberta Star
Cardston Globe
Cardston News
Cardston Record
Family Herald
Kamloops Standard-Sentinel
Lethbridge Herald
Lethbridge News
Macleod Advertiser
Macleod Gazette
Macleod News
Macleod Spectator
Macleod Times
Pincher Creek Rocky Mountain Echo
Raymond Chronicle
Raymond Leader
Raymond Recorder
Raymond Rustler
UID News
Western Native News

Index

protective presence of North West Mounted Police, 31

The Blackfoot Confederacy 1880–1920 (Samek), 71

'failure of reservation economies,' 4

Blood cattle owners. *See* Blood ranchers and cattle owners

Blood competitiveness, 87–88, 98, 102, 164, 168

    assisted by DIA and local agent, 100

    backlash against, 73, 98, 100

    in coal mining, 74

Blood freighters. *See* freighting

Blood haymakers. *See* haying

Blood indebtedness. *See* debt

Blood labour, 103–25. *See also* Aboriginal labour

    abandonment of beet harvest, 112–13

    day labour, 73

    field labourers, 110

    not susceptible to divide and conquer, 123

    pivotal to survival of Knight Sugar Co., 122

    refusal to become captive labour, 111, 118

    significance to sugar beet industry, 103, 105–11, 124–25

    sold to highest bidder, 119, 123

    strained relations with beet contractors, 113

    unwillingness to subsidize Knight Sugar, 121

    wage garnishees, 112

    wages, 109, 111–13

    work habits, 111–14

Blood ranchers and cattle owners, 152, 171

    grazing stock on Dominion lands, 43

    horse and cattle herds, 43, 49, 51, 125

Blood reserve, 24

    accommodation with rancher and farmer/settlers, 24

    expenditures, 139

farming, 171 (*See also* agriculture; haying)

income, 139

road allowances through, 136, 166

selection of, 26, 30, 128, 163–64

settlement patterns, 13

trails, 15

Blood reserve land, 13, 28

    abuse by ranchers and homesteaders, 56, 64

    Blood defense of their rights, 22, 36

    Cardston Mormons' use of, 50, 64–65

    carrying capacity, 51, 191n118

    closure to surrounding community, 49, 53–55

    decision making by Bloods concerning, 37, 57, 68

    environmental damage, 62, 64–66

    fencing, 49

    government manipulation to suit non-Native neighbours, 36, 59

    grazing, 44, 59, 62 (*See also* leases)

    grazing revenue difficulties, 45, 49–50, 54, 61, 168

    Greater Production Campaign, 57–60

    integration into non-Natives' land-use, 35–69

    leases, 49–50, 52–55, 64–66

    over-exploitation, 169

    overgrazing, 51, 62, 64

    perceived as underused and unproductive, 35, 57, 66–67

    refusal to surrender, 57 (*See also* alienation of Blood land)

    seen as open territory to which others had a right, 36, 43, 47, 56, 168

    significance to neighbours, 36, 47, 163, 168

    stock trespass on, 42, 44, 48–49, 51, 54–55, 189n84, 190n104

    treaty rights and, 43

Bloods, 21

in transition, 124

unprofitable in inflated wage circumstances, 121

wages, 113, 118, 123

sugar beet season, 105–6

Sun Dance, 22

Sweeting, John F., 120

Swinford, S., 75

T

T. Eaton Company, 129, 136, 207n33

Tanner, George, 142

Taylor, John W., 59, 103–5

Thistle, Paul C., *Indian-European Trade Relations*, 6

Thompson, John Herd, 12

Three Persons, Tom, 3, 132, 140

Tobias, John L., 20

Tough, Frank, 11, 72

Town Life (Wetherell/Kmet), 4

Trachtenberg, Alan, 5–6

traditional Native economic behaviours

adapted and altered, 172–73

rendered obsolete in Southern Alberta, 72

treaty promises, 92

treaties, 92

making land available to capital, 10

Native right to use of public domain, 48

written *vs.* oral accounts of, 127

Treaty 7, 31, 69, 127, 173

food crisis following, 32

government beef purchases, 138

leasing policies and, 60

promises that necessitated non-Native market economy, 139

supply of Indians with food and other goods, 24

treaty money issuance

altered to fit beet harvest, 107, 109, 111, 118, 123

merchants' interest in, 137–38

Trudeau, Pierre Elliott, 128

U

unauthorized credit, 140–44, 161, 209n75

Urquhart, M.C., *Historical Statistics of Canada*, 33

V

vagrancy laws, 10

Venne, Sharon, 127

Vibert, Elizabeth, 29

Views from Fort Battleford (Hildebrandt), 6–7

Voisey, Paul, 8, 24, 46, 129, 137

Vulcan, 24

W

wage garnishees, 112, 119

wages, 107–8, 112, 119

Walker, James St. G., 2

Wallace and Hauks, 49

War Measures Act, 58

Western Canada Irrigation Congress, 120

Western Lumber Company, 144

Wetherell, Donald G., 15

Town Life, 4

White Paper (1969), 128

White, Richard, 9

Whoop-Up Trail, 24

Wilson, James, 42–43, 49, 74, 81, 86, 98–100, 106–8, 111–12, 114, 138, 141, 166

arranging of freighting contracts, 88–89

assistance with debt collection, 142

www.ingramcontent.com/pod-product-compliance
Lightning Source LLC
Chambersburg PA
CBHW051958270326
41929CB00015B/2704